250 BICYCLE TOURS
in Maine

Coastal and Inland Rides from Kittery to Caribou

Howard Stone

THIRD EDITION

Backcountry Publications
Woodstock · Vermont

An Invitation to the Reader

Although it is unlikely that the roads you cycle on these tours will change much with time, some road signs, landmarks, and other items may. If you find that changes have occurred on these routes, please let us know so we may correct them in future editions. The author and publisher also welcome other comments and suggestions. Address all correspondence:

Editor, Bicycle Tours
Backcountry Publications
PO Box 748
Woodstock, Vermont 05091

Library of Congress Cataloging-In Publication Data

Stone, Howard, 1947–

25 Bicycle Tours in Maine : coastal and inland rides from Kittery to Caribou / Howard Stone. – 3rd Ed.

      p.   cm.

ISBN 0-88150-410-6 (alk. paper)

1. Bicycle touring–Maine–Guidebooks. 2. Maine–Guidebooks. I. Title

GV1045.5.M2S76 1998

796.6'4'09741–dc21

97-45164

CIP

Published by Backcountry Publications
A division of The Countryman Press, Inc.
PO Box 748, Woodstock, VT 05091

Distributed by W. W. Norton and Company
500 Fifth Avenue, New York, NY 10110

Text design by Sally Sherman
Cover design by Sue Wheeler
Cover photograph of Pemaquid Point, Maine, by Jeff Greenburg/New England Stock Photo
Interior photographs by the author
Maps by XNR Productions © 1998 Backcountry Publications

Printed in the United States of America
10 9 8 7 6 5 4 3 2 1

Acknowledgments

I'd like to give special thanks to those people who accompanied me while I researched the book, often enduring days that began and ended at 3 AM. In alphabetical order, they are Becky Burns, June Comeau, Carla Kerber, Leesa Mann, Dick Oliveira, and Gayle Yarrington. Gayle also helped me proofread the manuscript. Kevin and Anita Clifford allowed me to stay overnight numerous times, even though they had a newborn baby to take care of.

I would like to express my thanks to Donald Bumpus, of the Maine State Development Office—Division of Tourism, for offering me use of the department's photo collection. And to John Wojtowicz, who developed my photographs.

I am grateful to Chris Lloyd, Laura Jorstad, and Ann Kraybill of Backcountry Publications for their continued encouragement and support.

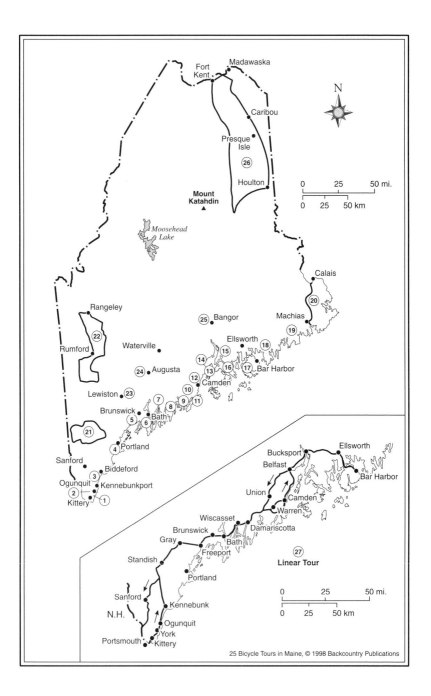

Fort Kent
Madawaska
Caribou
Presque Isle
(26)
Houlton
Mount Katahdin ▲
Moosehead Lake
Calais
(20)
Rangeley
(25) Bangor
Machias
(19)
(22)
Rumford
Waterville
Ellsworth
(15)
(18)
(14)
(16)
(17) Bar Harbor
(24) Augusta
(13)
Lewiston (23)
(12)
Camden
(10)
(7)
(9) (11)
Brunswick
(8)
(5) Bath
(6)
(21)
(4) Portland
Sanford
Biddeford
(3)
Ogunquit
(2) Kennebunkport
Kittery (1)

N

0   25   50 mi.
0   25   50 km

Bucksport
Ellsworth
Belfast
Bar Harbor
Union
Camden
Warren
Wiscasset
Damariscotta
Brunswick
Gray
Bath
Freeport
Standish
(27)
Linear Tour
Portland
Sanford
Kennebunk
N.H.
Ogunquit
York
Portsmouth
Kittery

0   25   50 mi.
0   25   50 km

25 Bicycle Tours in Maine, © 1998 Backcountry Publications

Contents

Introduction

Maine offers thousands of miles of safe and scenic bicycling. The state is blessed with an impressive network of secondary roads, most of them paved but not heavily traveled. Away from busy arteries like I-95 and US 1, an unspoiled landscape of weathered fishing villages, rolling farmland, and elegant New England towns beckons the cyclist. Most of Maine is rural enough to give the cyclist a sense of remoteness and serenity, but the nearest town, village, or grocery store is usually not more than a few miles away.

I've divided the state into four primary geographical areas: the southern coast, the midcoast region, the Down East coast, and inland Maine. The southern coast comprises the coastal region from the southern tip of Maine to Brunswick. This section of coastline is fairly smooth and contains most of the state's sandy beaches. However, some of the rockbound headlands like those at Cape Neddick, Cape Elizabeth, and Portland Head are as picturesque as any in the state. The southern coast is the flattest part of Maine, and therefore provides fairly relaxed bicycling.

The midcoast region covers the portion of the coast from Brunswick northeast to Bucksport at the northern tip of Penobscot Bay. This area contains the most jagged shoreline in Maine, with nine major peninsulas (and dozens of sub-peninsulas) jutting like fingers into the Atlantic. Between the peninsulas lie tidal estuaries and coves alive with watercraft ranging from graceful windjammers to hardy lobstering boats. At the heads of the estuaries and along the sheltered indentations of Penobscot Bay lie handsome towns with a rich architectural heritage from the 19th century, when they were prosperous seaports and shipbuilding centers.

The Down East coast extends from Bucksport to Maine's easternmost shoreline between Lubec and Calais. This is the least populated part of coastal Maine, and the least visited by tourists (except for glorious Acadia National Park, which is crowded during the summer). Unspoiled small towns and villages overlook harbors filled with lobstering and fishing boats, and rimmed by weatherbeaten wooden docks piled high with lobster traps. In general, the terrain is either rolling or gently rolling, with lots of short, sharp hills but not many long ones. Even in Acadia, where the highest mountains on the East Coast plunge headlong into the sea, the bicycling is surprisingly relaxed because nearly all the roads stay in the lower elevations and avoid steep grades.

I've defined inland Maine as any part of the state farther inland than about 15 miles from salt water. In general, inland Maine is hilly, forested, and laced with long rivers and dozens of unspoiled lakes. The eastern edge of the White Mountains extends into western Maine, providing the dramatic scenery of the Granite State without busy roads like the Kancamagus Highway or NH 16. A pleasant mixture of woods and rolling farmland with weathered barns and grazing dairy cows graces the land closer to the ocean. In the far northeastern reaches of the state, open potato farms undulate to the horizon, giving the landscape an Iowa-like appearance.

About the Rides

Ideally a bicycle ride should be a scenic, relaxing, and enjoyable experience that brings you into intimate contact with the landscape. In striving to achieve this goal, I've routed the rides along paved secondary and rural roads to avoid busy highways as much as possible. The tours include scenic spots such as dams, falls, ponds, ocean views, open vistas, and attractive villages.

Most of the rides fall between 25 and 45 miles in length, and a few have shorter or longer options. You can shorten any of the tours by examining the map and picking an alternative route. All the rides make a loop or figure eight rather than going out and then backtracking along the same road. I've included five overnight trips, which average 40 to 55 miles per day. The last ride is a continuous linear tour from the southern tip of Maine to Bar Harbor and back.

If you've never ridden any distance, the thought of riding 25 or, heaven forbid, 50 miles may sound intimidating or even impossible. I want to emphasize, however, that anyone in normal health can do it— and enjoy it—if you get into a little bit of shape first, which you can accomplish painlessly by riding at a leisurely place for an hour or two several times a week for about three weeks. At a moderate pace, you'll ride about ten miles per hour. If you think of the rides by the hour rather than by the mile, the numbers are much less intimidating.

Not counting long stops, a 25-mile ride should take about 3 hours at a leisurely speed and a 50-mile ride about 6 hours. However, I recom-

Stonington Harbor

mend that you start early and allow a full day for even the shorter rides because of the wealth of things to see and do along the way.

With the exception of the southern and extreme eastern coastal areas, Maine is rolling or hilly. As a result, biking the state involves some effort. Most of the rides ascend several hills, sometimes steep or long enough so that you will want to walk them. To compensate, however, there's a downhill run for every uphill climb. Except for a few difficult climbs in the northern and western parts of the state, no hills are long enough to be really discouraging. Most of the hills that you'll encounter are under a half mile long, with the steepest portion limited to a couple hundred yards or less.

It is obviously impossible to cover every scenic, historic, or popular spot in an area as large as Maine with only 25 rides—or even with the 27 rides of this expanded edition—so some well-known places are not represented in the book. Old Orchard is a fine beach and amusement area, but it is neither very safe nor scenic for bicycling. Portland's museums, architectural landmarks, and waterfront shops are best visited on foot. South Harpswell and Bailey Island are lovely, but bicycling to them involves extensive backtracking. To get to Boothbay Harbor you have to either ride at least a few miles on ME 27, a busy and unattractive road, or follow secondary roads from Damariscotta and then backtrack along the same route. The Moosehead Lake, Allagash, and Mount Katahdin areas are spectacular, but bicycling in this part of Maine involves riding for long distances on dirt roads with an entourage of lumber trucks and large recreational vehicles. With the exception of Islesboro, Maine's numerous islands either are too small to warrant inclusion in the book, or, surprisingly, they don't have many views of the water from the roads.

Bicycle paths, or bikeways, are few and far between in Maine. The two most popular—the Back Cove Recreation Path in Portland and the South Portland Greenbelt—are hemmed in by urban areas. Most other recreational trails in the state, often following abandoned railroads like the Jay to Farmington Trail or the Solon to Bingham Trail, have non-asphalt surfaces of dirt, gravel, crushed stone, or cinder. A 45-mile rail trail from Westbrook to Fryeburg, following the Presumpscot and Saco Rivers, is in the planning stage. Because I have given precedence to paved roads, Maine's hundreds of dirt roads and unpaved trails (except for the carriage roads in Acadia National Park) are beyond the scope of this book. Bicyclists looking for rail trails and unpaved roads may wish to consult *40 Great Rail-Trails in New York and New England* by Karen-Lee Ryan (Rails-to-Trails Conservancy, Washington, DC, 1996); or *The Mountain Biker's Guide to Northern New England* by Paul Angiolillo (Menasha Ridge Press, Birmingham, AL, 1993).

Helpful Hints

1. If you are not concerned with riding fast, the most practical bicycle for recreational riding is a mountain bike or a hybrid between a mountain bike and a road bike. Most people find the upright riding position comfortable. The gearing is almost always lower than it is on road bikes, which makes climbing hills much easier. The shift levers are mounted on the handlebars, so you don't have to move your hands when shifting gears. The fatter, thicker tires are resistant to punctures and unlikely to get caught in storm-sewer grates. Mountain bikes are more stable, rugged, and resistant to damage than road bikes. The only disadvantage of mountain bikes is that they are a little slower than road bikes because of their wider tires and less streamlined riding position.

If most of your riding is on pavement, you don't need standard mountain-bike tires, which are about 2 inches wide with a deep, knobby tread. Use narrower tires (often called city tires or cross-training tires), which are 1³/₈ or 1¹/₂ inches wide with a fairly smooth tread.

2. If you've never ridden any distance, start with a short, easy tour, and work your way up to the more difficult ones.

3. Use a firm, good-quality seat. A soft, mushy seat may feel inviting, but as soon as you sit on it the padding compresses to zero under your weight, so that you are really sitting on a harsh metal shell.

4. Adjust your seat to the proper height and make sure that it is level. With your pedals at six and twelve o'clock, put the balls of your feet directly over the spindles. Your extended leg should be slightly bent. Then put both heels on the pedals. Your extended leg should now be straight, and you should be able to backpedal without rocking your fanny from side to side. If it rocks, the seat is too high; if your extended leg is still bent with the pedal at its lowest point, the seat is too low.

5. Pedal with the balls of your feet, not your arches or heels. Toe clips or cleats are ideal for keeping your feet in the proper position on the pedals; they also give you added leverage when going uphill. The straps should be *loose* (or the spring tension on clipless pedals should be low) so that you can take your feet off the pedals effortlessly.

6. Spin your legs quickly in your low and middle gears, rather than grinding slowly in your higher ones. Using low gears is much more efficient and less tiring. Get used to riding at 70 revolutions per minute (RPM); then work your way up to above 80. If you find yourself pedaling below 70 RPM, shift to a lower gear. To count your RPM, use a watch with a second hand or, even better, a bicycle computer that measures cadence.

7. When approaching a hill, always shift into low gear *before* the hill, not after you start climbing it. If it's a steep or long hill, get into your lowest gear right away. I use a fairly low gear even on moderate hills.

8. If you have a 10- or 12-speed bike, you'll find it much easier to climb hills if you get a freewheel (the rear cluster of gears) that goes up to 34 teeth instead of the standard 28 teeth. (You may have to buy a new rear derailleur to accommodate the larger shifts.) For the ultimate in hill-climbing ease, you need a bicycle with 18 or more speeds. The

smaller the inner front chainwheel, the lower the low gear. I recommend a small chainwheel with 24 or 26 teeth.

9. Eat before you get hungry, drink before you get thirsty, and rest before you get tired.

10. To keep your pants out of your chain, tuck them inside your socks.

11. Don't wear jeans or cut-offs; their thick seams are uncomfortable. For maximum comfort, wear padded cycling shorts or pants, with no underwear. Stretchy, synthetic clothing designed for bicycling is comfortable, and wicks perspiration away from your skin better than cotton.

12. Use common courtesy with motorists and pedestrians. Hostility toward bicyclists has received national media attention; it is caused by the 2 percent of the riders who are discourteous (mainly messengers and groups hogging the road), who give the other 98 percent of responsible riders a bad image. Please do not join the 2 percent minority!

13. If you have to use the bathroom, the simplest solution is to get out of sight off the road. A footpath or one-lane dirt road that curves away from view into the woods is ideal. Most fast-food restaurants have easily accessible bathrooms. If a restaurant is of the "Please wait to be seated" variety or has facilities "for customers only," either walk in briskly or order a snack. Most gas stations have rest rooms; most convenience stores and country stores do not, but they will sometimes accommodate you if you ask urgently.

About the Points of Interest

Maine has a wealth of museums and historic sites. I have intentionally not listed their hours and fees because they are subject to change, often from one year to the next. Most of Maine's attractions are open only during the summer or, with luck, between May and October. Many of the historic houses and smaller museums are open only two or three days a week because they depend on voluntary contributions and effort. If you really want to visit a site, phone before the ride to find out the hours.

As you pedal through towns and villages, try to notice each building. Maine's communities abound with nineteenth-century architecture, including elegant wooden houses, Victorian commercial buildings, stately white churches, inviting brick or stone libraries, and bell-towered schoolhouses.

About the Overnight Tours

An overnight tour requires some preparation. It is important to reserve your accommodations at least a week in advance—it's no fun to pull into town at dusk and find that all the motels are full. When you reserve the place where you'll be staying the night before the tour, mention that you will be taking a bicycle trip and leaving your car there for a few days.

You will also need some extra equipment and clothing. It is essential to have a rear rack that sits above the back wheel and a pair of panniers that clip onto the rack. Be sure to bring raingear; the most effective is made of Gore-Tex®, a breathable synthetic fabric. (Many cyclists prefer a rain cape, which maximizes ventilation.) Bring an extra change of clothing and keep it in a closed plastic garbage bag, since even "water-repellent" panniers will leak in a heavy downpour. Wool clothing—or, even better, polypropylene—stays warm when wet, whereas cotton becomes cold and clammy, which can bring on hypothermia if the temperature is below 60 degrees. Don't forget a jacket; inland Maine can be chilly in the morning even during the summer. Bring three or four water bottles, a spare inner tube, brake cable, derailleur cable, and a few spare spokes (with nipples) fitted to your wheel. You should also bring a few additional tools (see *What to Bring With You, #4*).

Be sure that your bicycle is in good condition. Replace worn tires, tubes, and cables *before* the tour—if you break down in Aroostook County or the western mountains, there won't be a bike shop around the corner.

Safety

You will reduce your chances of having an accident by following these safety tips:

1. Ride on the right, with the traffic. Never ride against traffic.
2. Wear a helmet. Using a helmet is analogous to wearing a seat belt in a car. Most bicycle helmets are light, comfortable, and well ventilated. In addition to cushioning your head after a fall, a helmet also provides protection from the sun and the rain.
3. Be sure your bike is mechanically sound. Its condition is especially important if you bought the bike at a discount store, where it was probably assembled by an amateur with little training. Above all, be

sure that the wheels are secure and that the brakes work. Replace worn tires, tubes, and cables before you hit the road.

4. Use a rearview mirror. When you come to an obstacle—a pothole or a patch of broken glass—you can tell at a glance, without peeking back over your shoulder, whether or not it's safe to swing out into the road to avoid it. On narrow or winding roads you can always be aware of the traffic behind you and plan accordingly. Mirrors attach to your helmet, your eyeglasses, or the end of your handlebars.

5. Stop signs and traffic lights are there for a reason—obey them.

6. Pay attention to the road surface. Not all roads in Maine are silk-smooth. Often the bicyclist must contend with bumps, ruts, cracks, potholes, and fish-scale sections of road that have been patched and repatched numerous times. When the road is rough, slow down and keep alert, especially going downhill. On bumps, you can relieve some of the shock by getting up off the seat.

7. If you are bicycling in a group, ride single file and at least 20 feet apart.

8. Use hand signals when turning. To signal a right turn, stick out your right arm.

9. If you stop to rest or examine your bike, pull both you and the bicycle *completely* off the road.

10. Bring reflective legbands and a light with you in case you are caught in the dark. I like ankle lights; they're lightweight and bob up and down as you pedal for additional visibility.

11. Sleek black bicycle clothing is stylish, but bright colors are more visible, and light colors are safest at dusk.

12. Watch out for sand patches, which often build up at intersections, sharp curves, and the bottom of hills. Sand is very unstable if you're turning, so slow way down, stop pedaling, and steer in a straight line until you're beyond the sandy spot.

13. Avoid storm sewers with grates parallel to the roadway.

14. *Never* ride diagonally across railroad tracks—it is too easy to catch your wheel in the slot between the rails and fall. Either walk your bike across or, if no traffic is in sight, cross the tracks at right angles by swerving into the road. When riding across tracks, slow down and get up off the seat to relieve the shock of the bump.

15. In towns, beware of car doors opening into your path. To be safe, any time you ride past a line of parked cars, stay 4 or 5 feet away from

them. A car pulling to the side of the road in front of you is an obvious candidate for trouble.

16. Roads that are freshly oiled and sanded (to seal cracks before winter) are treacherous, and the only safe course is to slow down. If the oil is still wet or the sand is deep, walk.

17. A low sun limits visibility for drivers, especially those peering through a smeared or dirty windshield. Assume that anyone driving into a low sun may not see you, and give these cars the benefit of the doubt at intersections. Use your rearview mirror to monitor the traffic behind you if you're pedaling directly into the sun.

18. Little kids riding their bikes in circles in the middle of the road or shooting in and out of driveways aren't expecting you. Call out "Beep-beep" or "Watch out" as you approach.

19. In the fall, wet leaves are very slippery. Avoid turning on them.

20. If a dog chases you, try to outrun it—often you can, because most dogs are territorial and will only chase you a short distance. Keep your legs moving by pedaling quickly; it is hard for a dog to bite a fast-rotating target. If you can't outrun the animal, use dog repellent, or dismount and walk with your bike between you and the dog. Never swerve into the middle of the road or ride on the left to avoid a dog. Often, yelling "Stay!" or "No!" in an authoritative voice will make a dog back off. (For more about dog repellent, see *What to Take With You,* #6.)

21. Steel-decked bridges are extremely slippery when wet; there is a very real danger of falling and hurting yourself on the sharp metal grating. If the road is wet, or early in the morning when there may be condensation on the bridge, please walk across.

What to Take with You

You will enjoy the tours more if you add a few basic accessories to your bike and take a few items with you.

1. Bike rack. It's so much easier to whip your bike on and off a rack than to wrestle it into and out of your car or trunk. I prefer bike racks that attach to the back of the car—do you really want to hoist your bike over your head onto the roof? If you use a rack that fits onto the back of the car, make sure that the bike is at least a foot off the ground and

15

that the bicycle tire is well above the tailpipe. Hot exhaust blows out tires! (My thanks to Pam Jones for suggesting this.)

2. Handlebar bag with transparent map pocket on top. It's always helpful to have some carrying capacity on your bike. Most handlebar bags are large enough to hold tools, a lunch, or even a light jacket. It is easy to follow the route if the map or directions are readily visible in the map pocket. For additional carrying capacity, you can buy a metal rack that fits above the rear wheel and a pack that fits on top of the rack.

   Always carry things on your bike, not on your back. A knapsack raises your center of gravity and makes you more unstable; it also digs painfully into your shoulders if you have more than a couple of pounds in it.

3. Water bottle. On any ride of more than 15 miles you will be thirsty, and if you don't drink enough water you will dehydrate. It's a good idea to bring two or three water bottles and keep them filled. A good rule of thumb is to drink one bottle of water per hour. Put only water in your bottles—it quenches thirst better than any other liquid.

4. Basic tools. Tire irons, a 6-inch adjustable wrench, a small pair of pliers, a small standard screwdriver, and a small Phillips-head screwdriver are all you need to take care of virtually all roadside emergencies. A rag (or packaged moist towelettes) and a tube of hand cleaner are useful if you have to handle your chain. If your bike has any Allen nuts (nuts with a small hexagonal socket on top), carry metric Allen wrenches to fit them. Most bicycle shops sell a handy one-piece kit with several Allen wrenches, along with a standard and a Phillips-head screwdriver.

   On the overnight tours, it's a good idea to bring a few extra tools: a freewheel remover (make sure it fits your freewheel; there are different models), a chain-rivet remover, a spoke wrench, and a crank tool to tighten your crank bolt should it become loose (make sure it's the right size). Also bring a spare brake cable, a spare derailleur cable, and a few extra spokes and spoke nipples (be sure that the spokes fit your wheel). I tape the extra spokes to my pump.

5. Pump and spare tube. If you get a flat, you're immobilized unless you can pump up a new tube or patch the old one. On the road, it is easier to install a new tube than to patch the old one. Do the patching at home. Pump up the tire until it's hard, and you are on your way.

If you cycle a lot and don't use a mountain bike, you will get flats—it's a fact of life. Most flats are on the rear tire, because that's where most of your weight is. You should therefore practice taking the rear wheel off and putting it back on the bike, and taking the tire off and placing it back on the rim, until you can do it confidently. It's much easier to practice at home than to fumble by the roadside.

6. Dog repellent. When you ride in rural areas you will occasionally be chased by dogs. The best repellent is a commercial product called Halt, an extract of hot peppers that comes in a small aerosol can and is available in many bike shops. You also may be able to obtain it from your post office (many mail carriers use it) or from the manufacturer, ARI, PO Box 510, Orchard Hill, GA 30266. Another alternative is to carry a squirt gun or small plant sprayer filled with ammonia. Just make sure that the container doesn't leak. Repellent is effective only if you can grab it instantly when you need it—don't put it in your handlebar pack, a deep pocket, or anyplace else where you'll have to fish around for it. I clip Halt to the top of my handlebar pack.

7. Fenders. When the roads are wet, fenders prevent a plume of water and mud from streaming up your back and gumming up your brakes and front derailleur.

8. Bicycle computer. A bicycle computer (or cyclometer) is the best device to indicate distance traveled. Computers are very easy to read because they sit on top of your stem and have large, clear digits. Most computers indicate not only distance, but also speed, elapsed time, and cadence (revolutions per minute of the pedals). The solar-powered models last a long time before the batteries need replacement.

9. Bike lock. Common sense dictates locking your bicycle if you leave it unattended. The best locks are the rigid, bolt cutter–proof ones like Kryptonite® or Citadel®. The next best choice is a strong cable that cannot be quickly severed by a normal-sized bolt cutter or hacksaw.

10. Food. Always bring some food along when you go for a ride. Some of the rides go through remote areas with many miles between places to buy food, and that country store you were counting on may be closed on weekends or out of business. Fruit is nourishing and contains a lot of water. A couple of candy bars or pieces of pastry will provide a burst of energy for the last 10 miles if you are getting tired. (Don't

17

A road winds past the keeper's residence
for the Marshall Point Light in Port Clyde.

east sweets before then—the energy burst lasts only about an hour, then your blood-sugar level drops to below where it was earlier and you'll be really weak.)

For liquids, the best choice is plain old water, and the worst choice is carbonated beverages. Fruit juice is fine in conjunction with water.

11. Helmet. See *Safety*, #2.

12. Rearview mirror. See *Safety*, #4.

13. Bicycle lights and reflective legbands. See Safety, #10.

14. Bicycling gloves. Gloves designed for biking, with padded palms and no fingers, will cushion your hands and protect them if you fall. For maximum comfort, use handlebar padding also.

15. Kickstand. A kickstand makes it easy to stand your bike upright without leaning it against a wall or other object. Keep in mind that a strong wind may knock your bike over and that in hot weather a kickstand may sink far enough into asphalt to topple your bike.

16. Toe clips. See *Helpful Hints*, #3.

17. Roll of electrical tape. You never know when you'll need it.

Using the Maps and Directions

Unfortunately, a book format does not lend itself to quick and easy consultation while you're on your bike. The rides will go more smoothly if you don't have to dismount at each intersection to consult the map or directions. You can solve this problem by making a photocopy of the directions to carry in your map pocket. You will have to dismount occasionally to turn the sheet over or to switch sheets, but most people find it easier to follow the directions than the map.

The maps reflect the major intersections and the main side roads that you will pass. I have enlarged congested areas on the maps for the sake of legibility. The small arrows alongside the route indicate the direction of travel. The maps and directions indicate the names of roads if there was a street sign at the time I researched the route; I designated the road as "unmarked" if the street sign was absent. Street signs may appear or disappear at any time, and the name of a road may change at a town line or on the far side of an intersection. The spelling of road names also conforms to the street signs that I saw on the actual tour—other atlases and maps may have spellings that differ.

The directions indicate the distance to the next turn or major intersection, so it will be very helpful to have a bicycle computer. Each direction begins with the cumulative mileage that you have covered up to that point. The cumulation is meant to be only a guideline. No two computers are calibrated exactly the same, so most likely there will be a discrepancy between the cumulated mileages in the book and the reading on your own computer. The longer the ride, the greater the discrepancy will be.

In writing the directions, it is obviously not practical to mention every single intersection. Always stay on the main road unless the directions state otherwise.

In addition to distances and a description of the next intersection, the directions also mention points of interest and situations that require caution. Any hazardous spot, for example an unusually busy intersection or bumpy section of the road, has been clearly indicated by a **Caution** warning. It's a good idea to read over the entire tour before taking it, in order to familiarize yourself with the terrain, points of interest, and places requiring caution.

In the directions, certain words occur frequently, so let me define them to avoid any confusion.

To "bear" means to turn diagonally, at an angle between a right-angle turn and going straight ahead. In these illustrations, you bear from road A onto road B.

To "merge" means to come into a road diagonally, or even head-on, if a side road comes into a main road. In the examples, road A merges into road B.

To turn "sharply" means to turn at an angle greater than 90 degrees, in other words, to make a hairpin or other very sharp turn. In the examples, you turn sharply from road A onto road B.

In the directions, state highways are designated "ME" (for example, ME 103), and federal highways are designated "US" (for example, US 1).

Bicycle Clubs

If you would like to bike with a group and meet other people who enjoy cycling, join a bicycle club. Most clubs have weekend rides of comfortable length, with a shortcut if you don't want to ride too far. Some clubs hand out maps or directions before the ride, or mark the route by painting arrows in the road at the turns. The major clubs in Maine are: Casco Bay Bicycle Club, 37 Bernadette Street, Westbrook, ME 04092; Merrymeeting Wheelers Bicycle Club, 9 Bickford Avenue, Brunswick, ME 04011; Maine Wheels, 225 Paris Hill Road, South Paris, ME 04281; The County Pedalers, 124 Harvest Lane, Presque Isle, ME 04769; and Maine Freewheelers, Box 2037, Bangor, ME 04402. These clubs are affiliated with the League of American Bicyclists, the main national organization of and for bicyclists. The League has an excellent monthly magazine and a dynamic legislative-action program. Its address is 1612 K Street NW, Suite 401, Washington, DC 20006. The Bicycle Coalition of Maine, Box 5275, Augusta, ME, is a political advocacy group devoted to improving conditions for bicyclists.

Many bicycle shops run informal group rides. Ask your local shop if it runs any, or if any other shops in the area do. If there is no club within an hour's drive, consider starting one!

Further Reading and Resources

The *Maine Atlas and Gazetteer.* DeLorme Publishing Company, Freeport, ME. This is a superb resource that is updated every year. It divides the entire state into seventy quadrangles, each at a scale of 2 miles to the inch. This scale is large enough to show every back road, lake, stream, and most points of interest. In addition to the maps, the atlas contains lists and brief descriptions of beaches, nature preserves, parks, hiking trails, unique natural areas, waterfalls, canoe trips, lighthouses, museums, historic sites, and campgrounds.

Maine: An Explorer's Guide, by Christina Tree and Elizabeth Roundy. Eighth edition. The Countryman Press, Woodstock, VT, 1997. This is the best guidebook to the state in print. It describes points of interest, recreational areas, cultural events, fairs and festivals, places to shop, lodging, and restaurants.

Bicycling. DeLorme Publishing Company, Freeport, ME, 1994. This pamphlet includes 22 maps that indicate suggested rides. It covers several areas not included in this book, including South Harpswell–Bailey Island, the Boothbay Harbor region, the islands of Vinalhaven and North Haven, Ellsworth-Trenton-Lamoine, Bucksport-Bangor, Bangor-Orono-Old Town, the Belgrade Lakes region, Naples-Bridgton-Harrison, and others. There's even a Century (a 100-mile ride) northeast of Augusta.

A Pocket Guide to Biking on Mount Desert Island, by Audrey Minutolo.

Down East Books, Camden, ME, 1996.

A Pocket Guide to the Carriage Roads of Acadia National Park, by Diana F. Abrell. Second edition. Down East Books, Camden, ME, 1995.

Acadia's Biking Guide and Carriage Road Handbook, by Tom St. Germain. Second edition. Parkman Publications, Bar Harbor, ME, 1995.

Exploring Maine and *Maine Invites You*. Maine Publicity Bureau, Hallowell, ME. Two similar guides, each published annually, listing points of interest and accommodations in Maine.

Take a Ride (Road & Mountain) Guide. Kennebec Valley Tourism Council, 179 Main Street, Waterville, ME 04901.

Maine Geographic series. DeLorme Publishing Company, Freeport, ME, 1994. This series of pamphlets (*Bicycling* is one of them) covers numerous topics, including wildlife, historic sites, islands, lighthouses, natural sites, country inns, canoeing, and hiking.

THE SOUTHERN COAST

The Southern Tip: York–Eliot–Kittery

Distance: 29 miles
Terrain: Gently rolling, with several short hills and two long ones.
Special features: Historic York Village, rolling farmland, Piscataqua River, harbor views.

The southern tip of Maine, which is only an hour from Boston, is an excellent area for bicycling. It has historic villages, elegant old homesteads, quiet harbors, and peaceful country roads that wind across rolling meadows and along the broad Piscataqua River. Traffic on the secondary roads, and even on ME 103 along the coast, is pleasantly light, because most travelers entering Maine zip across the area on I-95 and do not visit the coast until they reach the beach areas north of where this ride starts. Even visitors to Kittery usually head directly to the factory outlets on US 1 without further sightseeing in the town.

The ride starts from York Village, a town steeped in history, about seven miles north of the bridges that link Maine and New Hampshire. York Village, which contains a National Historic District, is the southernmost of the several distinct communities within the township of York. (Newcomers always have trouble keeping all the Yorks straight.) Among the historic buildings, which were built between 1719 and 1760, are the Old Gaol (the chief museum for the Historic District, with original cells and dungeons; it's pronounced "jail"), Jefferds Tavern, the Old Schoolhouse, and the elegant Emerson Wilcox House and Elizabeth Perkins House. Guides in period costumes explain the history of the buildings to visitors. Across from the Old Gaol stands the stately First Parish Church, a latecomer built in 1862.

From York Village, the route heads west across the bottom of Maine a few miles inland from the coast and the Piscataqua River, which flows between Maine and New Hampshire. This section of the ride follows

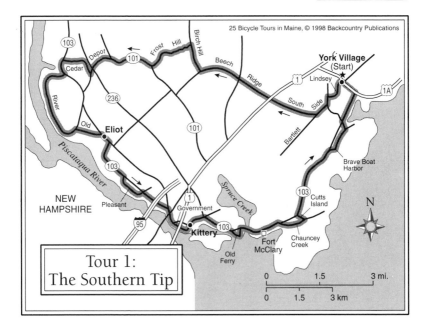

25 Bicycle Tours in Maine, © 1998 Backcountry Publications

Tour 1:
The Southern Tip

quiet back roads through gently rolling farmland into Eliot. A delightful lane hugs the river, which at this point is a wide tidal estuary. Just ahead, you'll glide into the center of Eliot, a gracious and thoroughly unspoiled town that is virtually undiscovered by tourists.

The route continues along the river into Kittery, the most southerly town in Maine. Kittery is the home of the massive and misnamed Portsmouth Naval Shipyard, which is on Seavey Island adjacent to the downtown area. It is closed to the public, but you can see it clearly from the road. Kittery is also a fierce retailing competitor with Freeport, an hour up the coast. Clustered along US 1 just north of town is a group of factory outlets and the sprawling Kittery Trading Post, a clothing and outdoor-sports store similar to L.L. Bean.

The final part of the ride between Kittery and York follows several inlets and coves that pierce the coast. This first bit of Maine's shoreline bears more of a resemblance to the midcoast area than to most of the southern coast. Two miles past downtown Kittery is Kittery Point, a tranquil village with Maine's oldest church, a cemetery with weathered slate headstones, and fine old houses overlooking Portsmouth Harbor. Just before York Village you'll cross the York River, a tidal estuary with a footpath along its north bank.

25

Sewall's Bridge, York Village, a replica of the original span built in 1761

Directions for the ride

Start from the parking lot next to the town hall on US 1A in York Village. There is usually room at the back of the lot, near the cemetery. If the lot is full, there is another lot across the road in the York Village Historic District (entrance on Lindsey Road).

If you're coming from the south, get off the Maine Turnpike at exit 4, the Yorks-Ogunquit exit. Bear right at the end of the ramp and go 0.2 mile to US 1. Turn right and go 0.25 mile to US 1A on the left, at the traffic light. Turn left and go 0.8 mile to the parking lot on the left.

From the north, get off the Maine Turnpike at the Yorks-Berwick exit, just after the toll booth. Turn left at the end of the ramp, and go 0.4 mile to the end (US 1). Continue with the directions from the south, beginning "Turn right and go 0.25 mile ..."

0.0 Turn left out of the parking lot and immediately right on Lindsey Road, passing the graveyard on your left. Go 0.8 mile to the end, passing through the York Village Historic District.

Notice the handsome granite library on your right as you leave the parking lot.

0.8 *Go left across the wooden-railed bridge, called Sewall's Bridge.*
It is a replica of the original one built at this site in 1761. The Elizabeth Perkins House is on your right after you cross the bridge.

0.9 *At the far end of the bridge, bear right on South Side Road. After 0.4 mile, the main road curves right and Bartlett Road goes straight. Stay on the main road for 1.6 miles to the cross-roads (US 1) and stop sign.*
You can see the York River on the right across the fields.

2.9 *Cross US 1 onto Beech Ridge Road and go 2.2 miles to Birch Hill Road on the right. It's after the main road curves sharply left downhill.*
This road and several following ones pass through rolling farm-land where cows and horses graze.

5.1 *Turn right on Birch Hill Road and go 0.8 mile to Frost Hill Road on the left.*

5.9 *Turn left and go 1.5 miles to the end (ME 101).*
You'll climb a steep hill, followed by a relaxing descent.

7.4 *Turn right on ME 101 and go 1.6 miles to Depot Road, which bears left.*

9.0 *Bear left and go 0.7 mile to the crossroads (ME 236) and stop sign.*
Eliot High School is on your left at the corner.

9.7 *Cross ME 236 and immediately turn right on Cedar Road. Go 0.8 mile to the end (ME 103), at a large traffic island.*

10.5 *Bear left and go 0.5 mile to River Road on the right.*

11.0 *Turn right and go 3 miles to Old Road, which bears right at a traffic island. (Signs may also say RIVER ROAD and FORE ROAD.)*
This is a delightful ride along the Piscataqua River, with New Hampshire on the opposite shore. You'll have good views of the arched bridge that carries I-95 across the river.

14.0 *Bear right on Old Road and go 0.7 mile to the end (merge right on ME 103).*

The lovely Eliot town green is on your left just before the end. Notice the handsome fieldstone library with a pillared portico on the left at the head of the green.

14.7 *Bear slightly right on ME 103 and go 0.5 mile to Moses Gerrish Farmer Road (still ME 103) on the right.*

You'll pass the town hall, an attractive wooden building on the right set back from the road, behind the fire station.

15.2 *Turn right on Moses Gerrish Farmer Road (still ME 103) and go 1.5 miles to Pleasant Street, which bears right. The sign may also say FERNALDS DRIVE.*

You'll pass a Baha'i school on the right, tucked off the road in a cluster of old buildings. The Baha'i faith, founded in Persia in 1863, emphasizes the spiritual unity of all mankind.

16.7 *Turn right on Pleasant Street and go 0.8 mile to a crossroads (ME 103 again, Main Street) and stop sign.*

There's a pizza shop on your left as soon as you turn. Some smaller roads branch off Pleasant Street, but stay on the main road.

17.5 *Bear right on ME 103 and go 1 mile to the end (Dennett Road), at a stop sign.*

18.5 *Bear right (still ME 103). Just ahead you'll go under a bridge. Just beyond the bridge, bear right at the traffic island (still ME 103) and stay on the main road for 0.25 mile to the end, at the stop sign.*

19.0 *Bear left (still ME 103, the most jagged road in Maine) and go 0.1 mile to the fork where Government Street bears slightly right uphill.*

19.1 *Bear right and go 0.2 mile to US 1, at the traffic light.*

19.3 *Go straight for 0.4 mile to another light, in downtown Kittery.*

At the traffic light, the Portsmouth Naval Shipyard is to your right, across the bridge.

19.7 *Continue straight at the light onto ME 103, passing the Victorian library on the right. Go 0.2 mile to Whipple Road on the right.*

19.9 *Turn right (still ME 103) and go 0.25 mile to the crossroads and stop sign.*

20.1 *Bear right at the crossroads (still ME 103, of course) and go 0.8 mile to Old Ferry Lane, a narrow lane that bears slightly right downhill.*

You'll pass a red wooden Victorian schoolhouse, built in 1873, on the left.

20.9 *Bear right on Old Ferry Lane and go 0.2 mile to the end.*

21.1 *Turn left and go 0.1 mile to the end (ME 103 again).*

21.2 *Turn right and go 1.8 miles to the fork where ME 103 curves left and Chauncey Creek Road, a smaller road, bears right.*

At the top of the hill past the bridge over Spruce Creek (a tidal inlet) is Maine's oldest church, built in 1730, on the left, with its graveyard facing it across the road.

Just 0.3 mile ahead you'll come to Fort McClary on the right. This is a small octagonal blockhouse mounted on a base of massive granite blocks, built in 1808 and 1809. Behind it is a fine view of Portsmouth Harbor, with the town of New Castle, New Hampshire, on the far side.

About 0.4 mile past the fort is Frisbee's Market, owned by the same family since 1828. Behind the store, in its original building, is Cap'n Simeon's Galley, a great lunch spot with a superb view of the harbor.

23.0 *Bear right on Chauncey Creek Road and go 0.9 mile to the second left, Cutts Island Lane. It's a sharp left up a steep hill.*

Here the loop route turns left, but if you continue straight for 0.6 mile to a fork and bear right, Seapoint Beach, a small unspoiled crescent, is just ahead. Beyond Seapoint Beach is Crescent Beach, equally unspoiled.

23.9 *Make a sharp left on Cutts Island Lane and go 0.3 mile to the end (ME 103 again).*

24.2 *Turn right and go 2.3 miles to a fork where ME 103 curves left and Brave Boat Harbor Road goes straight ahead, uphill.*

26.5 *Go straight on Brave Boat Harbor Road for 0.8 mile to the point where the main road turns left at a traffic island and a dead end road goes straight.*

Here the loop route turns left, but if you go straight there's a lovely ride along the harbor for 0.5 mile.

27.3 Turn left at the traffic island and go 0.1 mile to the diagonal crossroads (ME 103).

27.4 Bear right on ME 103 and go 1 mile to the end (US 1A).

Immediately after the bridge over the York River, notice the small footbridge on your left. A footpath meanders along the riverbank on the far side of the footbridge.

28.4 Turn left onto US 1A and go 0.5 mile to the parking lot on your right.

You're back in York Village. Rick's All Season Restaurant, on the right just before the lot, is a good place to eat. The red gambrel-roofed building opposite the entrance to the parking lot is the Old Gaol.

Final mileage: 28.9

Bicycle Repair Services

Berger's Bike Shop, 241 York Street, York Village (363-4070)

Bicycle Bob's, 990 Lafayette Road, Portsmouth, NH (603-431-3040)

Peddler's Bicycle Shop, 1 Cate Street, Portsmouth, NH (603-436-0660)

Gus's International Bicycle Shop, US 1, North Hampton, NH (603-964-5445)

P.J. Gallagher's, 181 Lafayette Road, North Hampton, NH (603-431-7990)

Philbrick's Seacoast Sports, 181 Lafayette Road, North Hampton, NH (603-964-5581)

Stratham Hill Bicycle, 240 Portsmouth Avenue, Stratham, NH (603-778-8180)

2

The Southern Beaches: York–Ogunquit

Distance: *27 miles*
Terrain: *Gently rolling, with two short hills.*
Special features: *Long Sands Beach, Short Sands Beach, Cape Neddick Light, Perkins Cove, Marginal Way*
Caution: *Shore Road, between York Beach and Ogunquit, is very narrow, very winding, and heavily traveled on beach days. When this road is busy, it is difficult for traffic to pass a bicycle without either risking a head-on collision or squeezing the bicycle off the road. Please take this ride in the early morning or during the off-season.*

The coastline between York and Ogunquit, about 10 to 15 miles north of Kittery, is the most southerly of Maine's major beach areas. Long Sands Beach and Ogunquit Beach are long and straight, stretching for several miles along the shore. Between the beaches are rockbound coves and headlands where cliffs and ledges plunge to the sea. Cape Neddick Light, Perkins Cove, and Marginal Way, a dramatic oceanfront footpath, are as scenic as any spots in Maine, and are fine examples of the images that spring to mind when you think of "the Maine coast." In contrast, only 3 miles inland lies a completely different landscape of woods, ponds, soft green farms, and lonely country roads that hardly ever see a tourist. The three towns of York Harbor, York Beach, and Ogunquit have an early-20th-century ambience; Ogunquit also boasts about a dozen art galleries and an excellent museum of American art.

Unless you specifically wish to go to the beach on a hot day, the ride is infinitely more enjoyable when the beaches are not in use. During the off-season, or early on summer mornings, you can gaze calmly at the broad sweep of Long Sands Beach without dodging car doors as they open into your path, and you can enjoy the charm of Perkins Cove without

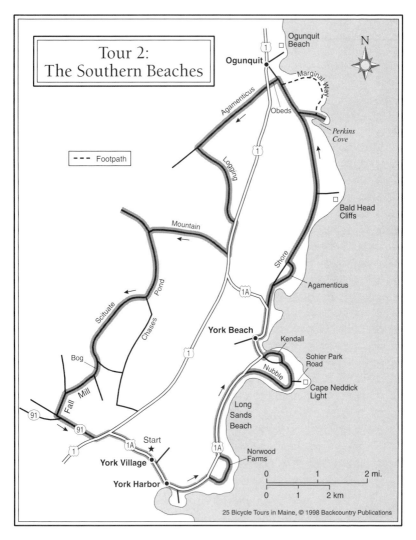

Tour 2:
The Southern Beaches

- - - Footpath

25 Bicycle Tours in Maine, © 1998 Backcountry Publications

jockeying your bike through hordes of tourists. Shore Road, a delightful ride when not busy, will be nearly deserted, and when you arrive at Ogunquit you won't have to ride in the gutter because of the mile-long line of cars inching its way to the beach.

If you decide to go to the beach, brace yourself: the water is cold. Not just brisk or chilly or invigorating, but frigid, arctic, the temperature at which beer should be served. If you throw an ice cube into the ocean, it's a wonder that it melts. Even on a 90-degree day, only a hardy few will actually be swimming. I've always been somewhat mystified that people go to the Maine beaches at all. It's fortunate that they do, otherwise the traffic to Cape Cod would back up all the way to Boston.

Directions for the ride

Start from the parking lot next to the town hall on US 1A in York Village. There is usually room at the back of the lot, near the cemetery. If the lot is full, there is another lot across the road in the York Village Historic District (entrance on Lindsey Road). To get there see the York-Eliot-Kittery ride (Tour 1).

0.0 *Turn left out of the parking lot onto US 1A.*

The York Village Historic District is opposite the town hall (see the York-Eliot-Kittery ride for more detail). It's worth visiting after the ride.

After 1 mile, US 1A curves left and Harbor Beach Road bears right. Here the route stays on US 1A, but if you bear right and go 100 yards you'll come to a small beach cupped between two headlands. The elegant Stage Neck Inn commands the headland on your right. The community just before the intersection is York Harbor.

1.0 *Continue on US 1A for 0.6 mile to Norwood Farms Road on the right. It's shortly after a handsome stone church on your left.*

1.6 *Turn right. After 0.3 mile, the main road curves sharply left. Continue for 0.6 mile to the end (US 1A again).*

2.5 *Turn right and go 2.2 miles to Nubble Road (unmarked), which bears right uphill. A sign points to Nubble Light.*

Caution: Watch for car doors opening into your path. The road hugs Long Sands Beach. On the left is an endless, congested row of beach houses. Cape Neddick rises ahead and to the right.

4.7 *Bear right on Nubble Road, which heads out to Cape Neddick. After 0.5 mile the main road bears right, following the ocean.*

Cape Neddick Light, York (also called Nubble Light), was built in 1873.

Continue on the main road for 0.4 mile to a fork where Sohier Park Road bears right.

Handsome cedar-shingled houses perch on the low bluff over-looking the sea.

5.6 *Bear right on Sohier Park Road and go 0.1 mile to the dead end and Cape Neddick Light.*

The lighthouse, also called Nubble Light, stands dramatically above a craggy ledge separated from the mainland by a narrow channel. Attached to the lighthouse is the white keeper's residence, and a small red outbuilding adds to the charm of this spot. The lighthouse was built in 1873.

5.7 *From the lighthouse, backtrack 0.1 mile to the main road.*

5.8 *Turn right and go 0.6 mile to Kendall Road on the right. It's immediately after Fort Hill Avenue on your right.*

6.4 *Turn right and go 0.5 mile to the stop sign at US IA (unmarked).*

Caution: There is a steep, curving descent shortly after you turn.

This is a beautiful narrow lane, with the rocky shore on the right and elegant wooden summer homes on the left.

6.9 *Turn right at the stop sign, following the ocean on your right, and go 0.3 mile to the end (US IA), in the center of York Beach. US IA turns right here.*

The road follows Short Sands Beach. Across from it is Ocean House, a rambling Victorian resort hotel. York Beach is cluttered with shops and snack bars: my favorite is the Goldenrod, a landmark since the turn of the century.

At the end of this road the ride turns right, but if you turn left and go 0.1 mile you'll come to York's Wild Kingdom, a combination zoo and amusement park.

7.2 *Turn right on US IA and go 0.6 mile to a fork where US IA bears left and Shore Road goes straight.*

7.8 *Go straight on Shore Road for 0.6 mile to Agamenticus Avenue, which bears right as you start to go uphill.*

8.4 *Bear right and go 0.6 mile to the end (Shore Road again).*

Agamenticus Avenue loops close to the coast, passing gracious wood and stone houses.

9.0 *Turn right on Shore Road and go 3.8 miles to a small road that turns sharply right at a stop sign and a traffic island. The main road curves left here. A sign in the traffic island says* TO PERKINS COVE.

After 1.8 miles you'll see a graceful stone Episcopal church on the right at the top of a hill. Immediately after the church a road on the right leads 0.4 mile to Bald Head Cliffs, which rise vertically from the ocean to a height of about 60 feet. The Cliff House, a sprawling old resort, stretches along the top of the cliff.

The Ogunquit Museum of American Art is on your right about 1.5 miles beyond the road to the Cliff House.

12.8 *Turn sharply right at the stop sign and go 0.3 mile to the tip of the small peninsula bordering Perkins Cove.*

Perkins Cove is a small inlet that is clogged with boats, spanned by a tall footbridge, and lined with a dense cluster of weathered fishing shacks that now house craft shops, restaurants, galleries, and artists' studios. Although commercial, the cove is picturesque, especially when it is not clogged with pedestrians and traffic.

A visit to Ogunquit is not complete without a stroll along Marginal Way, the mile-long footpath that hugs the rocky coastline from Perkins Cove almost to the center of town. Halfway down the road to the Cove, just before the narrow neck of land, the path begins on the left from the back of the parking lot. Lock your bike near the parking lot and savor the walk.

13.1 *From Perkins Cove, backtrack 0.3 mile to Shore Road.*

13.4 *Bear right and go 0.6 mile to Obeds Lane, a narrow lane on the left immediately before the Seacastles Resort on the left.*

Shortly before the intersection, notice the elegant fieldstone library, built in 1897, on the left.

The loop route turns left on Obeds Lane, but if you'd like to visit Ogunquit Beach, continue straight for 0.25 mile to the main square, turn 90 degrees right, and go 0.25 mile to the beach.

Einstein's, wedged into the triangle where Shore Road merges into US 1, is a good lunch spot that serves genuine bagels (a great biking food) slathered with cream cheese.

14.0 *Turn left on Obeds Lane and go 0.3 mile to US 1, at the traffic light.*

14.3 *Cross US 1 onto Agamenticus Road (**Caution** here). Go 1.9 miles to Logging Road, which turns left down a steep little hill.*

As soon as you cross US 1, the traffic disappears. Agamenticus Road, and the next few roads on the ride, are winding and wooded.

16.2 *Turn left and go 1.8 miles to the end (US 1).*

18.0 *Turn right and go 0.5 mile to Mountain Road on the right.*

18.5 *Turn right and go 1.5 miles to the end (Mountain Road on the right; Chases Pond Road on the left).*

You'll cross over the Maine Turnpike just before the end.

20.0 *Turn left on Chases Pond Road and go 1.3 miles to a fork where Scituate Road bears right.*

At the fork, Chases Pond is on the right.

21.3 *Bear right, following the pond, and go 2 miles to another fork where Bog Road bears right.*

You'll see Scituate Pond on the right 0.5 mile before the fork.

23.3 *Bear right and go 0.25 mile to another fork where Fall Mill Road (unmarked) bears right. You reach this intersection as you're going downhill.*

23.6 *Bear right on Fall Mill Road and go 0.5 mile to the end, at the stop sign.*

24.1 *Turn left (still Fall Mill Road) and go 0.5 mile to the end. You'll climb a short steep hill.*

24.6 *Turn left, and immediately merge head-on into ME 91 South. Go straight for 1 mile to the end (US 1), at the stop sign.*

You'll enjoy an exhilarating downhill ride through farmland to an inlet, part of the York River.

25.6 *Turn left on US 1 and go 0.3 mile to US 1A, which bears right.*

25.9 *Bear right, and stay on the main road for 0.8 mile to the parking lot on your left. It's just past the handsome granite library and the splendid First Parish Church on your left.*

The York Village Historic District is across the road from the parking lot. The large red gambrel-roofed building next to the graveyard is the Old Gaol, built in 1719. It serves as the museum for the historic area.

Final mileage: 26.7

Bicycle Repair Services

Berger's Bike Shop, 241 York Street, York Village (363-4070)

Bicycle Factory Outlet, US 1, Ogunquit (646-6642)

Bikes by the Sea, 315 Main Street, Ogunquit (646-5898)

Breton's Bike Shop, ME 9B, Wells (646-4255)

Wheels & Waves, US 1, Wells (646-5774)

3

Kennebunk–Kennebunkport

Distance: *24 miles*
Terrain: *Fairly flat with one short, steep hill.*
Special features: *Fine architecture in Kennebunk and Kennebunkport, Dock Square in Kennebunkport, George Bush's summer home, beaches and rocky coast, Seashore Trolley Museum.*
Caution: *During the summer, traffic along the coast is very heavy, especially in Dock Square and on Ocean Avenue, a narrow, curving road where it is difficult for a car to pass a bicycle safely. The best time to ride is early morning or during the off-season.*

The Kennebunk region, about midway between Kittery and Portland, contains a charming mixture of broad sandy beaches, rock-rimmed coves and headlands, and resort towns graced with 19th-century mansions and elegant beachfront hotels. During the summer, the coastal areas are jammed with traffic and pedestrians, but in the off-season they are refreshingly deserted. Just inland from the ocean, secondary roads abound that are relatively traffic-free even during midsummer.

The ride starts from Kennebunk, a small town that stretches from its traditional brick downtown area on US 1 to the ocean about 4 miles southeast. In the center of town is the Brick Store Museum, a cluster of 19th-century mercantile buildings with exhibits of local history and the decorative arts. As you pedal east out of town on ME 35, you'll pass gracious homes from the Federal and Victorian eras, many topped with cupolas and widow's walks.

A secondary road leads from the edge of town to the ocean and then follows the shore along Kennebunk Beach, passing rambling cedar-shingled homes overlooking the water and also the Narragansett, an enormous Victorian hotel that now houses condominiums. This road suddenly turns

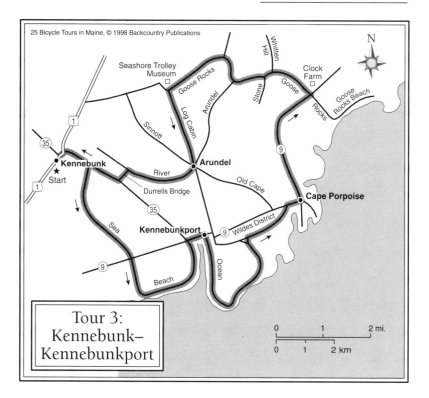

25 Bicycle Tours in Maine, © 1998 Backcountry Publications

N

Seashore Trolley
Museum

Goose Rocks

Whitten Hill

Clock
Farm

Goose Rocks Beach

Arundel

Stone

Goose

Rocks

Log Cabin

Sinnott

1

35

Kennebunk

★ Start

1

River

Arundel

Durrells Bridge

Old Cape

9

35

Sea

Kennebunkport

9

Wildes District

Cape Porpoise

9

Ocean

Beach

Tour 3:
Kennebunk–
Kennebunkport

0   1   2 mi.

0   1   2 km

inland along the Kennebunk River into Kennebunkport.

Kennebunkport is a lively, congested tourist mecca that is more attractive than most because it has not been despoiled by sterile new buildings, cutesy reproductions, tacky fast-food joints, or shantytowns of little beach cottages. The focal point of Kennebunkport is Dock Square, a compact nest of boutiques, antiques shops, galleries, and small restaurants, all in original 18th- and 19th-century buildings. Within several blocks of the square are numerous fine homes, many of which are now inns, built during the early 1800s by prosperous merchants and shipbuilders.

The route heads south and then east from Dock Square along famed Ocean Avenue, which follows the east bank of the Kennebunk River for a short distance to its mouth and then hugs the open sea past rocky coves and headlands. The road passes several large summer hotels from the Victorian era that maintain their turn-of-the-century elegance and

Kennebunkport is noted for its Victorian architecture.

dozens of smaller inns housed in charming old buildings with wide porches and bay windows. Kennebunkport boasts the largest concentration of traditional inns and resort hotels in New England.

From Ocean Avenue it's a mile and a half to Cape Porpoise, an attractive village that is partly a summer colony and partly a fishing port, rimming a small harbor lined with docks and weathered fishermen's sheds. Beyond, the route turns inland on tranquil wooded roads with very little traffic.

After several miles you'll come to the Seashore Trolley Museum, which maintains a collection of trolleys and antique buses from around the world. It also has a comprehensive bookstore relating to the history of trolleys and railroads. Admission to the museum includes a 20-minute ride on one of several trolleys that have been maintained in operating condition, complete with a conductor in period costume. The museum runs entirely on volunteer effort.

From the trolley museum, it's 2 miles to the small crossroads village of Arundel, where you can stop at the Cape-Able Bike Shop, and another 3 miles back to Kennebunk. About a mile before the end you'll pass the town's best-known landmark, the Wedding Cake House. This architectural curiosity, built during the 1820s, is a yellow mansion that is encased to the point of grotesqueness with ornate gingerbread trim. According to legend, the house was built by a sea captain who was called to duty during his wedding reception, before he could present the wedding cake to his bride. When he returned, he added the scrollwork to make up for his untimely departure.

Note: The route passes George Bush's summer home on Ocean Avenue. In general, bicycles are allowed to go through, even when the former president is in town. A security officer may tell you to proceed without stopping. However, the Secret Service may block the road at any time, for example when the former president is using the road or is outside the house. If this is the case, an alternative route is available.

Directions for the ride

Start from the free parking lot in the center of Kennebunk, on the west side of US 1. From the Maine Turnpike take exit 3. Turn left at the end of the exit ramp, and follow ME 35 for 1.7 miles to US 1, at a traffic light. Turn right and go 0.1 mile to the parking lot on your right, immediately after Bourne Street on your right.

0.0   Turn left on US 1, heading north, and go 0.1 mile to the traffic light (ME 35 on the left).

0.1   Continue straight for one block to another traffic light where ME 35 bears right.

The Brick Store Museum is on your right at the intersection.

0.2   Bear slightly right on ME 35 (Summer Street) and go 0.7 mile to Sea Road on the right, at a traffic light.

Notice the elegant homes along the road. The Taylor-Barry House, a Federal-style sea captain's mansion built in 1803 (at 24 Summer Street), is open to the public on weekday afternoons during the summer.

0.9   Turn right on Sea Road and go 2.4 miles to the traffic light (ME 9).

3.3   Continue straight for 2.8 miles to the traffic light (ME 9 again).

After about a mile the road curves left along the ocean and follows

Kennebunk Beach. After turning inland, you'll pass a Franciscan monastery on your right. It has an English Tudor main building, a vaulted stone shrine, and a footpath leading to the Kennebunk River.

6.1 **Turn right on ME 9 and go 0.3 mile to Dock Square, just after the bridge.**

Caution: The metal-grate bridge is very slippery when wet. It's safest to walk your bike on the sidewalk and enjoy the view, pedestrian traffic permitting.

In Dock Square the ride turns right, but it's worth exploring the immediate area to appreciate its fine architecture. Just beyond the square is White Columns, a splendid Greek Revival mansion with its original furnishings, and the graceful Congregational Church at the end of a side street. In Dock Square itself, the Book Port is a wonderful old bookstore where you can browse for hours.

6.4 **In Dock Square turn right on Ocean Avenue, following the river on your right, and go 3.6 miles to a road that bears right as you start to climb a steep, very short hill. If Ocean Avenue is blocked off in front of George Bush's summer home (after about 1.5 miles), backtrack to Dock Square. Turn right, and follow ME 9 about 2 miles to Cape Porpoise, where ME 9 turns left. (ME 9 jogs right and then left just past Dock Square.) Resume with mile 11.4. Caution: ME 9 is busy and fairly narrow.**

As soon as you turn onto Ocean Avenue, the side streets on the left are lined with handsome houses. After several blocks, you'll pass the finest of all, the Captain Lord Mansion, set back about 100 yards from the road at the head of a large lawn. It's a yellow Federal-style building, now an inn, with an octagonal cupola.

A mile from the square are two grand Victorian hotels, the Colony and the Breakwater. A short distance beyond, notice the fieldstone Episcopal church on the right, perched on the rocky shore. Shortly after the church is Walker Point; the road to it is blocked with RESTRICTED ACCESS signs and a gatehouse. On the point is the summer estate of former President George Bush. (For a lighthearted account of the former president's presence in

Kennebunkport, see *Bush Country, By George,* by Thistle McTavish and Allan Swenson. Portland, Maine: Guy Gannett Publishing Company, 1981. Unfortunately, it's out of print.)

Shortly before the intersection, a side road turns sharply right to the Shawmut Inn, another Victorian classic. Just ahead, notice the small stone church on the left.

10.0 *Bear right and go 50 yards to the end, turn right, and go 1.2 miles to the end, at the stop sign (merge right on ME 9).*

11.2 *Bear right on ME 9 (don't turn 90 degrees right). Go 0.2 mile to the intersection where ME 9 East turns left and a smaller road goes straight, in Cape Porpoise.*

Bradbury Brothers Market, on your right at the intersection, is a wonderful old-fashioned country store. Here the loop route turns left on ME 9, but if you either go straight or turn right and go 0.7 mile you'll hug the picturesque harbor. There's a seafood snack bar at the end of the road that goes straight.

11.4 *Turn left on ME 9 East and go 2.9 miles to a crossroads at Goose Rocks Road.*

On the far left corner is the Clock Farm, an unusual house with a clock tower above the barn.

Side Trip: Here the ride turns left, but if you turn right and go about a mile you'll come to Goose Rocks Beach, an attractive spot with the ocean on one side of the road and old wooden summer houses on the other. The beach is uncrowded because parking is very limited.

14.3 *Turn left at the crossroads and go 1.3 miles to a fork where Stone Road bears left. Ignore Whitten Hill Road on the right 0.2 mile before the fork.*

15.6 *Bear right and go 0.7 mile to another fork where Arundel Road bears left and the main road bears right.*

16.3 *Bear right and go 0.5 mile to another fork.*

16.8 *Bear left and go 1.5 miles to the end.*

The Seashore Trolley Museum is on your right at the intersection, about 100 yards down the road.

18.3 Turn left at the end (if you visited the museum, turn left when you leave it) and go 2 miles to a five-way intersection.

This is the village of Arundel. The Cape-Able Bike Shop is a sharp left at the intersection, 100 yards behind the church.

20.3 Bear right opposite the cemetery, passing a country store on your left. (Don't turn 90 degrees right opposite the church on Sinnott Road.) Go 1.5 miles to Durrells Bridge Road on your left, at a stop sign.

21.8 Turn left and go 0.3 mile to the end (merge right on Routes 9A and 35).

You'll cross the Kennebunk River.

22.1 Bear right and go 1.6 miles to the second traffic light (US 1).

The Wedding Cake House is on the right after 0.5 mile.

23.7 Bear left at the light on US 1. Just ahead is another light. Continue straight for 0.1 mile to the parking lot on your right.

Final mileage: 23.9

Bicycle Repair Services

Cape-Able Bike Shop, Arundel Road, Kennebunkport (967-4382)

Sanford-N-Sun, 480 Main Street, Sanford (324-1381)

Goodrich's Bicycle Shop, 111 School Street, Sanford (324-1381)

Quinn's Bike and Fitness, 140 Elm Street (US 1), Biddeford (284-4632)

Bicycle Habitat, 294 Main Street, Saco (283-2453)

4

Lighthouse Loop: Scarborough–Cape Elizabeth–South Portland

Distance: 31 miles (36 with side trip to Prouts Neck)
Terrain: Fairly flat, with two moderate hills.
Special features: Lighthouses, Crescent Beach, views of the Portland skyline.

The square peninsula that juts east from the Scarborough River to Cape Elizabeth, immediately south of Portland, provides pleasant and relaxed bicycling. The shoreline contains a varied mixture of salt marshes, gently curving beaches, craggy headlands, and busy port areas. Most of the region is suburban with well-spaced houses, landscaped grounds, and tree-lined streets. Even in South Portland, the most urban part of the region, the route follows residential side streets without much traffic. Along the southern and southwestern fringes, the suburban areas become almost rural, with tracts of woodland, expanses of farmland, and large estates that sweep down to the water's edge.

The ride starts from Scarborough, a large township that extends from the rural farmland west of the Maine Turnpike to the ocean. As you head south toward the coast, you'll skirt the vast salt marshes surrounding the mouth of the Scarborough River. A side trip leads down the beach-lined promontory to Prouts Neck, a staid, private enclave where the well-to-do have summered for years. The route heads east to Cape Elizabeth, passing gentleman farms, country estates, and Crescent Beach State Park, which is the closest good beach to Portland.

In Cape Elizabeth the shoreline turns abruptly north and changes in character from flat and sandy to rugged and rocky. Cape Elizabeth is a wealthy community that commands most of the eastern shore of the peninsula, with fine houses and two picturesque lighthouses perched on

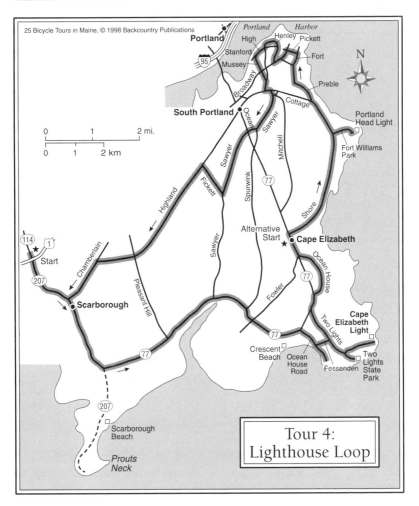

Tour 4:
Lighthouse Loop

the ledges above the ocean. Commanding the high headland where the coastline turns from east to north is Two Lights State Park, formerly a gun emplacement during World War II, with dramatic views and footpaths along the cliff tops. Just north of the park, at the peninsula's most easterly point, is Cape Elizabeth Light. Four miles north, guarding a spectacular rocky promontory, stands Portland Head Light, my favorite lighthouse in Maine. With its splendid setting in a large park, it is hard to believe that it is only 4 miles from Portland. The graceful white tower, built in 1791, is connected to a handsome keeper's dwelling (now a museum) with a peaked maroon roof. On windy days, the waves crash with dramatic force against the adjoining ledges.

From Portland Head Light it's only 3 miles to Portland Harbor, at the northern tip of the peninsula in South Portland. From the shore are good views of the Portland skyline on the opposite shore. The return trip to Scarborough heads southwest on quiet side streets and then along secondary roads through a mostly wooded area.

Directions for the ride

Start from Burger King in Scarborough, at the junction of US 1 and ME 114, about 5 miles south of the bridge between Portland and South Portland.

From the Maine Turnpike, take the Scarborough exit (exit 4). Continue past the toll booth and go 1.5 miles to US 1, at a traffic light. Turn left and go 1.4 miles to Burger King on your left.

If you're heading south on I-290, take exit 2 toward Scarborough, and stay on the main road for 3 miles to Burger King on your right.

An alternative starting point is the IGA supermarket on ME 77 in Cape Elizabeth, 4 miles south of the Million Dollar Bridge between Portland and South Portland. Starting from here shortens the ride by 2.6 miles, eliminating the section of ME 207 between US 1 and Chamberlain Road. Directions for the ride starting from Cape Elizabeth are at the end of this tour (see page 52).

0.0 *Turn left out of the parking lot onto ME 114, and just ahead cross US 1 at the traffic light onto ME 207. (**Caution** here: this is a very busy intersection.) Stay on the main road for 3 miles to ME 77 (Spurwink Road) on your left.*

Side Trip: The loop route turns left on ME 77, but to visit Prouts Neck, continue straight for 2.6 miles until the road becomes private, and backtrack to ME 77 on your right. You'll skirt Maine's largest salt marsh on the right and Scarborough Beach on the left. At the tip of the peninsula the road hugs the ocean, passing the Black Point Inn, a classic Victorian resort hotel.

3.1 *Turn left on ME 77 (right if you're coming from Prouts Neck)*

Portland Head Light, Cape Elizabeth, is Maine's first
lighthouse. The tower was built in 1791.

*and go 5.4 miles to Ocean House Road on the right. It's just
after Ocean Avenue and a small snack bar on the right.*

This stretch is pleasantly rural, lined with bucolic farms, well-
tended fields, and woodlots.

After about 3.5 miles, notice Sprague Hall, an old wooden
Grange hall, on the right at the corner of Fowler Road. Crescent
Beach State Park will be on your right a mile farther on.

8.5 *Turn right on Ocean House Road and immediately curve left,
following the main road. Go 0.7 mile to the dead end.*

This is an inspiring ride along the rocky shore to Kettle Cove, a
tiny beach hemmed in by outcroppings, with a grassy ribbon
between the road and the beach.

9.2 *From the dead end, backtrack 0.25 mile to Fessenden Road,
the first right.*

9.5 *Turn right and go 0.25 mile to the end, at the stop sign (merge right).*

9.7 *Bear right and go 0.3 mile to a fork (the sign says* TWO LIGHTS STATE PARK).

The route will explore both branches of the fork.

10.0 *Bear right and go 0.3 mile to the parking lot at the end. After exploring the park, backtrack to the fork.*

The park has dramatic views from the headland that are worth seeing. There is a small fee for bikes.

10.6 *Take a sharp right, following the other branch of the fork, and go 0.7 mile to the dead end.*

There's a snack bar here, open in warm weather. You can walk out onto the rocky ledges of the small peninsula; Cape Elizabeth Light is to the left, on the other side of the cove.

11.3 *At the dead end, make a U-turn and go 1.6 miles to the end, at a stop sign (merge right on ME 77).*

There's a hill heading away from the peninsula. You can see a second lighthouse on your right after less than 0.2 mile. It has been restored and is privately owned.

12.9 *Bear right and go 0.3 mile to Old Ocean House Road on the right, opposite a small cemetery.*

13.2 *Turn right and go 1.3 miles to a crossroads and a stop sign (ME 77 again).*

This is upper-crust suburbia, with gentleman farms and shorefront estates at the end of long driveways.

14.5 *Turn right and go 0.4 mile to the traffic light (Shore Road on the right).*

You'll pass the Cape Elizabeth town hall, a simple wooden building, on the right. There's a snack bar in the small shopping center on the left.

14.9 *Turn right on Shore Road and go 2.4 miles to the main entrance to Fort Williams Park on the right (a sign points to Portland Head Light).*

This is a pleasant ride with some views of the ocean, passing more fine houses.

17.3 *Turn right into the park and go 0.5 mile to Portland Head Light on the left, and backtrack to Shore Road.*

Fort Williams was founded in 1873 to defend Casco Bay and remained an active military base until 1964, when it became a city park.

18.3 *Turn right on Shore Road and go 0.8 mile to Preble Street, which bears right immediately before a gas station on your right.*

The road passes seaside estates.

19.1 *Bear right on Preble Street and go 0.5 mile to the end, where you merge right at a stop sign. Pillsbury Street, unmarked, is on your left at the intersection.*

You are now in South Portland.

19.6 *Bear right (still Preble Street) and go 0.3 mile to a fork where Fort Road bears right. It's a block after Beach Street, which also bears right.*

19.9 *Bear right on Fort Road and go 0.2 mile to Pickett Street on your left, at a stop sign (dead end if you go straight).*

Here the ride turns left, but just beyond the intersection is Southern Maine Technical College, a cluster of buildings overlooking Casco Bay. A footpath along the shore provides good views of the bay and its islands. The road continues 0.25 mile to the Spring Point Lighthouse and Museum at the tip of the peninsula. Next to the museum are the remains of Fort Preble, which was originally built in 1808, and later expanded and modernized several times through World War II.

20.1 *Make a left on Pickett Street and go less than 0.2 mile to a crossroads (Broadway) and stop sign.*

20.3 *Turn left and go 0.4 mile to Stanford Street on the right.*

20.7 *Turn right, and just ahead curve right on the main road (Henley Street). Continue for 0.8 mile to a crossroads (High Street, unmarked) and a stop sign.*

You'll go along Portland Harbor, with views of downtown Portland on the opposite shore.

21.6 *Turn right on High Street and go 0.25 mile to Mussey Street, which bears left at the stop sign.*

There's a Coast Guard station on the right at the intersection.

21.8 *Bear left on Mussey Street and go 0.3 mile to a traffic light (Broadway, unmarked).*

After 0.2 mile you'll cross the South Portland Greenbelt, a short bikeway that follows an abandoned railroad. If you turn right on the bikeway and go 0.3 mile you'll come to an unobstructed view of the Portland skyline across Mill Cove. (The bike trail continues west for about another mile, running parallel with Broadway, but it is less scenic).

22.1 *Continue straight for 0.3 mile to the end (merge right opposite a cemetery).*

22.4 *Bear right and go one block to the end (Cottage Road, unmarked).*

22.5 *Turn left and go one block to Mitchell Road, which bears right.*

22.5 *Bear right, passing the brick church on the left, and go 0.1 mile to the crossroads (Sawyer Street) and a stop sign.*

22.6 *Turn right and go 0.7 mile to the intersection where Spurwink Avenue goes straight and Sawyer Street turns right uphill.*

23.3 *Turn right (still Sawyer Street) and go 0.25 mile to the traffic light (ME 77, Ocean Street).*

23.5 *Continue straight and go 0.4 mile to a fork where Stillman Street bears right and the main road bears slightly left.*

23.9 *Bear slightly left and go 1.1 miles to the end (Sawyer Road on your left, Fickett Street on your right).*

The landscape thins out pleasantly.

25.0 *Turn right (uphill) and go 0.8 mile to the end. You are now in Scarborough.*

25.8 *Turn left and go 2.2 miles to the crossroads (Pleasant Hill Road) and a stop sign.*

28.0 *Continue straight for 0.8 mile to the end, at the stop sign (Chamberlain Road).*

28.8 Turn left and go 1 mile to the end (ME 207, Black Point Road).

29.8 Turn right and go 1.2 miles to US 1, at the traffic light.

Burger King is on the far right side of the intersection. **Caution** crossing US 1.

Final mileage: 31.0.

Directions for the ride: Cape Elizabeth start

Start at the IGA on ME 77 in Cape Elizabeth.

0.0 Turn left out of the parking lot and go 0.2 mile to the traffic light (Shore Road is on the right).

0.2 Follow the route from mile 14.9 through the directions for mile 28.8 (ME 207, Black Point Road).

15.1 Turn left on ME 207 and go 1.7 miles to ME 77 (Spurwink Road) on the left.

For **Side Trip** to Prouts Neck, see mile 0.1.

16.8 Follow the route from mile 3.1 through the directions for mile 13.2 (ME 77).

28.2 Bear right on ME 77 and go 0.2 mile to the IGA on the left.

Final mileage: 28.4

Bicycle Repair Services

Allspeed Bicycle & Ski, 1041 Washington Avenue, Portland (878-8741)

Back Bay Bicycle, 333 Forest Avenue, Portland (773-6906)

Bicycle Habitat, 240 Main Street, Saco (283-2453)

Charlie's Bicycle Repair, 14 Spring Street, Scarborough (883-6894)

Cycle Mania, 59 Federal Street, Portland (774-2933)

Ernie's Cycle Shop, 105 Conant Street, Westbrook (854-4090)

Gearheads, 84 Warren Avenue, Westbrook (854-6243)

Haggett's Cycle Shop, 34 Vannah Avenue, Portland (773-5117)

Joe Jones Ski & Sports, 456 Payne Road, Scarborough (885-5635)

New England Mountain Bike, Falmouth Shopping Center, Falmouth (781-4882)

Quinn's Bike & Fitness, 140 Elm Street (US 1), Biddeford (284-4632)

Rodgers Ski & Sport, 332 US 1, Scarborough (883-3669)

Seger's Cycle, 865 Bridgeton Road, Westbrook (854-5108)

Yarmouth Bicycle Shop, 49 Main Street, Yarmouth (846-1555)

5
Freeport–Brunswick
(or Brunswick–Freeport)

Distance: *33 miles (22 omitting South Freeport loop, 11 omitting Brunswick loop)*
Terrain: *Rolling, with several short steep hills.*
Special features: *L.L. Bean, Desert of Maine, harbor at South Freeport, Bowdoin College.*

The area between Freeport and Brunswick is superb for bicycling, with a network of back roads winding along the Harraseeket River (a tidal inlet) and Maquoit Bay and through rich farmland just north of the coast. Thousands of motorists speed between the two communities on I-95 or US 1, unaware of the serene country roads just a couple of miles to the south.

The ride starts from Freeport, a town about 15 miles northeast of Portland. Freeport is virtually synonymous with L.L. Bean, the camping–outdoor life–sporting goods–clothing store that is the most-visited man-made attraction in Maine. L.L. Bean is legendary for merchandise that is practical, of good quality, fairly priced, and that comes with a money-back guarantee. Stories abound of customers returning items several weeks or even months after purchase and receiving a refund with no questions asked. Besides functional, comfortable clothing, the store also carries an excellent selection of bicycles, cycling accessories, and bicycle clothing.

From Freeport, the route heads inland briefly to one of the state's more unusual natural attractions, the Desert of Maine. It is comprised of long strips of rippled sand, about a tenth of a mile wide, surrounded by pine trees. This desert, still growing, is the result of poor farming practices that depleted the topsoil and uncovered the sand underneath, which drifted and spread until it buried entire trees.

54

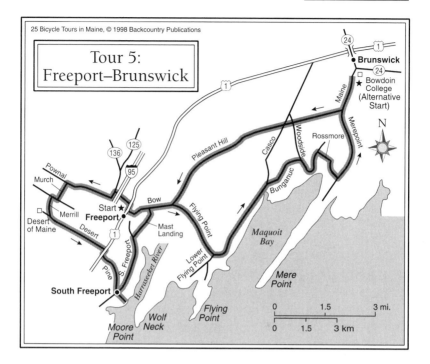

25 Bicycle Tours in Maine, © 1998 Backcountry Publications

Tour 5:
Freeport–Brunswick

From the Desert of Maine, it's not far to the coast at South Freeport, a charming fishing port on the Harraseeket River, which is actually a small bay. The ride follows narrow back roads that run close to the water, passing through haystack-dotted fields that slope gently to the shore. The tour heads inland for about 3 miles into Brunswick, which marks the beginning of the midcoast area. North and east of Brunswick, the coast becomes much more jagged, with a succession of peninsulas, sub-peninsulas, and countless coves and inlets until Penobscot Bay.

Brunswick (the alternative starting point) is the epitome of the gracious New England college town, and the first of the handsome coastal communities that grace US 1 about every 10 miles until Searsport, about 75 miles up the coast. The focal point of Brunswick is Bowdoin College with its lovely campus shaded with elm trees. Bowdoin is home to two excellent museums: the Bowdoin College Museum of Art and the Peary-MacMillan Arctic Museum. Robert Peary, the first person to reach the North Pole (in 1909) was a Bowdoin graduate, as was his chief assistant, Donald MacMillan. Next to the campus stands the splendid, cross-shaped

First Parish Church, which was built in 1846 in Gothic style. Downtown Brunswick, with an unusually wide main street, is just north of the college and the church. Adjacent to the downtown area are numerous fine homes from the early 19th century, including the Harriet Beecher Stowe House, where the author wrote *Uncle Tom's Cabin* between 1850 and 1852.

From Brunswick, it's about 9 miles back to Freeport. Most of this section follows Pleasant Hill Road, a quiet secondary road that runs parallel to US 1, passing through broad expanses of farmland.

Directions for the ride: Freeport start

Start from—where else?—L.L. Bean, on the north side of US 1 in the center of town. If the parking lot is full, there are more lots on the south side of US 1. Directions for the ride starting from Brunswick are at the end of this tour (see page 59).

The first part of the ride encompasses the western loop, which visits the Desert of Maine and South Freeport. You can shorten the ride to 22 miles by omitting this loop. If you wish to do so, start by heading east on Bow Street, which is directly opposite L.L. Bean. Go 1.5 miles to a fork where Pleasant Hill Road bears left. Pick up the tour at mile 12.0.

0.0 *Turn left out of the parking lot, heading east on US 1, and go 0.3 mile to ME 125 on the left, at a blinking light (a sign says TO INTERSTATE 95).*

0.3 *Turn left and go 0.6 mile to the end (ME 125 turns right).*

0.9 *Turn left and go 1.7 miles to Murch Road on the left.*
You'll pass the Pine Tree Academy, a Seventh-Day Adventist school.

2.6 *Turn left and go 0.6 mile to the end (Hunter Road, unmarked).*

3.2 *Turn right and go 0.2 mile to the first left, Merrill Road. You'll reach this intersection while you're going downhill.*

3.4 *Turn left and go 0.5 mile to the end, at a stop sign (merge left on Desert Road).*

3.9 *Make a sharp right and go 0.3 mile to the Desert of Maine at the dead end.*

4.2 *From the Desert of Maine, follow Desert Road for 2.2 miles to US 1, just past the I-95 interchange.*

The road goes through farmland with grazing horses and cows, up and down several short hills.

6.4 *Turn right on US 1 and go 100 yards to Pine Street on the left.*

6.4 *Turn left onto Pine Street and go 1.4 miles to a crossroads (South Freeport Road, unmarked) and a stop sign.*

Caution: Be careful when turning left from US 1, which is very busy. There are two short, steep hills on Pine Street. When you get to the crossroads, there is a grocery on the right. This is South Freeport.

7.8 *Continue straight for 0.4 mile to the dead end, passing gracious homes.*

At the end is a picturesque dock and the Harraseeket Lunch and Lobster Company, a great spot for a snack, with excellent homemade pies.

8.2 *From the dock, backtrack 0.4 mile to South Freeport Road at the second stop sign.*

8.6 *Turn right and go 1.5 miles to Mast Landing Road (unmarked) on the right, just after a bridge over a little inlet. A sign says* TO PORTERS LANDING.

10.1 *Turn right and go 1.2 miles to the end.*

At the end, the loop route turns right, but you can shorten the ride to 11 miles by turning left and riding 0.8 mile to the end (US 1), opposite L.L. Bean.

11.3 *Turn right and go 0.7 mile to a fork where Pleasant Hill Road bears left.*

12.0 *Bear right at the fork (a sign says* TO WOLF NECK WOODS STATE PARK*). Go 2.1 miles to another fork where Lower Flying Point Road turns right and Flying Point Road (unmarked) curves left.*

This stretch has several short, steep ups and downs.

Side Trip: After 0.8 mile, Wolf Neck Road on the right leads about 3 miles to Wolf Neck Woods State Park, a scenic preserve with hiking trails at the tip of the peninsula.

14.1 *Curve left on Flying Point Road and go 2.8 miles to a fork just*

Hay bales dot a field sloping down to Maquoit Bay, Brunswick.

beyond the top of a steep hill. (Casco Road bears left and Bunganuc Road bears right.)

This is a lovely road, winding through broad fields with views of the bay in the distance.

16.9 *Bear right at the fork and go 1.3 miles to the end (Woodside Road), at the stop sign.*

18.2 *Turn right and go 1.3 miles to Rossmore Road on the right.*

Again the road passes through large fields that slope gently down to the bay.

19.5 *Turn right on Rossmore Road and go 1.1 miles to the end.*

You'll pass a marker on the left indicating the site of the home of Matthew Thornton, a signer of the Declaration of Independence.

20.6 *Turn left and go 3.3 miles to Bowdoin College on the right.*

The Art Museum has its own building; the Arctic Museum is in Hubbard Hall. Opposite the far end of the campus is Bowdoin Pines, a stately grove. The snack bar in Moulton Union is a good lunch spot.

23.9 *From the college, backtrack 1 mile to Pleasant Hill Road on your right. It's just after the hospital on your left.*

24.9 *Turn right and go 1.8 miles to a diagonal crossroads (Casco Road) at a yield sign.*

The land quickly becomes rural, with large tracts of farmland.

26.7 *Continue straight for 4.4 miles to the end (merge right at a yield sign).*

This section is rolling, with several short hills. You'll pass an old cemetery with weathered headstones on the right.

31.1 *Bear right and go 1.6 miles to the end (US 1), opposite L.L. Bean.*

After 0.6 mile, a small road that goes uphill is on your right. If you turn onto it, the Mast Landing Audubon Sanctuary is just ahead on the right. The 150-acre preserve has foot trails through woods and fields and along a small tidal river.

There's a tough hill about 0.25 mile long just before Freeport.

Final mileage: 32.7

Directions for the ride: Brunswick start

Start from Maine Street, which borders Bowdoin College on the west side of the campus.

0.0 *Head south on Maine Street, with the college on your left, and go 1 mile to Pleasant Hill Road on your right. It's just after the hospital on your left.*

1.0 *Follow the ride from mile 24.9 to the end, opposite L.L. Bean.*

At this point you can shorten the ride to 22 miles, omitting the eastern loop past the Desert of Maine and South Freeport, by backtracking on Bow Street for 1.5 miles to the fork where Pleasant Hill Road bears left, and resuming the tour at mile 12.0.

8.7 *Turn right on US 1 (left if you visited L.L. Bean). Go 0.3 mile to ME 125 on the left, at a blinking light (a sign says TO INTERSTATE 95).*

9.0 *Follow the tour from mile 0.3 to the college.*

Final mileage: 32.7

Bicycle Repair Services

L.L. Bean, US 1, Freeport (865-4761)

National Ski & Bike, US 1, Freeport (865-0523)

Center Street Cycles, 11 Center Street, Brunswick (729-5309)

New England Mountain Bike, Falmouth Shopping Center, Falmouth (781-4882)

Yarmouth Bicycle Shop, 49 Main Street, Yarmouth (846-1555)

THE MIDCOAST REGION

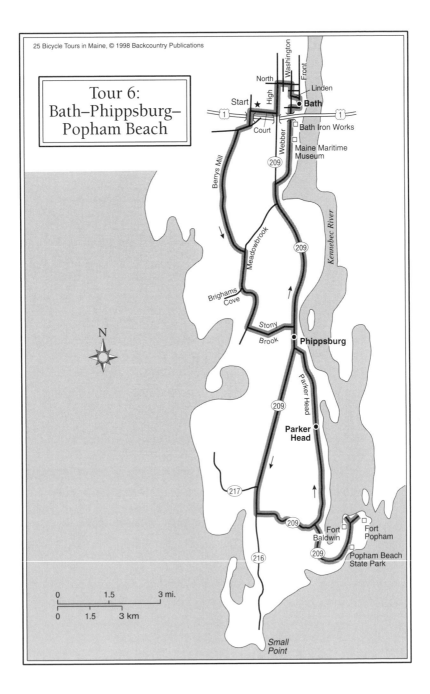

25 Bicycle Tours in Maine, © 1998 Backcountry Publications

Tour 6:
Bath–Phippsburg–
Popham Beach

Washington
Front
North
Linden
Start
High
Bath
1
1
Court
Bath Iron Works
Webber
Maine Maritime
Museum
209
Berrys Mill
209
Kennebec River
Meadowbrook
Brighams
Cove
Stony
Brook
Phippsburg
Parker Head
209
**Parker
Head**
217
209
Fort
Baldwin
Fort
Popham
209
Popham Beach
State Park
216

N

0   1.5   3 mi.
0   1.5   3 km

*Small
Point*

6

Bath–Phippsburg–Popham Beach

Distance: 36 miles (16 omitting the Popham Beach Loop)
Terrain: Rolling, with several short, steep hills.
Special features: Popham Beach State Park, Fort Popham, Fort Baldwin, Maine Maritime Museum, elegant sea captains' homes in Bath.
Caution: On hot weekends, traffic on ME 209 heading to and from Popham Beach is very heavy. It's best to take this ride when it's not a beach day, or during the week.

The peninsula extending from Bath south to Small Point is the third of the nine peninsulas that characterize the midcoast region between Brunswick and Penobscot Bay, and this peninsula is the most westerly in the book. Most of the landscape consists of low, forested hills interspersed with a few small farms. The broad tidal estuary of the Kennebec River flows along the eastern edge of the peninsula. Narrow secondary roads run parallel to ME 209, the main north-south road, enabling the cyclist to complete two short loops between Bath and Popham Beach with very little backtracking. The short ride on this tour consists of the northern loop only.

The ride starts from the western edge of Bath, a small city boasting many gracious 19th-century homes, a handsome downtown area, and the superb Maine Maritime Museum. Bath blossomed into a thriving shipbuilding center and seaport during the mid-1800s, and the well-maintained houses of successful sea captains and merchants are testimony to the city's prosperous history. Shipbuilding still dominates Bath's economy at the massive Bath Iron Works, where large naval vessels and submarines are constructed. The tall crane at the Iron Works can be seen all over the city. You'll explore Bath at the end of the ride.

From Bath, the route quickly enters rural, wooded countryside. The first few miles on secondary roads snaking down the center of the penin-sula are the hilliest. After about 8 miles you'll arrive at the eastern shore in the little fishing village of Phippsburg. The route now heads north, running parallel to the Kennebec River back to Bath.

The long ride continues south, looping around the southern half of the peninsula. The southern tip, Small Point, is not on the route because it is an out-and-back trip of several miles each way, with limited views of the ocean. On the southern shore you'll come to Popham Beach State Park, one of Maine's most attractive coastal areas, with a broad, sandy beach unmarred by cottages and condominiums. Just past the beach, at the eastern tip of the peninsula, are two forts, Fort Popham and Fort Baldwin. The latter, commanding the top of a hill, provides an inspiring view. Next to the forts is the small summer community of Popham Beach, where you can take advantage of a good seafood restaurant. Heading north, the route follows a narrow lane, hugging the Kennebec River, to Phippsburg, where you'll rejoin the short ride.

Directions for the ride

Start from McDonald's, Bath Shopping Center, on the north side of US 1. If you're coming from the south on US 1, you can't turn left into McDonald's because the highway is divided. Take the exit for Western Avenue and Congress Avenue. Turn right at the end of the exit ramp, take your first right on Congress Avenue, and your first right again on Shopping Center Drive. McDonald's is at the far end of the shopping center.

0.0 *Leave the parking lot at its western end, farthest from McDonald's (don't get on US 1). Turn left at the end of the entrance road onto Congress Avenue and go 0.2 mile to the end.*

Congress Avenue crosses a bridge over US 1.

0.4 *Turn right and go 0.25 mile to Berrys Mill Road, which bears left.*

0.6 *Bear left and go 3.6 miles to the end (Campbells Pond Road, unmarked, on the left).*

This is a lovely narrow road winding through the woods, up and down several short steep hills.

4.2 *Turn right and go 1 mile to a fork where Brighams Cove Road bears right and the main road bears left.*

5.2 *Bear left and go 1.4 miles to an unmarked road on the left at the bottom of a hill.*

This is another narrow back road with a steep hill halfway along, and some shorter ups and downs.

6.6 *Turn left and go 1.7 miles to the end (ME 209).*

This is the toughest road on the ride, with two steep hills; but hang in there! The rest of the ride is much easier. When you come to ME 209, note the fine brick house on the corner.

Here the long ride turns right. To do the short ride, turn left on ME 209 and go 4.1 miles to Webber Avenue, which bears right. There's a grocery 0.5 mile before the intersection, just after a small bridge. Resume at mile 32.1. **Final mileage:** 16.4.

8.3 *Turn right on ME 209 and go 4.7 miles to the fork where ME 217 bears right.*

At the beginning of this section the road hugs the bay as it approaches the small village of Phippsburg.

13.0 *Bear left at the fork (still ME 209) and go 0.7 mile to the intersection where ME 209 turns left and ME 216 goes straight.*

13.7 *Turn left, staying on ME 209. After 3.3 miles, you'll pass the entrance to Popham Beach State Park on the right. Continue for 1.5 miles to the dead end.*

Shortly before the end is the small summer community of Popham Beach. Spinney's Restaurant, a reasonably priced eatery serving fresh seafood, is a great place for a halfway stop. At the end is Fort Popham, a semicircular granite fort that was begun in 1861 and never completed. It was designed to protect the mouth of the Kennebec River during the Civil War.

18.5 *From Fort Popham, backtrack 0.4 mile to Fort Baldwin Road, a narrow lane on the right. The main road curves left at the intersection.*

18.9 *Make a sharp right and go 0.2 mile to the end of the paved road.*

Fort Popham commands the tip of a peninsula in Phippsburg.

Walk your bike another few hundred yards along the series of batteries and embankments that comprise Fort Baldwin. The views are superb. At the very top of the hill is a lookout tower with the best view of all. The fort was built between 1905 and 1912 and manned during World Wars I and II.

This was also the site of the Popham Colony, which in 1607 was the first English colony north of Virginia. After a year the settlers became discouraged, built the first ship in the New World, and sailed back to England.

19.2 *Backtrack to the main road.*

19.5 *Bear right on ME 209 and go 2.7 miles to the point where ME 209 curves 90 degrees left and a smaller road is on the right.*

22.2 *Turn right on the smaller road and go 5.1 miles to the end, where you'll merge right on ME 209.*

The lovely narrow road winds along the Kennebec River, bobbing up and down small hills, to the unspoiled fishing village of Parker Head. You'll pass an old cemetery and several handsome wooden houses, and ride through Phippsburg at the end. When you come to the end, notice the Phippsburg Public Library, a small wooden building built in 1923. There's also a grocery at the intersection.

27.3 *Bear right on ME 209 and go 4.8 miles to Webber Avenue, which bears right.*

Hawks soared overhead while I was bicycling along this section. You will pass a general store about 0.5 mile before the intersection, just after a small bridge.

32.1 *Bear right on Webber Avenue and go 2.2 miles to the traffic light just past the endless Bath Iron Works, a green metallic building a quarter-mile long.*

You'll pass the Thomas Plant Memorial Home, an elegant, white home for the elderly overlooking the river. Further along is the fascinating Maine Maritime Museum, constructed on the site of a former shipyard. The museum has exhibits showing how the tall ships from the age of sail were constructed and an actual shop (called the Apprenticeshop) where craftsmen learn the trade of building small wooden boats. Immediately after the Iron Works, notice the fine wooden church on the left, contrasting with the industrial bleakness across the street.

At the traffic light, the road passes underneath US 1.

34.3 *Go straight at the light for one block to the next traffic light (Centre Street).*

Caution: There are diagonal railroad tracks at the beginning of this block. Please walk across them.

34.4 *Turn right and go 0.1 mile to the end, Front Street, at the top of the hill.*

The Bath City Hall, a graceful concrete building with a cupola, stands in front of you.

34.5 *Turn left and go 0.25 mile to Linden Street on the left, just past a small park.*

Front Street passes through the central business district, with proud redbrick buildings from the Victorian era on both sides of the street. In the 1970s, after a long period of neglect, the downtown area was refurbished to its original luster.

34.7 *Turn left on Linden Street and go one block to the end (Washington Street).*

Notice the yellow-brick library on the left and the Gothic-style church across the street, built in 1844.

34.8 *Turn right and go 0.2 mile to the second crossroads (North Street, unmarked).*

You'll see an impressive 30-room sea captain's mansion on your right just before the intersection. It was built in 1844 in grand Federal style.

Washington Street boasts the largest concentration of Bath's elegant homes. You may want to cruise slowly down to US 1 and up to the far end of the street, admiring this showpiece of 19th-century architecture.

35.0 *Turn left and go 0.2 mile to the second crossroads (High Street), at a blinking light.*

35.2 *Turn left and go 0.5 mile to Court Street, a crossroads on the far side of the redbrick courthouse on the right.*

35.7 *Turn right onto Court Street and go 0.4 mile to the end. McDonald's is in front of you.*

Final mileage: 36.1

Bicycle Repair Services

Bath Cycle & Ski, US 1, Woolwich (442-7002)

7
Wiscasset–Head Tide–Newcastle–Sheepscot

Distance: *32 miles*
Terrain: *Rolling, with several short steep hills.*
Special features: *Fine architecture in Wiscasset, historic villages, idyllic rolling countryside, unique country store.*

Just north of US 1, between Wiscasset and Damariscotta, is an area that is ideal for bicycling. Vacationers clog ME 27 to get to and from Boothbay Harbor or speed through on US 1 itself, leaving the secondary roads to the north virtually untraveled. The region, though slightly inland, is still coastal in character, with tidal inlets, patches of salt marsh, and serene rolling countryside sloping to the Sheepscot and Damariscotta Rivers.

The ride starts from Wiscasset, an architectural jewel of a town about 45 miles northeast of Portland. The sign that says WELCOME TO WISCASSET, PRETTIEST VILLAGE IN MAINE greeting you as you enter the town from the south on US 1, does not exaggerate. Wiscasset is highlighted by a large number of elegant mansions gracing the hillside above the Sheepscot River. Most of them were built by wealthy merchants and sea captains during the early- and middle-19th century, during Maine's heyday as a shipbuilding center and seaport. One of the more unusual mansions is the Musical Wonder House, a Greek Revival house with a collection of antique music boxes, player pianos, and other mechanical musical instruments. Two other mansions worth visiting, both built in 1807, are Castle Tucker, renowned for its graceful elliptical staircase, and the Nickels-Sortwell House, a superb Federal-style residence.

From Wiscasset, the route heads north on quiet back roads, through rolling farmland with sturdy old barns, to the historic village of Head Tide. This is a small, well-preserved 19th-century community on the National Register of Historic Places, best known as the birthplace of poet Edward Arlington Robinson in 1869.

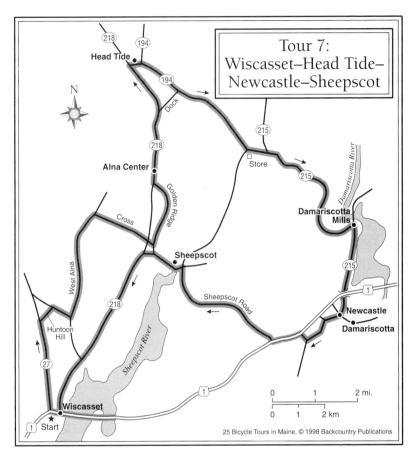

Tour 7:
Wiscasset–Head Tide–
Newcastle–Sheepscot

25 Bicycle Tours in Maine, © 1998 Backcountry Publications

From here, the route turns east to Damariscotta Mills, another pic-turesque village clinging to the steep hill above the Damariscotta River. On the way, a colorfully named country store is a good halfway stop.

You'll now head south, hugging the shore of Salt Bay, a wide tidal pool on the Damariscotta River that's a great spot to observe migrating shore birds. The route follows the bay and river to Newcastle (and its twin town of Damariscotta, just off the route), and curves west through idyllic rolling farm country to Sheepscot, another meticulously preserved 19th-century village. The final section of the ride follows the Sheepscot River back to Wiscasset, passing handsome white houses perched on the hill above the river.

Directions for the ride

Start from the Lincoln County Courthouse, US 1, Wiscasset. It's on the south side of US 1, immediately east of ME 27. The courthouse is a handsome brick structure built in 1824.

0.0 *Turn left out of the parking lot and immediately turn right on ME 27. Go 2 miles to Huntoon Hill Road on the right, at the top of the hill (sign says TO HUNTOON HILL GRANGE).*

It's a steady but gentle climb out of Wiscasset.

2.0 *Turn right and go 0.5 mile to the end.*

2.5 *Turn right and go 0.6 mile to the end.*

This is a flying downhill run.

3.1 *Turn left and go 2.6 miles to Cross Road on the right.*

It's your first right, and it comes up suddenly as you start to go down a hill. You'll pass the Wiscasset Speedway, a small oval track, shortly after you turn.

5.7 *Turn right and go 1.3 miles to a crossroads (ME 218).*

You'll pass Sheepscot Station, a replica of the original train station built in 1895, on your left just before the intersection. In front of the station is a squat little locomotive built in 1902. This is the type of engine used in mines, shipyards, and other heavy industries during the early part of the century.

When you come to ME 218 the route goes straight, but you can shorten the ride to 12 miles by turning right on ME 218 for 4.6 miles to US 1, and right for 0.2 mile to the courthouse on the left.

7.0 *Go straight for 0.1 mile to the first left, Golden Ridge Road.*

7.1 *Turn left and go 1.7 miles to the end (merge right on ME 218).*

This is a lovely narrow road, ascending onto a ridge with fine views, followed by a long downhill run.

Caution: Watch for sandy spots on the descent.

8.8 *Bear right on ME 218 and go 1.4 miles to a fork (ME 218 bears left).*

There's a store at the fork. Just after you merge onto ME 218, you will see a lovely little schoolhouse with a bell tower on your left,

71

built in 1795, and a green-shuttered meetinghouse, built in 1789. This is Alna Center. Beyond, the road traverses a ridge with sweeping views.

10.2 *Bear left at the fork, staying on ME 218, and go 1.3 miles to an unmarked road at the bottom of a hill.*

11.5 *Turn right and go 0.25 mile to ME 194, which goes both to the left and straight ahead, in Head Tide.*

Just after you turn there's a small dam on the left. The pool above the dam is smothered with alewives during their spring spawning run. A path on the right leads up a short hill to a fine white church built in 1838.

11.7 *Go straight on ME 194 East for 3.2 miles to a small country store on the right, at an intersection.*

This corner has a rather earthy name, as stated on the store. This is a great halfway stop where you and your cycling companions can take pictures of each other, with the store in the background. Don't forget to buy a T-shirt.

14.9 *From the store, continue on ME 194. After 0.5 mile you'll merge head-on into ME 215. Continue straight for 3.7 miles to the end, at a yield sign at the bottom of a steep hill. ME 215 turns sharply right here.*

Caution: Watch for potholes on the descent. The village of Damariscotta Mills lies at the bottom of the hill. As you start to descend, notice the lovely Federal-era mansion on your left. Several smaller roads fork off the main road, but stay on ME 215.

19.1 *Make a sharp right (still ME 215) and go 2 miles to a crossroads and a stop sign, in the center of Newcastle. **Caution:** You encounter diagonal railroad tracks after 0.4 mile—walk across them.*

As soon as you turn, notice the weathered church on your right. The road hugs the shore of Salt Bay, bobbing up and down little hills. After going underneath US 1, you'll pass gracious homes and an old schoolhouse with a cupola that has been renovated into apartments.

At the crossroads, the large brick church on the left on the far

Sheepscot: a tranquil New England village tucked away from the bustle of Route 1

side of the intersection is the first Catholic church in Maine, built in 1808.

At the crossroads the ride goes straight, but if you turn left and go 0.2 mile you'll come to downtown Damariscotta (see the Damariscotta–Pemaquid Point ride, Tour 8, for more detail).

21.1 *Continue straight at the crossroads onto Business US 1. Go 0.2 mile to River Road, a smaller road that bears left as you start to go uphill.*

21.3 *Bear left and go 0.6 mile to the fork (a sign points right to US 1).*

The road follows the shore of the Damariscotta River.

21.9 *Bear right and go 0.2 mile to the end (US 1).*

22.1 *Turn left and go 0.8 mile to Sheepscot Road, which turns right up a short hill.*

22.9 *Turn right and go 3.1 miles to a crossroads as you come into Sheepscot. The main road turns left here.*

26.0 *Turn left and go 0.8 mile to a fork where the main road bears left.*

Sheepscot is a classic New England village tucked away from the bustle of US 1. Look for a map of the historic district just before the bridge over the river. There's a tough climb after the bridge.

26.8 *Bear left at the fork and go 0.25 mile to the end (ME 218).*

27.1 *Turn left and go 4.4 miles to US 1, at the stop sign, back in Wiscasset.*

About 0.5 mile before US 1, you'll pass the Lincoln County Museum and Old Jail on the left. The jail, with massive granite walls more than 3 feet thick, was built in 1837 and used until the 1950s.

When you come to US 1, the Nickels-Sortwell House is on your left, and a small sunken flower garden is on your right. The center of town is to your left on US 1.

31.5 *Turn right on US 1 and go 0.2 mile to the courthouse on the left.*

If you bear left after 100 yards onto High Street, the Musical Wonder House is just ahead, and Castle Tucker just beyond, opposite the end of the street.

Final mileage: 31.7

Bicycle Repair Services

Auclair Cycle & Ski, Boothbay House Hill, Boothbay Harbor (633-4303)

Bath Cycle & Ski, US 1, Woolwich (442-7002)

8
Damariscotta–Pemaquid Point–Round Pond

Distance: *40 miles*
Terrain: *Gently rolling, with several gradual hills and one very steep one.*
Special features: *Remains of a fort and colonial settlement, rock-bound Pemaquid Point, lighthouse, Fishermen's Museum.*

The Pemaquid Peninsula, extending from Damariscotta and Waldoboro south to Pemaquid Point, is the sixth of the nine fingers of land between Brunswick and Penobscot Bay. It's an enjoyable place for bicycling, with primarily gently rolling terrain and moderate traffic. Most tourists either don't get beyond Boothbay Harbor, on the next peninsula to the west, or they bypass the Pemaquid region by zipping along US 1 toward Bar Harbor.

The ride starts from Damariscotta, an attractive town at the head of the Damariscotta River, which is a long tidal inlet. In the center of town, handsome brick mercantile buildings from the late 19th century line both sides of the main street, which slopes upward to a graceful white church. In town is the Chapman-Hall House, a pre-Revolutionary dwelling built in 1753, with furnishings from the Colonial era and an herb garden.

From Damariscotta, the route follows the river along the western shore of the peninsula to Pemaquid Point, at the bottom. You'll have nice views of the river and some of the small coves that branch off it. On a small promontory about 3 miles north of the bottom are two adjacent historic sites, Fort William Henry and Colonial Pemaquid.

Fort William Henry, a round granite building, was built in 1692. It claimed to be the largest and strongest fort in North America, but was destroyed by the French four years later. The present structure is a replica.

Colonial Pemaquid is a collection of cellar holes from a small settlement going back to the early 1600s, including several dwellings, the

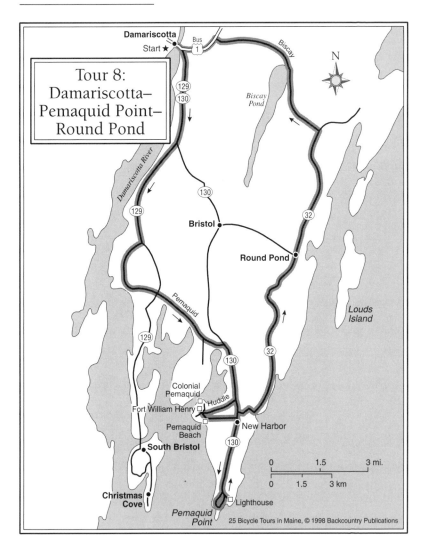

Tour 8:
Damariscotta–
Pemaquid Point–
Round Pond

25 Bicycle Tours in Maine, © 1998 Backcountry Publications

town hall, a tavern, forge, and stockade. It's surprising how small the houses were—only about 10 feet on each side. The other buildings aren't much bigger. Next to the cellar holes is a museum displaying a large collection of artifacts dug up from the site. If you're an archaeology buff, leave time to explore and enjoy yourself. For those less enthusiastic about artifacts, just south of the historic sites is sandy Pemaquid Beach.

Pemaquid Point is a splendid example of the tried-and-true phrase "rockbound coast of Maine." The surf crashes against windswept ledges of flat rocks, while pointed firs stand sentinel on the shore. Perched next to the rocks is the small, simple Pemaquid Point Light, built in 1824. It is connected to a white house that was originally the quarters of the lighthouse keeper and is now a museum of the fishing industry. Standing behind the lighthouse, on a clear day you can see Monhegan Island, 15 miles out to sea.

From Pemaquid Point, the route follows the eastern shore of the peninsula before cutting west back to Damariscotta. Two miles north of the point is the charming village of New Harbor, fronting on a small inlet smothered with lobster boats and sailing craft and docks piled high with neatly stacked lobster traps. About 7 miles up the coast is the unspoiled lobster port of Round Pond.

Directions for the ride

Start from the municipal parking lot on Business US 1 in the center of Damariscotta. It's on the south side of the road behind the brick business buildings, immediately east of the bridge connecting Damariscotta and Newcastle. Park in the blue-lined 8-hour parking spaces along the water.

0.0 *Turn right out of the parking lot onto Business US 1. Go 0.1 mile to ME 129 South, which bears right at the church at the top of the hill.*

0.1 *Bear right and go 3 miles to the fork where ME 129 bears right and ME 130 bears left.*

The road follows a ridge with views of the bay down below. It's a pleasant ride.

3.1 *Bear right on ME 129 and go 3.4 miles to an unmarked road on the right, shortly after a small church on the right. A sign says* TO DARLING MARINE CENTER.

Notice the apple orchard on the far corner. The road goes up and down some gentle hills, through a mixture of woods and farmland.

6.5 *Turn right on the unmarked road and go 2.8 miles to a crossroads (ME 129 again).*

77

The road dips down to a cove, and then climbs steeply up the toughest hill of the ride. You will come to the crossroads while going down a steep hill.

After 1 mile you'll pass the entrance to the Darling Marine Center, a research center run by the University of Maine. The extensive grounds (but not the laboratories) are open to the public.

Side Trip (about 14 miles): At the crossroads the loop route goes straight, but if you turn right on ME 129 you'll come to South Bristol and Christmas Cove, picturesque fishing and yachting villages at the tip of a smaller peninsula just west of the main one. After 5 miles you'll come to South Bristol, where the road crosses a small drawbridge. At the top of the tough hill after the bridge, turn right on West Side Road and go 1.4 miles, following the shore of Rutherford Island, to the end (ME 129 again). Turn right and go 1 mile to the dead end, going through Christmas Cove. At the point where the road forks into private dead-end roads, turn around and follow ME 129 for about 6.5 miles back to the loop route.

9.3 *Go straight at the crossroads (right if you visited Christmas Cove) for 2 miles to a fork where Pemaquid Harbor Road bears right and the main road curves left.*

You'll pass the Harrington Meeting House, a simple church built in 1772, containing exhibits of local history.

11.3 *Curve left at the fork and go 0.9 mile to the end (ME 130, Bristol Road).*

There's an old-fashioned country store on the right just before the end.

12.2 *Turn right on ME 130 and go 1.8 miles to Huddle Road on the right (a sign says TO COLONIAL PEMAQUID).*

There's a variety store on the right just before the intersection.

14.0 *Turn right and go 1.1 miles to a crossroads where Old Fort Road turns right and the main road turns left.*

Here the ride turns left, but to visit Fort William Henry and Colonial Pemaquid, turn right and immediately right again on the gravel road. The fort is just ahead on the left, and Colonial Pemaquid is 0.3 mile beyond the fort.

The sea crashes against rocky ledges near New Harbor.

15.1 *Turn left at the crossroads (straight if you visited the historic sites) and go 1 mile to the end (ME 130, Bristol Road), in New Harbor.*

Pemaquid Beach, the only sand beach on the peninsula, is on your right at the beginning of this stretch, set back from the road.

16.1 *Turn right on ME 130 and go 2.5 miles to a fork where ME 130 curves sharply left and a smaller road bears right.*

There's a sign for the Bradley Inn at the intersection.

18.6 *Bear right and go 0.9 mile to the end (ME 130 again).*

This is a lovely narrow road hugging the rocky coast at the extreme southern tip of the peninsula. You'll pass gracious homes and estates and get a view of Pemaquid Point Light across a small cove. At the end, the Hotel Pemaquid, an ornate Victorian classic, stands in front of you.

19.5 *Turn right and go 0.1 mile to the dead end, at the lighthouse and Fishermen's Museum.*

Spend some time exploring the ledges. The dark rocks are striped with narrow, light-colored bands.

19.6 *From the lighthouse, follow ME 130 for 2.9 miles to ME 32 on the right.*

Just before the intersection is the center of the lovely village of New Harbor, set back from the road on the right. An elegant cedar-shingled church fronts on the small green. There is also a grocery and snack bar.

22.5 *Turn right on ME 32 and go 6.5 miles to the village of Round Pond.*

Shortly after you turn onto ME 32, the road hugs the shore of New Harbor, a small inlet crammed with lobster craft, sailboats, and perhaps a tall-masted schooner.

Round Pond is an attractive lobster port with a grocery, big white houses, and a traditional New England church.

29.0 *Continue on ME 32 for 4.3 miles to Biscay Road on your left (a sign says* TO DAMARISCOTTA*).*

33.3 *Turn left and go 5.2 miles to the end (Business US 1). A McDonald's is on your left at the intersection.*

This is a smooth secondary road bobbing up and over short wooded hills. Halfway along you'll pass Biscay Pond on the left. The small beach here is a good spot for a swim before the end of the ride.

38.5 *Turn left on Business US 1 and go 1.2 miles to the parking lot on the left.*

Final mileage: 39.7

Bicycle Repair Services

Auclair Cycle & Ski, Boothbay House Hill, Boothbay Harbor (633-4303)

Bath Cycle & Ski, US 1, Woolwich (442-7002)

9

Wyeth Country:
Waldoboro–Friendship–Cushing

Distance: *33 miles (29 with shortcut)*
Terrain: *Rolling, with several short, steep hills and three long, steady ones.*
Special features: *Unspoiled coastal towns, bay views, side trip to the Olson House (scene of many paintings by Andrew Wyeth).*

Here is a tour of the peninsula pointing south between Waldoboro and Thomaston. This is a region that possesses the quiet charm of antique towns that are not commonly visited and the serenity of pastures of grazing horses and cows, silhouetted by tottering barns and old farmhouses. With the exception of US 1, the roads in the region are lightly traveled, because nearly all tourists heading up the coast stay on US 1 to Thomaston without venturing south.

The ride starts from Waldoboro and follows the western shore of the peninsula to Friendship, on one of the three sub-peninsulas that form its southern edge. The Friendship peninsula is the eighth and the chubbiest of the nine closely spaced promontories between Brunswick and Penobscot Bay. Its landscape is common to most of the midcoast region's peninsulas, with continuous short rolling hills and open ridges with views of the bay in the distance.

Waldoboro is a marvelous Victorian town that clings to the steep hillside rising from the east bank of the Medomak River. It is virtually unvisited because it is bypassed by US 1 a mile to the north. A short row of 19th-century brick buildings forms the business district. Friendship is an equally sleepy village with some gracious homes rimming the tip of the peninsula and a small harbor bobbing with sailing craft, lobster boats, and perhaps a couple of Friendship sloops. The latter, first built in

81

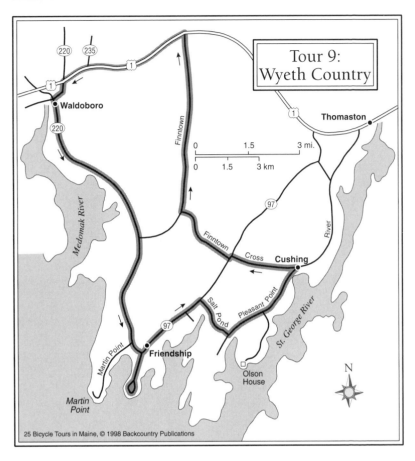

Tour 9:
Wyeth Country

25 Bicycle Tours in Maine, © 1998 Backcountry Publications

the town in the 1870s, are renowned for their seaworthiness, speed, and grace.

From Friendship you'll head halfway along the eastern shore of the peninsula, bordered by the broad St. George River, to Cushing. Cushing is a tiny hamlet with an old-fashioned general store and a few fishermen's houses surrounded by large fields undulating across the landscape. The community is best known as the locale of many of Andrew Wyeth's paintings, including his well-known work *Christina's World,* which portrays a woman lying on a broad, sloping field with a lonely house on the horizon. This dwelling, called the Olson House, is open to visitors Wednesday through Sunday. It is about 2 miles off the route.

The rest of the ride heads inland across the middle and then along the spine of the peninsula, climbing gradually onto a ridge with fine views and descending to South Pond. The last few miles follow US 1, which has a wide, smooth shoulder.

Directions for the ride

Start from the center of Waldoboro on ME 220, 0.6 mile south of US 1. There's a free parking lot with no time restrictions behind the brick commercial buildings on the west side of ME 220.

Moody's Diner, at the corner of US 1 and ME 220, is a great place to eat before or after the ride, and it's very reasonably priced. It's a classic wooden 1930s diner that has been a US 1 landmark for more than 50 years.

0.0   Head south on ME 220, passing the brick business buildings on your right. Go 9.4 miles to the end (ME 97), in Friendship, at the top of the steep hill.

At the beginning, behind the church on the right, notice the wooden Victorian factory with a cupola. As you head toward Friendship, the road ascends onto a ridge with fine views of the bay in the distance.

After 9 miles, at the intersection where Martin Point Road bears to the right, there's a one-room brick schoolhouse, built in 1857, that is now the Friendship Museum. It contains early local artifacts, marine exhibits, and material on the Friendship sloop.

Side Trip: Martin Point Road leads 2.6 miles to the tip of Martin Point. The road hugs the shore of Hatchet Cove, passing docks stacked with lobster traps, pine groves, and gracious homes nestled in the pines at the end of the peninsula.

9.4   Turn right at the end of ME 220 and go 0.9 mile to a fork where a smaller road, Davis Point Loop Road, bears right.

10.3   Bear right on the smaller road. After 0.6 mile the main road curves left uphill. Continue for 0.9 mile to the stop sign. You're back in Friendship.

You'll pass handsome shingled houses along the rim of the small peninsula just south of the center of town.

The Olson House in Cushing, the setting for many
of Andrew Wyeth's paintings

11.8 *Go straight onto ME 97 and go 2.7 miles to Salt Pond Road
on your right. It's 0.6 mile after Wadsworth Point Road on
your right.*

At the beginning you'll ride through the center of Friendship and
pass a small grocery. When you come to Salt Pond Road the ride
turns right, but you can cut 4.1 miles off the route by continuing
straight for 1.6 miles to Finntown Road on your left (it's immediately before Cross Road on your right). Turn left, go 2.2 miles to
the end, and resume with mile 22.4.

14.5 *Turn right on Salt Pond Road and go 1.4 miles to the end
(Pleasant Point Road).*

The road dips down to an inlet and then climbs a short, steep hill.

15.9 *Turn left and go 2.7 miles to the country store on your left, in
Cushing.*

Side Trip (1.9 miles each way): If you'd like to visit the Olson
House, turn right after 1.3 miles on Hathorne Point Road and go
1.9 miles to the house on your left, at the end of the paved road.
The terrain is very rolling.

The country store, a Maine classic, is a great halfway stop.

18.6 *Turn right as you leave the store, and just ahead go straight up the hill (don't curve left). Go 1.6 miles to the end (ME 97, Cushing Road).*

This section is very rolling, with several steep ups and downs through prosperous farmland.

20.2 *Jog left and immediately right on Finntown Road. Go 2.2 miles to the end.*

You'll pass a red, one-room schoolhouse on your right toward the end.

22.4 *Turn right and go 5.4 miles to the end (US 1).*

You'll climb gradually onto a ridge with a sweeping view, and see South Pond on your right near the end.

Caution: After about 5 miles, slow down for bumpy railroad tracks while you're going downhill.

27.8 *Turn left and go 4.3 miles to ME 220, at a blinking light. Moody's Diner is on your left at the intersection.*

This portion of US 1 has a wide, safe shoulder. You'll have two long climbs and a flying descent; the second climb is fairly steep.

32.1 *Turn left on ME 220 and go 0.6 mile to the crossroads where ME 220 turns left, in the center of Waldoboro.*

Caution: The descent into Waldoboro is very steep.

At the beginning, you'll pass the Waldoboro Historical Society Museum on the right. It contains a cluster of buildings, including an old barn, a one-room schoolhouse built in 1857, a cattle pound, and a turn-of-the-century farm kitchen. As you start down the long hill, notice the fine white church on the left. Just before the crossroads you'll see the small, yellow-brick library on your right.

Final mileage: 32.7

Bicycle Repair Services

Maine Sport Outfitters, US 1, Rockport (236-7120)

Fred's Bikes, Chestnut Street, Camden (236-6664)

Oggibike, 29 Mountain Street, Camden (236-3631)

10

Thomaston–Warren–Union–Cushing

Distance: *37 miles*
Terrain: *Rolling, with several short, steep hills.*
Special features: *Unspoiled old towns, beautiful rolling farmland, ponds nestled in valleys.*

As US 1 threads through the heart of the midcoast region near Thomaston, the back roads just to the north and south of it promise superb bicycling. The three small towns of Warren, Union, and Cushing seem hardly changed from the years between the world wars. Outside the towns, quiet secondary roads wind through prosperous rolling farmland and along several ponds with views of wooded hills in the distance.

The ride starts from Thomaston, a gracious coastal town. In the center of town are a graceful white church and a compact business block of three-story brick buildings, built at the turn of the century, which face each other across US 1. Elegant wooden Federal-era and Victorian houses, originally built by sea captains, grace US 1 on both sides of downtown. The most impressive house is Montpelier, a replica of the mansion built in 1794 for Henry Knox, the nation's first secretary of war. The Federal-style residence boasts a bowed front and a large, glassed-in widow's walk. In contrast, the Maine State Prison, at the west end of town, seems out of place.

From Thomaston you'll head northwest for several miles to Warren, a completely unspoiled Victorian town that clings to both sides of a steep, narrow valley. Although only a mile northeast of US 1, the center of town is virtually undiscovered by visitors because it lies along an unnumbered secondary road. The ride continues north toward Union through rich farmland and along Seven Tree Pond. Union is another museum-piece New England town perched on a hillside, built around a large, sloping green with a bandstand on one side and a monument on

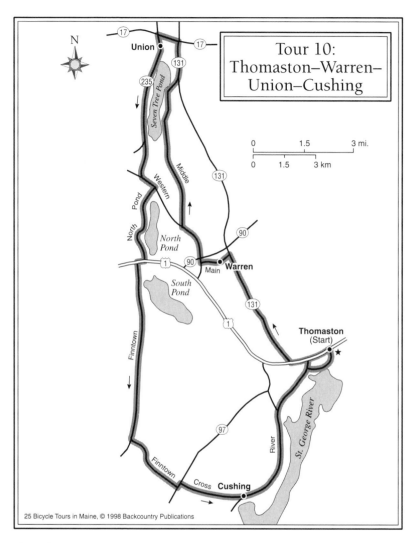

Tour 10:
Thomaston–Warren–
Union–Cushing

25 Bicycle Tours in Maine, © 1998 Backcountry Publications

the other. The town hosts a traditional agricultural fair in late August. The fascinating Matthews Museum of Maine Heritage, which features an extensive collection of early artifacts and crafts from the region, is next to the fairgrounds about a half mile off the route.

From Union you'll head south through idyllic rolling farmland, following the opposite shore of Seven Tree Pond and enjoying views of the Camden Hills across the water. You'll dip several miles south of US 1 to

Cushing, a tiny hamlet with an inviting country store and a few old houses. After leaving Cushing, you'll follow the St. George River, a tidal estuary between two peninsulas, for about 6 miles back to Thomaston.

Directions for the ride

Start from the municipal parking lot in the center of Thomaston, behind the business block on the north side of US 1.

0.0 *Turn right (west) on US 1 and go 1.1 miles to ME 131, which bears right.*

You'll pass the state prison on your left.

1.1 *Bear right on ME 131 and go 3.6 miles to Main Street on your left. It's immediately after Montgomery Avenue on your right. If you come to ME 90 you've gone 0.2 mile too far.*

ME 131 rolls up and down low ridges with good views.

4.7 *Turn left and go 0.9 mile to a fork with a monument in the middle.*

The road drops very steeply into Warren. Immediately after the bridge you pass an old wooden mill on your left. As you start to climb the short, steep hill out of Warren, notice the fine fieldstone library on the right and the two white churches farther on.

5.6 *Go straight at the fork (don't bear left) for 50 feet to the end, and then go right for 0.1 mile to the crossroads (ME 90) and a stop sign.*

5.7 *Continue straight for 1.4 miles to the second paved right, Middle Road. It's just past the top of a hill.*

7.1 *Turn right and go 4.4 miles to the end, at the top of the hill (merge left on ME 131).*

The road winds through rich farmland, rolling up and down several short steep hills. You'll see Seven Tree Pond on your left near the end.

11.5 *Bear left on ME 131 and go 1.2 miles to the crossroads (ME 17) and a stop sign.*

At the beginning, notice the small dam with a gorge at the bottom on the left.

12.7 *Turn left on ME 17 and go 0.7 mile to a crossroads (ME 235 on the left).*

A restaurant and convenience store are on the far side of the intersection.

13.4 *Turn left on ME 235 and go 0.25 mile to the Union town green, at a stop sign.*

Caution: The stop sign comes up suddenly while you're going downhill. Notice the large, wooden Masonic Temple on your left. On the right, a map on the green shows the town as it existed during the early 1800s.

Side Trip: Here the ride goes straight, but if you turn right and go 0.4 mile and then left on Fairgrounds Lane for 0.2 mile you'll come to the Matthews Museum of Maine Heritage.

13.6 *Continue straight on ME 235 and go 3.1 miles to a fork where the main road curves right and Western Road goes straight.*

The road follows Seven Tree Pond on your left, with views of the Camden Hills on your left. The best views are back over your left shoulder.

16.7 *Go straight onto Western Road for 1.8 miles to the second right, North Pond Road, which is unmarked. (The first right is a sharp right.)*

18.5 *Turn right and go 2.6 miles to the end (US 1, Atlantic Highway).*

The terrain is very rolling, with several short, steep hills with fine views from their summits. You'll see North Pond on your left.

21.1 *Turn right and go 0.1 mile to Finntown Road on your left.*

21.2 *Turn left and go 5.4 miles to the first paved left (still Finntown Road, unmarked here).*

You'll have two gradual climbs and descents as you pass through a mixture of woods and farmland. You'll see South Pond on your left at the beginning.

26.6 *Turn left and go 2.2 miles to the end (ME 97, Cushing Road).*

This section is mostly wooded. Look for a red, one-room schoolhouse on your left after 0.4 mile.

28.8 *Jog left and immediately right on Cross Road. Go 1.6 miles to a yield sign where you merge head-on into a larger road.*

This section is very rolling, with two steep hills each about 0.2 mile long.

30.4 *Go straight for 5.7 miles to Water Street on your right, immediately after the bridge over the St. George River.*

At the beginning, you'll ride through the hamlet of Cushing and pass the general store on your left. Beyond, the road winds through large farms with the St. George River in the distance. As you approach Thomaston you can see the prison to your left.

36.1 *Turn right and go 0.8 mile to the end at US 1, in the center of Thomaston. The parking lot is behind the business buildings in front of you.*

You'll climb gradually at first, following the harbor. You'll pass handsome white houses with dark shutters as the ride ends.

Final mileage: 36.9

Bicycle Repair Services

Maine Sport Outfitters, US 1, Rockport (236-7120)

Fred's Bikes, Chestnut Street, Camden (236-6664)

Oggibike, 29 Main Street, Camden (236-3631)

11
Lighthouses and Lobsters:
Thomaston–Port Clyde–Owls Head

Distance: *50 miles with Port Clyde loop; shorter loop: 30 miles*
Terrain: *Gently rolling, with a few moderate hills. This is one of the easier peninsula rides.*
Road surface: *0.4 mile of dirt road each way to Owls Head Light.*
Special features: *Historic mansion, Owls Head Transportation Museum, lighthouses.*

The peninsula extending from Thomaston and Rockland south to Port Clyde is the most easterly of the nine closely spaced fingers of land jabbing the coast between Brunswick and Penobscot Bay. North of Rockland the coastline suddenly smoothes out along the bay's western shore. Traffic on this ride is refreshingly light—much of it doesn't get beyond Boothbay Harbor, and many northbound travelers bypass Thomaston by shortcutting to Camden on ME 90.

Starting from Thomaston (see Tour 10 for more detail), the route heads south along the St. George River, passing large farms with views of the water in the distance. Just beyond the tiny community of St. George, the ride cuts east across the peninsula and then northeast along the opposite shore to the fishing village of Owls Head. A back road leads to Owls Head Light at the eastern tip, a spectacular spot with high, sheer cliffs rimmed by pines.

A worthwhile side trip, a little more than a mile off the route, is a visit to the Owls Head Transportation Museum, which has a collection of antique cars and airplanes. A unique feature of the museum is that many of the exhibits are kept in working order, with demonstrations given on weekends.

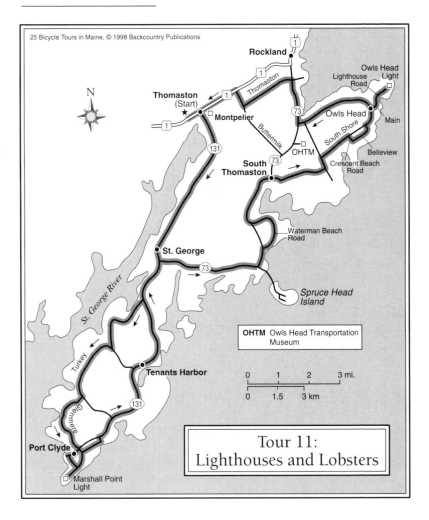

25 Bicycle Tours in Maine, © 1998 Backcountry Publications

OHTM Owls Head Transportation Museum

Tour 11:
Lighthouses and Lobsters

The longer ride continues south from St. George to Port Clyde, at the southern tip of the peninsula. Port Clyde is a classic Maine village, with rickety wharves perched on pilings, a small harbor filled with lobster boats, and stacks of lobster traps everywhere. The ferry to Monhegan Island, 11 miles out to sea, leaves from here. At the extreme tip is Marshall Point Light, a small white lighthouse next to a gambrel-roofed keeper's residence (the lighthouse is now automated).

From Port Clyde, the road winds north along the opposite shore of the peninsula to Tenants Harbor, another attractive lobster port. Smaller than Port Clyde, the compact village contains a simple white church, an old wooden schoolhouse, and a cluster of neat wooden houses with peaked roofs. The route continues north to St. George, where it rejoins the shorter ride.

Directions for the 50-mile ride

Start at the municipal parking lot in the center of Thomaston, behind the business block on the north side of US 1.

0.0 Turn left (east) on US 1 and go 0.6 mile to ME 131 on the right, at a traffic light.

Montpelier is on the far side of the intersection. The large industrial building in the distance is a cement plant.

0.6 Turn right on ME 131 and go 5.5 miles to ME 73 on the left. (Here the short ride turns left.)

There are good views of the bay across fields.

6.1 Go straight on ME 131 for 1.5 miles to a smaller road that bears right.

7.6 Bear right and go 2.5 miles to the end, at a stop sign. Here the road merges left, but you will turn sharply right.

This is a lovely narrow road with views of the bay.

10.1 Make a sharp right and go 2.2 miles to the first right, just after a small cove.

12.3 Turn right and go 2.3 miles to the crossroads (ME 131) and a stop sign in Port Clyde.

14.6 Turn right and go 0.3 mile to the dead end.

Just before the end are the Monhegan ferry terminal, an old general store, and an ice cream shop.

14.9 Backtrack 0.1 mile to the first right, at the top of the steep hill.

15.0 Turn right and go 0.4 mile to the end.

You'll follow Port Clyde Harbor at the beginning.

15.4 Turn right and go 0.6 mile to the dead end.

At the end, the road hugs the rocky coast to Marshall Point Light.

16.0 *At the lighthouse, make a U-turn and go 0.9 mile to the end of this road.*

16.9 *Turn right and go 1 mile to the end (ME 131).*

17.9 *Turn right and go 7.8 miles to ME 73 on the right.*

The road passes through Tenants Harbor, where there's a grocery.

25.7 *Turn right and go 3.5 miles to the point where ME 73 curves 90 degrees left and a smaller road goes straight.*

Side Trip: Here the loop route turns left, but if you go straight for 1.5 miles you'll come to Spruce Head Island. It's a lovely ride, hugging the coast, passing docks and weathered lobster sheds. Just before the end, turn right at Island Road at a stop sign and ride along the water. At the end of the paved road you'll see tiny Burnt Island, linked to Spruce Head by a private wooden bridge. On the return trip, go straight at the fork (don't bear left) back to ME 73.

29.2 *Turn left on ME 73 (right if you're coming from Spruce Head) and go 0.6 mile to Waterman Beach Road on the right, at the top of a short hill.*

29.8 *Turn right and go 1.9 miles to the end (ME 73).*

The narrow lane winds through a pastoral landscape of old barns and pastures of grazing cows and horses.

31.7 *Turn right and go 1.8 miles to the point where ME 73 turns left and a smaller road goes straight.*

There is a grocery on the corner. This is the village of South Thomaston.

33.5 *Go straight on the smaller road for 2.2 miles to the end (Ash Point Drive).*

You are now in Owls Head, where the road names are marked on tall square pillars.

35.7 *Turn left and go 0.4 mile to South Shore Drive on the right.*

36.1 *Turn right and go 1.1 miles to Crescent Beach Road on the right, as you start to climb a short hill.*

37.2 *Turn right and go 0.2 mile to the first left, Belleview Street.*

Marshall Point Light, Port Clyde

37.4 *Turn left and go 1.1 miles to the end (South Shore Drive again).*
You will pass gracious shingled homes overlooking the ocean.

38.5 *Turn right and go 0.7 mile to Main Street, which bears right at a grassy traffic island in the center of Owls Head.*

39.2 *Bear right and go 0.2 mile to Lighthouse Road on the left.*
Here the ride turns left, but if you go straight for 0.1 mile you'll come to the Owls Head dock.

39.4 *Turn left on Lighthouse Road. After 0.6 mile, the road turns to dirt. Go 0.4 mile to Owls Head Light.*

40.4 *From the lighthouse, backtrack 1 mile to Main Street.*

41.4 *Turn right and go 0.2 mile to the end, South Shore Drive.*

41.6 *Turn right and go 2.6 miles to ME 73.*
Side Trip: Here the ride turns right, but to go to the Transportation Museum, turn left on ME 73 and go 0.8 mile to the entrance road on the left. The museum is 0.5 mile down this road.

44.2 *Turn right on ME 73 and go 1.4 miles to a crossroads at railroad tracks. Crescent Street is on the right, and Thomaston Street is on the left.*

There is a grocery on the right just before the intersection.

45.6 *Turn left at the crossroads and go 1.9 miles to the end at Buttermilk Lane. **Caution:** Avoid the tracks as you turn left.*

The large building in the distance on your right is the cement plant that you saw at the beginning of the ride. You'll pass it later on the route.

47.5 *Turn right and go 0.5 mile to the end (US 1).*

48.0 *Turn left and go 2 miles to the center of Thomaston.*

The parking lot is behind the business block on the right.

Final mileage: 50.0

Directions for the 30-mile ride

0.0 *Follow the first two directions of the long ride, to the point where ME 73 turns left off ME 131.*

6.1 *Turn left on ME 73 and go 3.5 miles to the point where ME 73 curves 90 degrees left and a smaller road goes straight.*

For the side trip to Spruce Head Island, see mile 25.7 of long ride.

9.6 *Follow directions for the long ride from mile 29.2 to the end of the tour.*

Final mileage: 30.4

Bicycle Repair Services

Maine Sport Outfitters, US 1, Rockport (236-7120)

Fred's Bikes, Chestnut Street, Camden (236-6664)

Oggibike, 29 Mountain Street, Camden (236-3631)

12
Rockport–Camden

Distance: 27 miles
Terrain: Gently rolling, with several short, steep hills and two long, steady ones.
Road surface: 0.9 mile of dirt road, which can be avoided.
Special features: Picturesque harbors at Rockport and Camden, windjammer fleet, craft shops, Megunticook Lake, side trip to Mount Battie.

The Camden area, on the western shore of Penobscot Bay, about halfway between Portland and Acadia National Park, has a special appeal. Small harbors with sleek yachts and tall-masted sailing craft are framed by the wooded Camden Hills, which rise abruptly just behind the shore. Craft shops and galleries in 19th-century mercantile buildings line the streets fronting on the harbor. A few miles inland is Megunticook Lake, with its shoreline convoluted by an infinity of little coves and promontories, surrounded by green hills and meadows sloping to the water's edge.

The ride starts from Rockport, a quiet coastal town that is 2 miles south of Camden, its livelier and better-known neighbor. Tourists making the pilgrimage along US 1 have to seek Rockport out or know about it in advance, because one must leave the highway onto an unmarked side street to get to the town. Rockport's small, teardrop-shaped harbor is a gem, with a waterfront park and a boatbuilding school called the Artisans School (open to visitors) on the western shore. The idyllic Vesper Hill Chapel, set on a hilltop overlooking the bay, is about a mile outside of town.

From Rockport, you'll follow small roads that hug the shore of Penobscot Bay to Camden, a pearl on the necklace of the midcoast towns along US 1. In contrast to Rockport, Camden is packed with visitors to

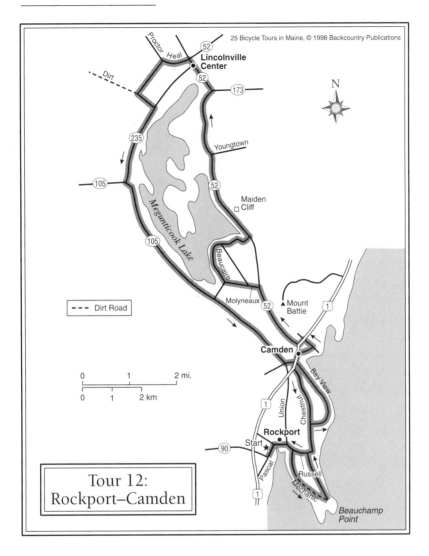

25 Bicycle Tours in Maine, © 1998 Backcountry Publications

Tour 12:
Rockport–Camden

the well-stocked craft shops, galleries, and restaurants lining the harbor. Camden's main street is US 1 itself, which means that nearly every vacationer heading up the coast stops in town. With its backdrop of rugged hills, Camden Harbor is unusually picturesque. Many of Maine's windjammers, the graceful schooners that take vacationers on week-long cruises up and down the coast, are based here. Camden is also host to one of Maine's fine summer theaters, the Camden Civic Theatre.

Although crowded, Camden is compact. The route heads inland away from the town on a secondary road, and within a half mile the traffic suddenly disappears. After about 3 miles, you'll come to Megunticook Lake and follow its shore, passing cozy waterfront cottages nestled in the pines. At the northern tip of the ride is the tiny village of Lincolnville Center, which consists of a few rambling old farmhouses and an old-fashioned country store. The route now turns south, paralleling the opposite shore of the lake back to Camden. Here you'll pick up a side road back to Rockport that runs along a hillside with views of the bay in the distance.

Directions for the ride

Start from the Rockport Baptist Church on Pascal Avenue, 0.2 mile east of US 1. Park on Pascal Avenue. If you're coming from the south or west, approach Rockport on ME 90. Cross US 1 and go 0.2 mile to the end (Pascal Avenue). Turn left, and the church is just ahead. If you're coming from the north, follow US 1 to ME 90 on the right, at a crossroads, 2 miles south of Camden. Turn left and go 0.2 mile to the end (Pascal Avenue). Turn left, and the church is just ahead.

0.0 *Head north on Pascal Avenue, with the church on the left and Rockport Harbor on the right. Go 0.2 mile to the end, on the far side of the bridge.*

From the bridge, there's a good view of the boat-filled harbor on the right.

0.2 *Turn right on the far side of the bridge and go 0.2 mile to the intersection at the top of the hill where Union Street turns left and Russell Avenue bears right.*

You'll go through the center of Rockport.

0.4 *Bear right and go 100 yards to Mechanic Street on your right.*

At this point the ride turns right and soon reaches a dirt stretch that is 0.9 mile long. If you want to avoid it (shortening the ride by 1.9 miles), continue straight for 0.9 mile to Bay View Street on your right, immediately after a cemetery on your right. Resume with mile 3.3.

0.5 Turn right on Mechanic Street. After 0.4 mile the road becomes dirt. Continue for 0.9 mile to where the road curves sharply left and becomes paved again.

Caution: The dirt section has some steep pitches where the surface may be loose.

1.8 Continue on the paved road for 0.9 mile to the end.

The Vesper Hill Chapel is on your left after 0.3 mile (turn left onto a dirt road, immediately bear left and go 100 yards to reach the chapel).

2.7 Turn right and go 0.6 mile to Bay View Street on your right, immediately after a cemetery on your right.

3.3 Turn right on Bay View Street and go 1.7 miles to the end, in Camden (merge right on US 1).

Craft shops, galleries, and antiques shops line the road at the end. The harbor behind the shops usually has a few windjammers at anchor.

5.0 Bear right on US 1 and go 0.1 mile to the first right (Atlantic Avenue, unmarked).

Notice the handsome redbrick library on the far corner.

5.1 Turn right and go 0.2 mile to the end.

You'll pass the Camden Amphitheatre on your left, a lovely terraced area overlooking the harbor, where concerts and productions of the Camden Civic Theatre are held.

5.3 Turn left and go 0.1 mile to the crossroads (US 1).

Side Trip: The loop route turns left on US 1, but if you'd like to climb Mount Battie, turn right on US 1 and go 1.4 miles to the entrance to Camden Hills State Park on the left. You'll pass Norumbega on the right, an ornate mansion, now an inn, that looks like a castle. Turn left into the park. Just past the entrance booth, turn left and go 1.5 miles to the top. The climb is quite steep. At the top, the stone observation tower provides an unparalleled view of Camden, the bay and its islands, and Megunticook Lake.

5.4 Turn left on US 1 (straight if you're coming from Mount Battie) and go 0.2 mile to ME 52 (Mountain Street) on the right.

Camden Harbor, framed by rugged hills, is unusually picturesque.

5.6 *Turn right and go 1.8 miles to Molyneaux Road on the left, at a traffic island.*

There's a long, gradual climb to get out of Camden and a good view of the Camden Hills on the right just before the intersection.

7.4 *Turn left on Molyneaux Road. Stay on the main road for 0.7 mile, to a fork where Beaucaire Avenue bears right.*

8.1 *Bear right at the fork. After 0.8 mile Start Road bears right, but curve slightly left on the main road and go 0.9 mile to the end (ME 52).*

This is a delightful wooded road hugging Megunticook Lake. On the hillside on the opposite shore is Maiden Cliff, a dramatic 800-foot plunge.

9.8 *Turn left on ME 52 and go 1.8 miles to a fork where Youngtown Road bears right and ME 52 curves left.*

The road follows the lake closely, passing beneath Maiden Cliff.

11.6 *Curve left and go 1.5 miles to a stop sign where ME 173 South bears right and ME 52 (Main Street) turns left.*

A convenience store is on the far side of the intersection, but there's a more appealing country store less than a mile ahead.

13.1 *Curve left (still ME 52) and go 0.8 mile to the crossroads where ME 52 (Belfast Road) turns right and Heal Road turns left in Lincolnville Center.*

The country store on the right just before the intersection is a good halfway stop.

13.9 *Turn left at the crossroads and go 0.6 mile to a fork where Proctor Road bears right.*

14.5 *Bear left. After 0.8 mile, the main road curves 90 degrees left at the bottom of the hill. Continue for 0.6 mile to the end (ME 235, Hope Road).*

There's a tough hill after the fork. At the top, the wooded hill in front of you is Hatchet Mountain. After the road curves left, you'll have dramatic views of the Camden Hills.

15.9 *Turn right on ME 235 and go 1.7 miles to the end (ME 105).*

17.6 *Turn left and go 5.3 miles to the crossroads (a sign says DO NOT ENTER if you go straight).*

You're back in Camden. This section has a few moderate hills. At the end, a millstream flows beneath the buildings on both sides of the road.

22.9 *Turn left at the crossroads and go 0.1 mile to another crossroads (US 1).*

23.0 *Jog right on US 1 and then immediately left on Chestnut Street and go 2.2 miles to a fork and a stop sign, in Rockport (Union Street bears right).*

Caution: Be careful making the left turn onto Chestnut Street. This street has diagonal parking, so watch for cars backing up.

Just after you turn left on Chestnut Street, notice the classic white church on the right, and then a handsome stone one just ahead.

25.2 Bear left downhill at the fork and go 0.2 mile to Pascal Avenue (unmarked) on the left, at the bottom of the hill.

25.4 Turn left across the bridge and go 0.2 mile to the starting point.

Final mileage: 25.6

Bicycle Repair Services

Maine Sport Outfitters, US 1, Rockport (236-7120)

Fred's Bikes, Chestnut Street, Camden (236-6664)

Oggibike, 29 Mountain Street, Camden (236-3631)

13
Islesboro

Distance: *28 miles*
Terrain: *Rolling, with two short, steep hills and two long, steady ones.*
Special features: *Bay views, fine summer homes, fishing village.*

Of the dozens of islands that dot the Maine coast, Islesboro is by far the finest for bicycling. It has everything that you would hope to see on a Maine island—small roads winding along the shore, stately summer homes perched on hills above the bay, coves with lobster boats and spindly piers, and peaceful villages with trim white houses. Traffic on the island is very light because the ferry can carry only about 30 cars. Islesboro is also easy to get to—it's only a 20-minute ride on the ferry, and there are several boats a day.

Islesboro is a stringbean-shaped island, about 10 miles long, in the middle of Penobscot Bay. The island lies about 2 miles from the bay's western shore and 3 miles from its eastern shore. The ride starts from the ferry dock on the island's western side and heads to the southern tip, Pendleton Point. After 5 miles, you'll arrive in the wealthy summer enclave of Dark Harbor, one of the three communities on the island. The center of town contains a few modest buildings, in contrast with the large, gracious houses along the shore as you come into and then leave the village. South of Dark Harbor, the road follows a ridge with views of the bay and summer estates on both sides.

North of Dark Harbor, the character of the island changes. The summer estates give way to modest, well-kept houses where lobstermen, carpenters, and other year-round residents live. Three miles north of Dark Harbor is Islesboro, the island's other community of any size. The rest of the ride loops around the northern half of the island, which is thinly populated except for the hamlet of Pripet. The road climbs onto gradual hills, with views of the bay in the distance. You'll pass the Islesboro

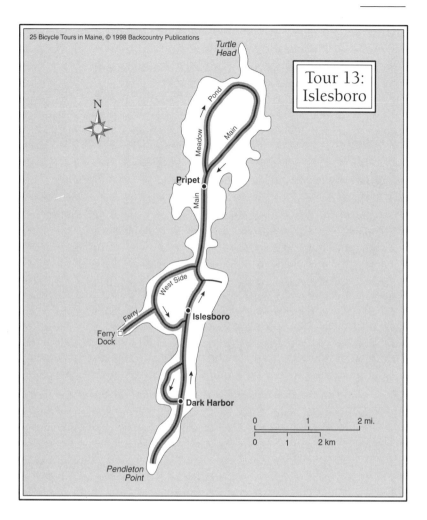

Historical Society Museum, a fascinating place to visit. The last 3 miles hug the coast, with dramatic views of the Camden Hills across the bay.

Directions for the ride

The ferry leaves from Lincolnville, which is 5.5 miles north of Camden. The ferry dock is just off US 1.

0.0 *From the ferry dock on the island, head away from the dock and go 1.1 miles to the end.*

1.1 *Turn right, following the sign for Dark Harbor, and go 1.2 miles to the end.*

This road is mostly wooded. You'll dip down to a small cove halfway along.

2.3 *Turn right and go 1 mile to the first right, almost at the top of a hill. It's a small road that's easy to miss.*

3.3 *Turn right and go 1.6 miles to the end, in Dark Harbor.*

The narrow road passes shorefront estates, with views of the Camden Hills on the other side of the bay. After 1 mile, a dirt road on the right (at a crossroads) leads for 0.3 mile onto a small point lined with elegant summer residences.

4.9 *Turn right at the end. After 2.1 miles the road becomes dirt. Continue for 0.2 mile to the dead end, at Pendleton Point.*

As soon as you turn right, the pool-like harbor, with only a narrow opening to the bay, is on your left. Just ahead are two short, steep hills. As you start to climb the second hill, notice the handsome brown church, with a belfry, on the right. At Pendleton Point there's a little beach tucked between rocky, spruce-rimmed headlands.

7.2 *From Pendleton Point, follow the main road for 5.9 miles to a fork.*

You'll pass a restaurant on your left in Dark Harbor. The village of Islesboro, with a few houses and a simple church, is about 1.5 miles before the fork. Notice the graceful fieldstone library with a small portico on your right a mile farther on. Just after the library, a side road on the right hugs the harbor for 0.6 mile to a dead end.

13.1 *Bear right at the fork and go 2.7 miles to another fork.*

You'll immediately pass the Historical Society Museum and a Masonic hall on your left, both traditional white buildings with peaked roofs. Beyond is a narrow isthmus with broad fields sloping to the bay. There's a grocery on the right about 0.5 mile before the fork in the hamlet of Pripet.

15.8 *Bear left at the fork and go 8.8 miles to a road on the right immediately after the Masonic hall and Historical Society*

A church in Dark Harbor

Museum on the right.

This section of the ride loops clockwise around the northern part of the island. Notice two whimsical metal sculptures on your right after about 1.5 miles. After a long but gradual climb, you'll enjoy a swooping downhill run to Turtle Head Cove. (Turtle Head, the extreme northern tip of the island, is private.)

24.6 *Turn right and go 2.1 miles to the first right (a sign indicates the way to the ferry).*

The road hugs the water, going past well-maintained houses and fields sloping down to the bay.

26.7 *Turn right and go 1.1 miles to the ferry dock.*

Final mileage: 27.8

Bicycle Repair Services

Fred's Bikes, Chestnut Street, Camden (236-6664)

Oggibike, 29 Mountain Street, Camden (236-3631)

Maine Sport Outfitters, US 1, Rockport (236-7120)

Solar Cycles, 64 Anderson Street, Belfast (338-6338)

14
Belfast–Northport

Distance: 23 miles
Terrain: Rolling, with several short, steep hills.
Special features: Fine architecture in Belfast, coastal scenery, Victorian gingerbread cottages in Temple Heights and Bayside.

The western shore of Penobscot Bay just south of Belfast, along with the countryside a short distance inland, is ideal for bicycling. Secondary roads hug the coastline between Northport and the center of Belfast, enabling the cyclist to avoid US 1 except for a short section that has a good shoulder. To the west of US 1, a network of country roads with very little traffic weaves through a harmonious mixture of forests and working farms.

The ride starts from the outskirts of Belfast, a beautiful coastal town that boasts a superb variety of 19th-century architecture. The center of town contains several handsome brick business blocks from the 1880s and 1890s, making the town seem larger than a community of only 6,500. Within a few blocks of the downtown area are elegant homes originally owned by sea captains and shipyard owners, two fine churches, and a Gothic-style library. Because the town center is about a half mile from US 1, traffic is limited primarily to local residents. You'll go through the center of Belfast at the end of the ride.

You'll cross US 1, heading inland, and quickly proceed into rural countryside. The route heads southwest and then southeast on quiet back roads that wind up and down past dairy farms and sturdy wooden barns. Eventually you'll come to the shore of Penobscot Bay in the small village of Northport, and follow the coastline back to Belfast on a small road etched into a hillside that rises sharply from the bay.

The coast road passes through two small summer communities of gingerbread Victorian cottages, Temple Heights and Bayside (both part of

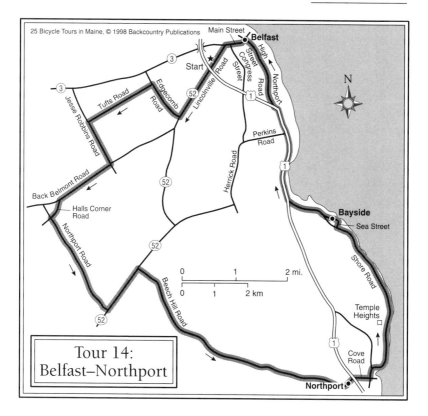

Tour 14:
Belfast–Northport

Northport). Temple Heights, which was founded in 1882, is a Christian Spiritualist camp. Spiritualism is based on the doctrine that the spirits of the dead can communicate with the living through intermediaries, who are called mediums. Two miles ahead is the larger community of Bayside, where small cottages with ornately carved trim and steeply pitched roofs are built around a central green that slopes down to the shore. Bayside was founded in 1849 as a Methodist Episcopal Church campground; most of the cottages were built between 1870 and 1900. From Bayside it's about 4 miles to the center of Belfast and another mile to the starting point.

The excellent Penobscot Marine Museum, 6 miles northeast of the starting point on US 1 in Searsport (a major shipbuilding center during the 19th century), is worth a visit after the ride.

Directions for the ride

Start from Shop 'n Save at the junction of US 1 and ME 52 (Lincolnville Road), in Belfast. The supermarket is on the northeast corner of the intersection, and the entrance is on Lincolnville Road.

0.0   *Turn right out of the parking lot and go 0.1 mile to US 1, at the traffic light.*

0.1   *Go straight on Lincolnville Road (ME 52) for 1 mile to Edgecomb Road on your right.*

1.1   *Turn right and go 0.7 mile to Tufts Road on your left.*
You'll ride through gently rolling farmland.

1.8   *Turn left and go 1.6 miles to the end of Tufts Road.*
The road passes through a harmonious mixture of woods and farmland, with forested hills rising in the distance.

3.4   *Turn left onto Jesse Robbins Road (unmarked) and go 0.9 mile to a crossroads and a stop sign (Back Belmont Road).*

4.3   *Turn right onto Back Belmont Road and go 1.1 miles to Halls Corner Road, which bears left (the road name is written vertically along a tall wooden signpost).*

5.4   *Bear left and go 0.4 mile to a crossroads (Northport Road).*

5.8   *Turn left onto Northport Road and go 2.2 miles to the end at ME 52.*
You'll have a gradual climb followed by a steady descent. **Caution:** Watch for potholes. The descent is bumpy, with sections of broken pavement.

8.0   *Turn left onto ME 52 and go 0.8 mile to Beech Hill Road on your right.*

8.8   *Turn right onto Beech Hill Road, and stay on the main road for 5.3 miles to the end at US 1.*
You'll climb steeply for 0.3 mile; then the terrain is very rolling as you wind past dairy farms with wooded hills in the background.

    Caution: For the first half of this section, watch for potholes and broken pavement, and take it easy on the descents. Some of

Victorian cottages in Bayside, a village in Northport

Northport's back roads need repaving.

The last two miles are mostly downhill on smoother pavement. Look for the Northport town hall, an old wooden building on your left just before the end.

14.1 *Cross US 1 onto Cove Road, bearing right as you go through the intersection. Go 0.3 mile to a crossroads and a stop sign (Shore Road, unmarked).*

14.4 *Turn left onto Shore Road and go 0.25 mile to a fork where a smaller road bears left and the main road curves right.*

Watch for bumps as you descend sharply.

14.7 *Curve right and go 3.4 miles to Sea Street on the right, in Bayside.*

The narrow road hugs the coast. There's a short, steep hill at the beginning and several similar hills farther along. You'll pass Temple Heights Spiritual Camp on your left after about a mile.

18.1 *Turn right onto Sea Street and go 0.4 mile to a stop sign where you merge right.*

You'll descend steeply to a small park in the center of Bayside, and climb another short, sharp hill.

18.5 *Bear right and go 0.8 mile to the end, where you merge right on US 1.*

19.3 *Bear right and go 1.8 miles to Northport Road (unmarked), which bears right. A sign says* TO DOWNTOWN BELFAST, WATER-FRONT.

US 1 is busy, but there's a good shoulder. The ride bears right on Northport Avenue, but you can cut 0.6 mile off the route (and bypass downtown Belfast) by staying on US 1 for 1.6 miles to the supermarket on your right, immediately after the traffic light.

21.1 *Bear right and go 1.5 miles to Main Street, at the traffic light in the center of Belfast.*

You'll pass gracious 19th-century houses as you approach the center of town. Notice the Gothic-style library, built in 1887, on your left two blocks before the light.

22.6 *Turn left onto Main Street and go 0.3 mile to Lincolnville Road on your left, just past the steep part of the hill.*

22.9 *Turn left onto Lincolnville Road and go 0.4 mile to Shop 'n Save on your right.*

Final mileage: 23.3

Bicycle Repair Services

Solar Cycles, 64 Anderson Street, Belfast (338-6338)

Birgfeld's Bicycle Shop, US 1, Searsport (548-2916)

Fred's Bikes, Chestnut Street, Camden (236-6664)

Oggibike, 29 Mountain Street, Camden (236-3631)

15

Castine Ride: Orland–Castine–Penobscot

Distance: 41 miles
Terrain: Rolling, with several steep hills.
Special features: Historic sites and fine architecture in Castine, lighthouse, Maine Maritime Academy, ocean and bay views.

This is a tour of the beginning of the Down East coast, which extends from the eastern shore of Penobscot Bay to the Canadian border. Penobscot Bay is bordered on the east by the large, triangular Blue Hill Peninsula, which extends from Bucksport and Ellsworth on the north to Stonington at the southern tip. The northwestern section of this region is a smaller peninsula with Castine at the bottom. The smaller peninsula has a different flavor than the rest of the region, seeming more midcoastal than Down East in character. Few tourists visit Castine, so traffic on this ride is pleasantly light.

Starting from the northern tip of Penobscot Bay, the ride follows the bay shore for about 15 miles to the small head on which Castine is located. The landscape is a pleasant mix of woods and open farmland with views of the bay.

Castine is a quiet, gracious, unspoiled town with a tumultuous history. Founded by Plymouth Pilgrims, it changed hands between the French, British, Dutch, and American colonists before the Revolutionary War. In 1779, a fleet of nearly 40 American ships, attempting to wrest control of Castine from the British, was destroyed by them. During the mid-19th century, the town's fortune improved as shipbuilding and maritime commerce flourished. Successful sea captains and traders built elegant homes on the hillside slanting back from the bay. While bicycling through the town, you will see numerous historic markers that trace its past. You'll pass the Maine Maritime Academy, which maintains a large

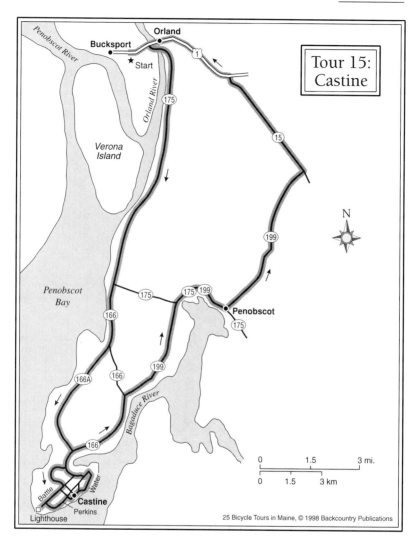

World War II troop ship as a training vessel.

From Castine, the route follows the Bagaduce River up the eastern side of the peninsula to the tiny village of Penobscot at the river's northern end. The route continues north, heading inland, across rolling open landscape with extensive views, and finally turns northwest back toward the start. There's a glorious downhill run approaching US 1.

Dice Head Light in Castine

Directions for the ride

Start from the Bucksport True Value Hardware on US 1 in Bucksport. It's about a mile east of the bridge between Verona Island and Bucksport, and just west of ME 46.

0.0 Turn right (east) out of the parking lot and go 0.8 mile to ME 175, which bears right.

0.8 Bear right and go 8.1 miles to the point where ME 175 turns left and ME 166 goes straight.

Near the beginning of this stretch, the road drops sharply to a bridge over a stream, and then climbs steeply for 0.3 mile. Beyond, you'll follow a ridge with views of the bay in the distance, and then descend gradually to the water's edge.

When you get to the intersection you can shorten the ride to 25 miles (and bypass Castine, of course), by cutting across the peninsula on ME 175.

8.9 Go straight on ME 166 for 1.9 miles to the fork where ME 166 bears left and ME 166A bears right.

10.8 Bear right and go 3.9 miles to the point where the main road curves right, merging onto ME 166.

Most of this section is inland from the bay, but halfway along you'll descend to the shore and climb away from the water again.

14.7 Curve right on ME 166 and go 0.5 mile to the first right, at the bottom of the hill, opposite a small cove.

15.2 Turn right and go 1.2 miles to the end.

There's a steep 0.3-mile climb on this road. At the end, Fort George, a series of earthen embankments, is on your right. It was built by the British in 1779 and occupied until the end of the war. Opposite the intersection are the redbrick buildings of the Maine Maritime Academy, with traditional collegiate architecture.

16.4 Turn right at the end and go 1 mile to Dice Head Light, at the end of the paved road.

The road traverses a hillside sloping sharply to the bay on your left, passing handsome mansions. A footpath leads 100 yards to a small, pine-covered point behind the lighthouse, and a wooden stairway at the end of the path leads down to the rocky shore. The lighthouse, built in 1829, is no longer in use.

17.4 Backtrack 0.1 mile to the first right, Perkins Street.

17.5 Turn right and go 1 mile to a crossroads and a stop sign (Pleasant Street, unmarked).

The road hugs the coast, passing sea captains' homes standing guard above the waves. You'll pass Fort Madison, some grassy embankments dating from 1811 that overlook the bay. Just ahead, on your right, is the brick Wilson Museum, with Indian artifacts, period furnishings, and a blacksmith shop. Beyond are two small, attractive churches, one of wood, and the other of stone.

18.5 Turn right and go 0.1 mile to another stop sign in the center of Castine (Main Street is on the left).

You'll see a concrete overlook on the right from which you can observe the State of Maine, the training ship of the Maine Maritime Academy. The ship is open to the public when it is in port during the summer.

When you get to Main Street, there's a snack bar and grocery at the intersection—the last food on the ride. Look along the street, which climbs steeply to the ornate Pentagoet Inn and a fine white church.

18.6 *Continue straight for 0.2 mile to a fork (Dyer Street bears left uphill).*

18.8 *Bear right along the water. After 0.5 mile, the main road turns 90 degrees left at the top of the hill. Continue for 0.2 mile to the first right, State Street.*

Dramatic views of the bay unfold on your left from the hilltop.

19.5 *Turn right, up a short steep hill, and go 0.2 mile to a stop sign (ME 166 North goes straight).*

19.7 *Continue straight on ME 166 and go 3.6 miles to the fork where ME 199 bears right and ME 166 bears left.*

This is an inspiring road, following a ridge high above the bay, with panoramic vistas.

23.3 *Bear right on ME 199 and go 5.5 miles to the point where ME 199 turns left and ME 175 goes straight, in the tiny hamlet of Penobscot.*

The road is very rolling, passing through open countryside with views of the bay. There's a snack bar on your right just before the intersection.

28.8 *Turn left on ME 199 and go 5 miles to the end (ME 15), at the top of the hill.*

The large solitary hill to your right is Blue Hill, about 8 miles away.

33.8 *Turn left on ME 15 and go 3.8 miles to the end (US 1 and ME 3).*

You'll climb steadily onto a high open ridge with views of distant hills, and then enjoy a long, fast descent to US 1.

37.6 *Turn left on US 1 and ME 3. Go 3.4 miles to the hardware store on the left.*

The road is busy, but there's a wide shoulder.

Final mileage: 41.0

Bicycle Repair Services

Bar Harbor Bicycle Shop, 193 Main Street, Ellsworth (667-6886)

Bergfeld's Bicycle Shop, US 1, Searsport (548-2916)

Pat's Bike Shop, 373 Wilson Street, Brewer (989-2900)

Ski Rack Sports, Maine Square Mall, Hogan Road, Bangor (945-6474)

Solar Cycles, 64 Anderson Street, Belfast (338-6338)

Wight's Sporting Goods, 930 Stillwater Avenue, Bangor (945-4455)

16

The East Penobscot Tour: Blue Hill–Deer Isle–Stonington

Distance: *79 miles in 2 days—40 the first day, 39 the second. For a shorter ride that can be done as a day trip, you can take the mainland loop only (44 miles), or the Deer Isle–Stonington loop only (31 miles). Directions for the 31-mile ride are at the end of this tour.*
Terrain: *Continuously rolling, with numerous steep hills—a challenge! The Deer Isle–Stonington loop is gently rolling with several short, steep hills.*
Road surface: *1 mile of dirt road near Deer Isle.*
Special features: *Unspoiled small towns and fishing villages, numerous coves and inlets, reversing falls.*
Accommodations *(all on Main Street, Stonington): Inn on the Harbor (367-2420); Boyce's Motel (367-2421); Pres Du Port Bed and Breakfast (367-5007); Ocean View House (summer only: 367-5114). Near the start of the ride, in Blue Hill: Blue Hill Inn, Union Street (374-2829); Heritage Motor Inn, ME 172 (374-5646); Captain Isaac Merrill Inn, 1 Union Street (374-2555); John Peters Inn, Peters Point (374-2116).*

The large, triangular peninsula between Penobscot Bay and Mount Desert Island is ideal for bicycling if you're willing to tackle a challenging landscape of continuously rolling hills. The scenery is superb: an ever-changing landscape of sheltered coves filled with lobster boats; sleepy villages; and boulder-strewn hills with dramatic views of the bay in the distance. Traffic is light as virtually all vacationers zip across the top of the peninsula on US 1 on their way to Acadia National Park. The peninsula is divided into two distinct portions: the mainland on the north, and the island of Deer Isle, with the town of Stonington at its southern tip, on the south. The coastline of both sections is some of the most jagged in Maine, twisting around a little harbor, snaking out to a spruce-lined point, and working its way back inland to the next inlet.

The ride starts from the lovely town of Blue Hill, which is on the eastern shore of the peninsula about a third of the way down. From the small town center overlooking the harbor, several roads fan outward up the neighboring hillsides, passing elegant white houses with dark shutters and fanlights above the door. Just north of the town is the round, blueberry-covered hill for which the community is named. During the summer, Blue Hill is a crafts and cultural center, with chamber music concerts at Kneisel Hall. The annual Blue Hill Fair, an authentic old-time agricultural fair, is held on Labor Day weekend.

From Blue Hill, the route heads west across a narrow segment of the peninsula to the Bagaduce River, a long tidal inlet. You'll cross it at Bagaduce Falls, a reversing falls popular with canoeists. The route curves south to the narrow, high-arched suspension bridge between the mainland and Deer Isle, passing through the small villages of West Brooksville and Brooksville. On Deer Isle, the ride follows an untraveled back road along the western shore to Stonington.

Stonington, at the bottom of the island, is a classic Maine lobster port. Weathered docks on tall pilings poke into the small harbor; old warehouses and fishing shanties line the shore; and a potpourri of simple houses with peaked roofs clamber up the steep hillside behind the harbor. Plan to stay overnight here, and head up the other side of the island the next day. Once back on the mainland, the road winds through the unspoiled villages of Sargentville, Sedgwick, and Brooklin before turning north to Blue Hill. The last several miles hug the shore of Blue Hill Bay, passing Blue Hill Falls, another reversing falls.

Directions for the 79-mile and 44-mile rides

FIRST DAY: 40 miles

Start from the junction of ME 15 and ME 177, in the center of Blue Hill. The town hall, a handsome building with an arched portico, built in 1896, is at the intersection. If you're doing the day trip, you can also start from Blue Hill Park, on Water Street 0.2 mile south of the intersection.

0.0 *With the town hall on your right, follow ME 15 South and go 0.6 mile to the crossroads at the top of the hill (ME 172 and ME 175 on the left).*

The hill leading out of town is a tough one. The brick library and a white church will be on your left at the beginning.

0.6 *Continue straight for 4.2 miles to the end, where ME 15 turns left and ME 176 turns right.*

The road ascends a ridge with a sweeping view.

4.8 *Turn right and go 2.4 miles to ME 175 on the left (a sign says TO BROOKSVILLE).*

The landscape has a distinctive Down East flavor—a blend of scrubby woodlands and fields peppered with boulders and blueberry bushes, and not as prosperous as southern and midcoast Maine. When you come to ME 175, a grocery is just beyond the intersection on your left.

7.2 *Turn left and go 1.1 miles to the end, in the hamlet of North Brooksville.*

The road descends to the Bagaduce River, crossing it next to the reversing falls. There's a snack bar at the bridge serving delicious fried clams. At the end, ME 175 turns left and ME 176 turns right.

8.3 *Turn right on ME 176. After about 10 miles, ME 176 runs head-on into ME 175, in Brooksville. Continue straight for 0.7 mile to a crossroads and a stop sign.*

The road weaves up and down a continuous succession of short but steep rolling hills, through farmland and blueberry fields with glimpses of the bay in the distance. After 2 miles you'll pedal into the tiny village of West Brooksville, where a small church stands all alone on a little rise. The road descends delightfully into South Brooksville, another minuscule village with a cove on the right and a small store on the left, set back from the road. There's a steep climb out of the village.

Shortly before the end is Brooksville, where you can visit the Brooksville Historical Society Museum. Housed in a building dating

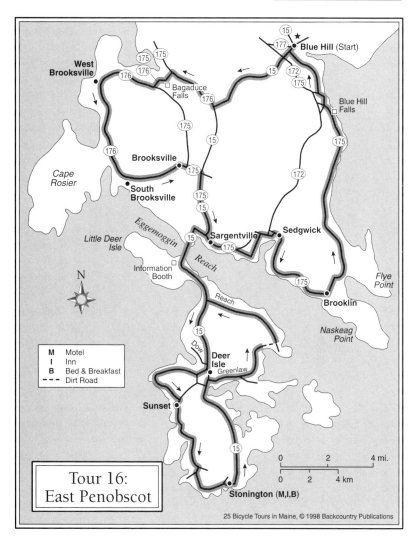

Tour 16:
East Penobscot

25 Bicycle Tours in Maine, © 1998 Backcountry Publications

from 1817, it displays farm implements, household articles, and clothing from the 18th and 19th centuries.

19.1 *Turn right at the stop sign (still ME 175) and go 2.9 miles to the end, in Sargentville.*

Halfway along there's a tough climb up Caterpillar Hill, but you'll be rewarded by a dramatic view across miles of boulder-strewn blueberry barrens with the bay glistening below. The rest area at the top is a great picnic spot.

When you get to the end, the long ride turns right on ME 15, and the 44-mile ride turns left on ME 175. To go 44 miles, turn left and go 1.5 miles to a smaller road that bears right. You'll go through the attractive village of Sargentville. Resume with mile 18.8 of the second day.

22.0 *Turn right on ME 15 and go 7.4 miles to an unmarked road on the right in the village of Deer Isle (a sign may point to Sunset). The road comes up just before you start to climb a hill.*

The road crosses the high bridge to Deer Isle after about a mile, and goes along a causeway a mile farther on.

29.4 *Turn right and go 0.5 mile to a fork where a smaller road bears right.*

There's a grocery store on the right at the beginning, and a cedar-shingled library just ahead.

29.9 *Bear right and go 4.1 miles to the end, in the hamlet of Sunset.*

The Salome Sellers House, built around 1830, with a collection of Indian artifacts, ship models, and period furnishings, is located here.

34.0 *Turn right and go 3.4 miles to a fork where Sand Beach Road, a smaller road, bears right. It's just after Whitman Road, which also bears right.*

The terrain is gently rolling with some short hills. At the fork, there's a grocery on the left.

37.4 *Bear right and go 0.3 mile to another fork, where Fifield Point Road bears right.*

37.7 *Bear left, uphill, and go 1.9 miles to the stop sign in Stonington.*

The road hugs the rocky shore, passing wharves, lobster shanties, and gaily decorated houses. The smell of fresh fish permeates the air.

39.6 *Turn right immediately after the stop sign, following the harbor on your right. Go 0.2 mile to another stop sign, in the center of Stonington.*

39.8 *Continue straight.*

Just ahead are the overnight accommodations, clustered together. The weathered, wooden commercial buildings house a fascinating variety of craft and antiques shops, galleries, and old-fashioned general stores.

SECOND DAY: 39 miles

0.0 *Continue in the same direction, with the ocean on your right, and just ahead bear left uphill on ME 15. Go 5.2 miles to an unmarked road on your right just after a cemetery on your right. There's a gas station on your left at the intersection.*

The first road that bears right as you go up the hill leads to the dock for the mailboat to Isle au Haut, a rockbound wooded island about 6 miles offshore, laced with hiking trails. Half the island belongs to Acadia National Park. Unless you have an off-road bicycle, the island is unsuitable for cycling—most of the road around its perimeter is loose, soft dirt.

After 0.1 mile, at the top of the hill, ME 15 curves left, but if you go straight on a smaller road for 0.6 mile you'll come to Ames Pond, a small pond smothered with pink water lilies. Farther on, ME 15 bobs up and down several short, steep hills.

5.2 *Turn right and go 1.3 miles to a fork where one road curves right and the other goes straight.*

6.5 *Go straight (don't curve right) for 2.9 miles to the end. The last mile is dirt.*

Caution: The stretch before the dirt road has bumpy and gravelly sections—take it easy.

9.4 *Turn left and go 3.7 miles to the end (ME 15).*

Caution: The first 0.5 mile is bumpy and gravelly. This is a little-used secondary road, winding through the woods.

13.1 *Turn right onto ME 15 and go 4.2 miles to the intersection where ME 15 turns left and ME 175 goes straight.*

You'll cross the bridge back to the mainland and then curse at the steep climb before the intersection.

17.3 *Go straight on ME 175 for 1.5 miles to a smaller road that bears right.*

Blue Hill rises above an inlet of Blue Hill Bay.

You'll go through Sargentville, an attractive village with fine old houses and a white church.

18.8 *Bear right and go 1.8 miles to the end (ME 175 again).*

The narrow road hugs the shore of an inlet.

20.6 *Turn right on ME 175 and go 0.7 mile to the end, in Sedgwick. ME 175 turns right at the intersection.*

You'll pass a general store on your right.

21.3 *Turn right (still ME 175) and go about 14 miles to a small crossroads shortly after the concrete arched bridge.*

After about 5 miles you'll come to Brooklin, a picturesque fishing village with a wonderful old-time general store, a three-story Odd Fellows hall, a large wooden schoolhouse, and a traditional white church built in 1853.

Three miles past Brooklin is a small square stone enclosure, originally a cattle pound, on your right. The last few miles hug the shore of Blue Hill Bay. Next to the unique arched bridge is Blue

Hill Falls, another reversing falls caused by the tide surging through the narrow inlet. This is a popular spot for canoeists and kayakers to test their whitewater skills. The crossroads is 0.4 mile after the bridge.

35.3 *Turn right and go 0.4 mile to a fork.*

35.7 *Bear right and go 2.7 miles to the end (ME 15) in Blue Hill.*

Near the end is a fine view of Blue Hill (the hill) rising across the harbor. When you come to the end, the center of town is to your right.

Final mileage: 38.5

Directions for the 31-mile ride (Deer Isle–Stonington loop)

Start from the visitors center on ME 15 in Deer Isle, 0.25 mile after the suspension bridge, on the right. You can also start from a dirt turnoff on your right 0.5 mile beyond the visitors center.

0.0 *From the visitors center, turn right (south) on ME 15 and go 5.2 miles to an unmarked road on the right in the village of Deer Isle (a sign may point to Sunset). The road comes up just before you start to climb a hill.*

5.0 *Follow the long ride from mile 29.4 of the first day through the directions for mile 9.4 of the second day, to ME 15.*

28.6 *Turn right on ME 15 and go 2 miles to the visitors center (or 1.5 miles to the dirt turnoff) on your left.*

Final mileage (to the visitors center): 30.6

Bicycle Repair Services

Bar Harbor Bicycle Shop, 163 Main Street, Ellsworth (667-6886)

17

Mount Desert Island–Acadia National Park

Distance: *Five suggested variations, 13 to 68 miles.*
Terrain: *Rolling to fairly flat.*
Special features: *Highest coastal mountains and headlands on the Eastern Seaboard, Somes Sound, fishing villages.*

Mount Desert Island has some of the most dramatic scenery in Maine. Very simply, it's a place where the highest mountains on the Atlantic coast north of Rio de Janeiro plunge into the sea. About 4 million visitors come to the island each year, and most are favorably impressed unless their entire stay is fogged in.

Mount Desert Island contains nearly all (but not 100 percent) of Acadia National Park (it's usually pronounced "dessert"; the word means "barren" in French); however, only half of the island consists of park land—the other half is privately owned.

Acadia National Park is land that is owned by the United States Government and managed by the National Park Service. The park's boundaries are highly irregular because the park land has been acquired bit by bit over a long period of time, chiefly by donation. The park contains enclaves surrounded or nearly surrounded by private land, and there are also enclaves of private land surrounded by park land. Several small pieces of the park are not on Mount Desert Island: the two largest are the tip of Schoodic Peninsula (the peninsula east of Mount Desert Island, on the far side of Frenchman Bay), and half of Isle au Haut (south of Stonington).

Bar Harbor is the largest town on Mount Desert Island. It is located on the island's northeast shore, about 3 miles from the National Park Visitor Center and a mile from the closest park land. Most of the island's motels, stores, restaurants, and other services are in Bar Harbor.

Much of Mount Desert's appeal stems from its small size and its lack of commercial development and exploitation. Many visitors to Acadia are surprised by how small the island is. Roughly circular in shape, it is about 13 miles wide and 16 miles long; however, it seems much larger because of its incredible wealth of scenery, and because it is nearly bisected by Somes Sound into two separate islands.

The town of Bar Harbor and the National Park Service deserve the highest commendation for limiting commercial development. Thanks to strict zoning, Bar Harbor has retained the ambience of a pre–World War II community. There are no fast-food chains here, no Holiday Inns, no condominiums, no shopping malls, no four-lane neon highways leading into town. For that, you have to go back to Ellsworth. The island's other towns are virtually unspoiled. The National Park itself has only one real commercial establishment, the tastefully designed Jordan Pond House (a restaurant).

Mount Desert Island is divided into two approximately equal-sized sections by Somes Sound, which extends from the southern coast most of the way back to the north shore. The two parts contrast dramatically in geography. The eastern half, where most of the park is located, contains most of the mountains and headlands, including the highest point, 1530-foot Cadillac Mountain. The western half is for the most part much gentler, with workaday fishing villages framed by lobster boats and docks stacked with lobster traps. Most visitors to the park do not see the western portion of the island.

Because Mount Desert is so special, it is impossible to do it justice with only one bicycle ride. At the same time, the island is so small that it is impossible to have more than two loops that do not duplicate each other to a large extent. I have therefore given directions for five rides, which do overlap in places: two on the eastern half, one on the western half, a "grand tour" covering both halves, and a carriage road ride along the dirt (but rideable) roads that are off-limits to motor vehicles.

In general, bicycling on the island is a pleasure. During the 10-week high season, from late June through Labor Day, traffic is very heavy, but the roads are wide enough to be safe, and the park is full of cyclists. An 11-mile section of the Park Loop Road is a one-way, two-lane road. To avoid traffic, simply go in the off-season. In April, May, late September, and October you'll have the island nearly to yourself, and you can enjoy its dramatic views without craning your neck around people in front of you. The visitors center on ME 3 is open only from May through October, but the park headquarters, on ME 233 near Eagle Lake, is open all year. The park roads are silk-smooth and well graded, with some long hills but none that are really steep, and the island's other roads are generally well maintained.

RIDE A: *Park Loop*

Distance: *26 miles (33 with side trip up Cadillac Mountain)*
Terrain: *Rolling, with several long, steady hills.*
Special features: *Rugged coast, glacial lakes, Cadillac Mountain, museum of Stone Age antiquities, wildflower garden.*
Food: *None, except at Jordan Pond House, an elegant restaurant.*
Caution: *Sections of Park Loop Road allow parking in the right lane. Watch for car doors opening in front of you.*

This ride follows Park Loop Road, which goes past the most frequently visited attractions of the park and its most rugged coastal areas. If you have time for only one ride, this is the one to do. Take as much time as you can—gaze from the overlooks, visit the museum and gardens, hike along the cliffside trails or up rugged Champlain Mountain, go down to the ocean and poke among the tidal pools to observe sea urchins and marine plants. It's not difficult to stretch the ride over most of the day—Mount Desert is too special to rush through.

Start from the Acadia National Park Visitor Center on ME 3, about 3 miles northwest of Bar Harbor.

Directions for the ride

0.0 *As you leave the parking lot, turn right on Park Loop Road. Go 3 miles to the intersection where Park Loop Road turns sharply left (a sign says* SAND BEACH).

At the very beginning, there's a steep hill 0.5 mile long. This is the worst hill on the entire island (except for Cadillac Mountain and the carriage roads), so don't get discouraged. At the top, an overlook provides a spectacular view of Frenchman Bay, dotted with

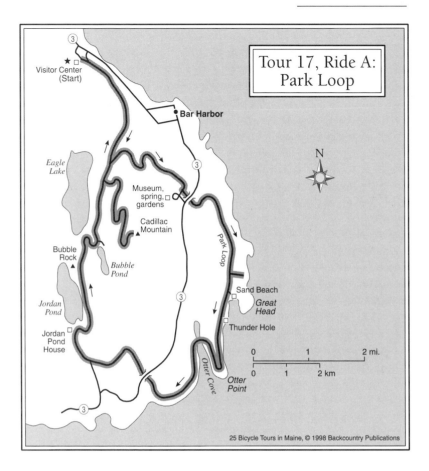

Tour 17, Ride A:
Park Loop

N

Visitor Center (Start)

Bar Harbor

Eagle Lake

Museum, spring, gardens

Cadillac Mountain

Bubble Rock

Bubble Pond

Jordan Pond

Jordan Pond House

Park Loop

Sand Beach

Great Head

Thunder Hole

0   1   2 mi.

0   1   2 km

Otter Cove

Otter Point

25 Bicycle Tours in Maine, © 1998 Backcountry Publications

islands. As you bicycle along, the barren mountains, which are immense granite rocks thinly covered with scrubby trees, loom in front of you.

Another overlook explains the cataclysmic fire of October 1947, which destroyed most of the northeastern quarter of the island. The fire roared to the coast just south of Bar Harbor, miraculously sparing the town itself, but destroying hundreds of palatial summer estates and resort hotels that America's financial barons had built during the Gilded Age of the late 1800s. As none of them were rebuilt, the fire contributed to transforming the island from an exclusive preserve of the wealthy to a place that can be comfortably enjoyed by all. In a wonderful example of nature's regenerative powers, the burned area is now reforested, with hardwoods replacing the original pine and spruce.

3.0 Make a sharp left (still Park Loop Road) and go 2.8 miles to a small road on the right that leads to Sieur de Monts Spring.

The spring, enclosed by a small portico, is 0.2 mile from the main road. Next to it are the Robert Abbe Museum of Stone Age Antiquities, a nature center, and the Wild Gardens of Acadia, a large collection of plants and wildflowers native to the park.

A trail climbs about 1.5 miles from the spring to the top of Dorr Mountain, 1270 feet high.

6.0 From the spring, backtrack to Park Loop Road (be sure it's this road and not ME 3).

6.2 Turn right on Park Loop Road and go 2.6 miles to a road on the left (a sign says SCHOONER HEAD OVERLOOK).

You'll climb along the side of Champlain Mountain, with spectacular views of the bay to your left. From the Champlain Mountain Overlook you can see Highseas, one of the few mansions to survive the 1947 fire.

From the next parking lot, the rugged Precipice Trail climbs very steeply for about 0.5 mile to the summit of Champlain Mountain, which towers a thousand feet above the sea. If you have time for only one hike, this is the most spectacular.

8.8 Turn left and go 0.3 mile to the dead end, and backtrack to Park Loop Road.

At the end is a headland rising sharply from the sea. A footpath leads 0.2 mile down to the shore, where at low tide you can see a small cave hollowed into the hillside. **Caution:** The footpath ends abruptly; beyond it are wet, slippery rocks.

9.4 Turn left on Park Loop Road and go 0.6 mile to Sand Beach on the left.

The entrance station to the park is at the beginning; the fee for bicycles is currently $3.00. There is no fee during the off-season or before 8 AM.

Sand Beach, tucked between two massive headlands, is actually composed of tiny, ground-up seashells as well as sand. The headland on the left, called Great Head, is a sheer cliff 145 feet high. Swim if you dare—the water is always freezing. An easy foot trail follows the shore for 1.8 miles from Sand Beach (from the upper parking lot, near the road) to Otter Point.

10.0 *Continue for 0.7 mile to Thunder Hole, a narrow crevice in the rock with vertical walls.*

When the sea is angry, and for a brief period in the middle of the incoming tide, the waves crash into the opening, compressing the air trapped inside with a thundering boom. On calm days there is no thunder, only the soft gurgle of the sea lapping meekly against the rocks. There's a short, steep hill when you leave Sand Beach.

10.7 *Continue for 7.4 miles to a road on the left (a sign says* TO ME 3, BLACKWOODS CAMPGROUND, NORTHEAST HARBOR).

Here the ride goes straight, but if you're doing the Grand Tour (Ride D) turn left.

The first half of this stretch hugs the shore along dramatic Otter Cliffs, down to Otter Point, and around Otter Cove. Otter Cliffs, an unbroken wall over 100 feet high, are the highest sheer cliffs on the Eastern Seaboard. The last 2 miles of this stretch, and the remainder of the ride, head inland through woods and along glacial lakes.

18.1 *At the intersection continue straight on Park Loop Road, following the sign to Jordan Pond. Go 0.6 mile to the Jordan Pond House on your left.*

This is an elegant restaurant, famous for tea and popovers. It replaces the original one, a farmhouse which was built in 1847 and burned in 1979. Be sure to look behind the building, where a broad lawn sweeps down to the shore of mountain-ringed Jordan Pond. Two hump-shaped hills, called the Bubbles, guard the opposite end of the pond.

18.7 *Continue for 2.9 miles to a small road on the right that leads to Bubble Pond, which is just off the main road.*

Bubble Pond is a smaller version of Jordan Pond, a sausage-shaped glacial lake hemmed in by granite mountains. A stream cascades from the end of the pond.

After you leave Jordan Pond House, the road climbs onto a hillside bordering the pond. Just past the pond, look to your left for Bubble Rock, a large boulder perched precariously on top of South Bubble. If you pedal furiously, you can probably get beyond it before it topples down the hill onto the road.

21.6 *From Bubble Pond, continue for 1.3 miles to the road to the summit of Cadillac Mountain, on your right.*

You'll ascend a hillside above Eagle Lake on your left, the largest of the three ponds on the ride.

Side Trip: You can tackle the 3.5-mile climb to the summit of Cadillac Mountain, which at 1530 feet is the highest in the park. The road climbs steadily but not steeply to the top, gaining a thousand feet in elevation over the 3.5 miles, for an average grade of 5.5 percent. (The hills at the beginning of the ride are steeper.) If you have fairly low gearing (a 32- or 34-tooth freewheel, or a bike with 15 or more speeds), and are in reasonable shape, you won't have any trouble. If you have standard 10- or 12-speed gearing you'll get to the top, but you'll push hard on the pedals, probably wanting to rest several times, and wishing you were riding in a vehicle that shares the mountain's name.

At the top, a footpath makes a short loop providing a nearly 360-degree panorama. Far below you can see Bar Harbor and the islands poised like stepping-stones across the mouth of Frenchman Bay. Just after you begin the descent, a short footpath on the right leads to Sunset Point, which provides an equally spectacular view to the west.

The descent, which is steady but not steep enough to be hairy, provides a relaxing reward for the effort of the climb. **Caution:** Take it easy on the hairpin turn halfway down.

22.9 *From the bottom of the road to Cadillac Mountain, continue straight (turn right if you went to the summit). Go 0.5 mile to a road that bears left (a sign says TO THE VISITOR CENTER).*

23.4 *Bear left and go 3 miles to the visitors center.*

Final mileage: 26.4

The Asticou Azalea Garden in Northeast Harbor

RIDE B: Jordan Pond–Seal Harbor–Northeast Harbor–Somes Sound

Distance: 23 *miles*
Terrain: *Rolling, with several long, steady hills.*
Special features: *Glacial lakes, Somes Sound, side trip to Cadillac Mountain.*

This ride explores the western portion of the eastern half of Mount Desert Island, between Somes Sound and Jordan Pond. The ride starts by heading south past Eagle Lake, Bubble Pond, and Jordan Pond, which are midway between the eastern shore and Somes Sound. On the island's southern shore, the route passes through the two old-moneyed, somewhat stuffy summer colonies of Seal Harbor and Northeast Harbor.

If you enjoy gardens, you can visit two exquisite ones about a half mile apart in Northeast Harbor. The Asticou Terraces and Thuya Garden crown a hillside with a stunning view of the harbor; a footpath zigzags up the steep slope past sheltered overlooks to an enclosed semiformal garden at the summit. The Asticou Azalea Garden, bordering a small pond, incorporates elements of Japanese landscape design.

As you leave Northeast Harbor you'll pedal north, hugging the shore of Somes Sound, with views of Saint Sauveur Mountain and Acadia Mountain rising sharply from the opposite shore. Because the ride starts by following the Park Loop Road in the opposite direction from which most visitors drive on it, traffic on this ride is much lighter than on the Park Loop ride.

Directions for the ride

Start from the Acadia National Park Headquarters on the south side of ME 233. It's 2.8 miles west of ME 3, 1.7 miles west of Park Loop Road, and 0.5 mile west of the carriage road parking area at Eagle Lake.

0.0 *Turn right on ME 233, heading east, and go 1.6 miles to the bridge where ME 233 passes underneath Park Loop Road.*

After 0.5 mile, Eagle Lake will be on your right. The two hump-shaped hills at the far end of the lake are called the Bubbles.

1.7 *Turn left just past the bridge, and just ahead bear left, following the sign to Cadillac Mountain. Go 50 yards to the end (Park Loop Road).*

1.9 *Turn left, heading south. After 0.4 mile Park Loop Road turns sharply left, but continue straight for 0.5 mile to the road that leads to the summit of Cadillac Mountain on the left.*

If you'd like to tackle the summit, it's 3.5 miles each way (see mile 21.6 of the Park Loop ride for more detail).

2.8 *Go straight (left if you're coming from Cadillac Mountain) for 1.3 miles to a small road on the left, at the bottom of a hill, that leads to Bubble Pond (see mile 18.7 of the Park Loop ride for more detail).*

You'll traverse a hillside high above Eagle Lake on your right. Bubble Pond is just off the main road.

4.1 *Continue on the main road for 2.9 miles to Jordan Pond House on the right (see mile 18.1 of the Park Loop ride for more detail).*

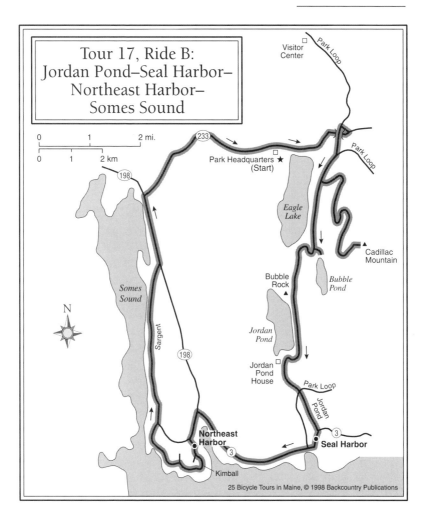

Tour 17, Ride B:
Jordan Pond–Seal Harbor–
Northeast Harbor–
Somes Sound

Be sure to go behind the building for the view of Jordan Pond and the Bubbles at the far end. About a mile after leaving Bubble Pond, look for Bubble Rock, a large boulder perched precariously on the hillside on your right.

7.0 *From the Jordan Pond House, continue for 0.6 mile to a traffic island where the road curves sharply right, at a yield sign. Continue 50 yards to Jordan Pond Road on the left (a sign says* NO THROUGH TRAFFIC).

7.6 Turn left and go 0.8 mile to the end (merge right on ME 3, at a stop sign), in Seal Harbor. A grocery and snack bar are just ahead.

8.4 Bear right on ME 3 and go 3.5 miles to the end (ME 198).

After about 0.5 mile you'll pass a vaulted stone Congregational church on the left. Beyond are some short, steep hills.

The parking lot for Asticou Terraces is on your left 1.8 miles beyond the church. The footpath begins across the road and leads a quarter mile to the Thuya Garden, which is entered through a gate immediately after the lodge.

At the end the ride turns left, but if you turn right you'll immediately come to the Asticou Azalea Garden on your right.

11.9 Turn left at the end and go 0.8 mile to a fork in the center of Northeast Harbor (Summit Road bears right, Main Street bears left).

12.7 Bear left at the fork and go 0.2 mile to another fork where Kimball Road bears left and Main Street bears right.

You'll go through the center of Northeast Harbor, passing old two- and three-story wooden buildings.

12.9 Bear left on Kimball Road and go 0.3 mile to the end (South Shore Road), opposite the stone church.

13.2 Turn right. After 0.4 mile the main road bears left along the water. Continue for 1.3 miles to the end (merge left at a stop sign). At the end, Millbrook Road is on your right and Sargent Drive is on your left.

South Shore Road becomes Manchester Road, passing rambling clapboard homes with wide porches standing guard above the sea.

14.9 Bear left at the end and go 3.3 miles to the end (merge left on ME 3 and ME 198).

This is one of the nicest rides on Mount Desert Island, clinging to the shore of Somes Sound, with views of the rugged Saint Sauveur and Acadia Mountains, both rising to a height of 680 feet, on the far side.

18.2 Bear left on ME 3 and ME 198 and go 1.2 miles to ME 233 on the right.

Here the ride turns right, but if you're doing the Grand Tour (Ride D), go straight, picking it up at mile 29.9.

19.4 **Turn right on ME 233 and go 3.1 miles to the Park headquarters on the right.**

Final mileage: 22.5

RIDE C: Western Loop

Distance: *28 miles*
Terrain: *Gently rolling.*
Special features: *Echo Lake, Mount Desert Oceanarium, ocean views, fishing villages, lighthouse, side trip to Swans Island.*

This ride loops around the western, and much less visited, half of Mount Desert Island. You'll start from the attractive village of Somesville, near the northern tip of Somes Sound, and head south along Echo Lake. Like most of the other lakes on Mount Desert Island, Echo Lake is slender and hemmed in by granite mountains. Beyond is Southwest Harbor, a colorful lobster port where weathered docks with little red shacks at the end jut into the boat-filled harbor. Here you can visit the Mount Desert Oceanarium, which is a combination of an aquarium, museum, and marine learning center.

Below Southwest Harbor, the route follows the circular bulge of land that forms the southern tip of Mount Desert Island. You'll enjoy ocean views from the quiet summer community of Manset and from the natural seawall a couple of miles south. Ahead is Bass Harbor, another classic Maine lobster village that is completely uncommercial. From here you can take the 30-minute ferry ride to Swans Island. The route now skirts the largely undeveloped western shore of the island, passing through the tiny villages of Tremont and West Tremont, on lightly traveled ME 102. Just before the end, you'll pass the northern end of Long Pond, the largest lake on the island.

Directions for the ride

Start from the Somesville Library, on the east side of ME 102, in Somesville. You can park in front of the library. Notice the lovely small dam behind it.

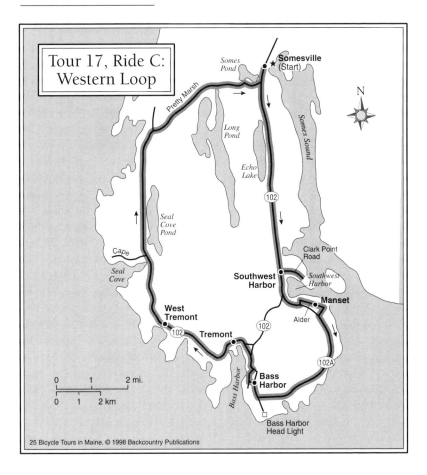

Tour 17, Ride C:
Western Loop

25 Bicycle Tours in Maine, © 1998 Backcountry Publications

0.0 *With your back to the library, turn left (south) on ME 102 and go 5.8 miles to Clark Point Road on the left, at a blinking light in the center of Southwest Harbor.*

Somesville is the oldest community on Mount Desert Island, dating back to 1761. Just after you start, notice the graceful white church and the fine old homes in the village.

You'll follow the shore of Echo Lake, which is 2 miles long. The lake is walled in by rugged Beech Cliff, which towers 600 feet above it on the opposite shore at its southern end.

5.8 *Turn left on Clark Point Road and go 0.7 mile to the dead*

end, following the harbor on your right, and backtrack to ME 102.

Southwest Harbor is a traditional Maine fishing village. At the end of the road are a Coast Guard station and the Mount Desert Oceanarium. This is more than an aquarium; it is also a museum and learning center, with exhibits on the lobster and the lobstering industry, boatbuilding, and how fishermen and seafarers have adapted to the tides and the weather. The building was formerly an old hardware store.

7.2 *Turn left on ME 102 and go 0.7 mile to the intersection where ME 102 bears right and ME 102A turns left.*

7.9 *Turn left and go 0.5 mile to Alder Lane, a narrow road on the left.*

8.4 *Turn left and go 1.2 miles to the end (ME 102A again, Seawall Road).*

This is a lovely loop along the harbor, passing through Manset, a gracious summer community and yachting center. You'll go past the Moorings, a well-known inn and restaurant, and a good lunch spot. As you're pedaling along the water, look back over your left shoulder for a view of the harbor and the mountains rising behind it.

9.6 *Turn left on ME 102A and go 4 miles to the point where ME 102A turns 90 degrees right and a smaller road turns left.*

Here the loop route turns right, but if you turn left and go 0.5 mile you'll come to Bass Harbor Head Light, at the southernmost point of Mount Desert Island. The lighthouse, perched on top of a high craggy ledge, is a small brick tower attached to a white keeper's house. It was built in 1858. The light was automated in 1974; the keeper's house is now a private residence. Behind the lighthouse, a walkway and stairs lead down to the rocks.

13.6 *Continue on ME 102A for 0.6 mile to McMullen Avenue on the left, in Bass Harbor (a sign says TO THE SWANS ISLAND FERRY).*

The road comes up while you're going downhill.

14.2 *Turn left and go 0.1 mile to the first right, at a stop sign.*

Side Trip: Here the loop route turns right, but to go to the Swans

Island ferry dock, go straight for 0.25 mile. Swans Island is a pleasant spot for bicycling, with about 12 miles of paved road (there aren't many loops, so most of the time you have to go out and back on the same roads). There are three tiny settlements on the island—Atlantic, Minturn, and Swans Island. There's a museum in Atlantic, an old general store in Minturn, and a lighthouse at the tip of the peninsula south of Swans Island. During the summer, several boats a day make the 30-minute crossing. The terrain on the island is hilly, but the hills are short.

14.3 Turn right (curve left if you're coming from the ferry dock) and go 0.2 mile to the end (ME 102A).

14.5 Turn left and go 0.6 mile to a road that bears left (a sign says TO SEAL COVE).

15.1 Bear left and go 0.3 mile to the stop sign (merge head-on into ME 102).

15.4 Go straight, and stay on the main road for 12.3 miles to the end (ME 102).

You'll go through the tiny villages of Tremont and West Tremont, which consist of a few simple houses. After 5 miles, you can bear left on Cape Road, which leads 0.5 mile to unspoiled Seal Cove. At the far end of the cove the road turns to dirt, so backtrack to ME 102.

Toward the end you'll pass the northern tip of Long Pond, which is 4 miles long, and the largest lake on the island. Just before the end, Somes Pond is on the left.

27.7 Turn left and go 0.4 mile to the library on the right. If you're doing the Grand Tour (Ride D), pick it up at mile 59.9.

Final mileage: 28.1

RIDE D: Grand Tour

Distance: *68 miles (39 omitting the Western Loop)*
Terrain: *Rolling, with several long, steady hills.*
Special features: *Rugged coastline, Somes Sound, fishing villages, lighthouse.*

Here is a tour around the entire circumference of Mount Desert Island. Starting from the visitors center, you'll follow Park Loop Road past the

A stretch of craggy coastline on Mount Desert Island

major coastal landmarks, including Thunder Hole, Sand Beach, Otter Cliffs, and Otter Cove. You'll then go through Northeast Harbor and along the eastern shore of Somes Sound into Somesville. The route now follows the entire Western Loop (Ride C). To finish, you'll head north to the village of Town Hill and return to the visitors center along a little-used back road.

143

Since the route forms a figure eight, you can shorten the ride to 39 miles by omitting the Western Loop.

Because of its length, this tour is designed for the enthusiastic and experienced cyclist who would like to see most of the island's scenery on one ride, without stopping for any length of time at points of interest. The tour will be enjoyed most by cyclists who already have some familiarity with the island and its attractions.

Directions for the ride

Start from the Acadia National Park Visitor Center on ME 3, about 3 miles northwest of Bar Harbor.

0.0   Follow the Park Loop ride (Ride A) through the directions for mile 10.7.

18.1   Turn left, following the sign for ME 3, Blackwoods Campground, Northeast Harbor. Go 50 yards, and turn left again onto Jordan Pond Road (a sign says NO THROUGH TRAFFIC). Go 0.8 mile to the end (merge right on ME 3 at the stop sign).

18.9   Follow the Jordan Pond ride (Ride B) from mile 8.4 through the directions for mile 18.2, to ME 233 on the right.

29.9   Continue straight on ME 198 and go 1.4 miles to the end (ME 102).

There are snacks at the garage on the right. Here the Grand Tour turns left, but if you want to shorten the ride to 39 miles , turn right on ME 102 and go 2.1 miles to Crooked Road on the right at the top of a hill, opposite the old wooden fire station with a bell tower (there's a country store on your right just past the intersection).

Turn right and go 4.9 miles to the end (ME 3), staying on the main road. Turn right on ME 3 and go 0.4 mile to the entrance to the visitors center on the right.

Final mileage: 38.9.

31.3   Turn left on ME 102 and go 0.5 mile to the Somesville Library on the left.

Notice the picturesque little dam behind the library.

31.8   Follow the entire Western Loop ride (Ride C).

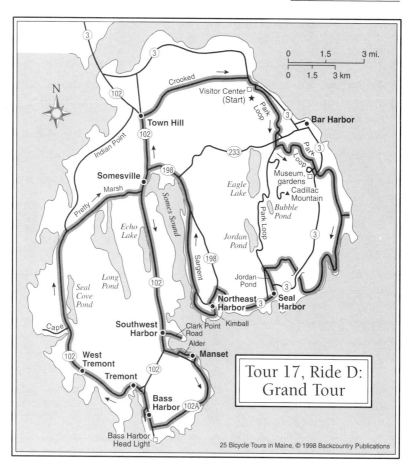

Tour 17, Ride D:
Grand Tour

25 Bicycle Tours in Maine, © 1998 Backcountry Publications

59.9 When you arrive back at the library, continue straight on ME 102 for 2.6 miles to Crooked Road on the right at the top of a hill, opposite the old wooden fire station with a bell tower.

There's a wonderful country store on your right just past the intersection. This is the village of Town Hill.

62.5 Turn right on Crooked Road and go 4.9 miles to the end (ME 3).

You'll pass a granite quarry shortly before the end.

67.4 Turn right on ME 3 and go 0.4 mile to the entrance to the visitors center on the right.

Final mileage: 67.8

RIDE E: Carriage Road Ride

Distance: *13 miles*
Terrain: *Gently rolling, with two long, steep hills.*
Road surface: *Hard packed gravel. A mountain bike is recommended.*
Special features: *Roads off-limits to motor vehicles, Eagle Lake, two smaller ponds.*
Caution: *Although the roads are generally hard-packed, there may be loose spots. Take it easy, especially on descents. Also watch for pedestrians and horses. In good weather the carriage roads are crowded with cyclists after 10 AM. On a sunny Saturday in mid-June (not yet the height of the season), I encountered cyclists every minute or two. Many of them were families with children, some of whom were riding on the wrong side of the road or too fast while going downhill. I suggest starting the ride before 8:30 AM so that you can enjoy it before the roads become busy.*

A unique feature of Acadia National Park is its network of dirt roads, called carriage roads, that wind through the interior forests and skirt the lakes and flanks of the mountains. The roads, on which motor vehicles are not allowed, are ideal for hiking, horseback riding, cross-country skiing, and bicycling. Construction of the 50-mile network was financed and directed by John D. Rockefeller, Jr., between 1917 and 1933. The roads are superbly engineered, with gentle grades, stone culverts, and retaining walls. The paths cross 16 graceful stone bridges, each one individually designed. The road surface is maintained in a firmly packed state, allowing ready passage by mountain bike.

This ride follows 13 miles of carriage roads. The southern portion of the ride goes along Eagle Lake, the second largest lake in the park. There are clearly numbered signposts at every intersection.

Directions for the ride

Start from the north end of the visitors center parking lot, where a dirt path heads away from the lot between two wooden fences. There's a sign with a bicycle on it at the beginning of the path.

   0.0 *Follow the path away from the parking lot and go 0.5 mile to the end, at signpost number 1.*

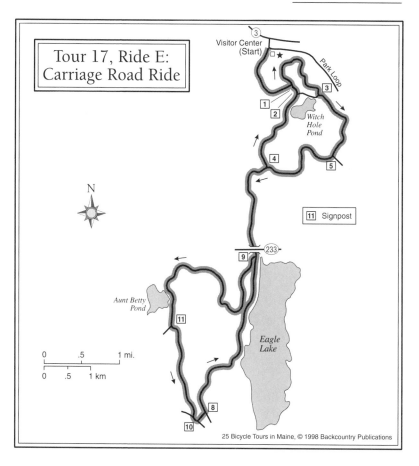

Tour 17, Ride E:
Carriage Road Ride

The entire way is uphill, with some steep pitches that you'll want to walk. This is the first of only two tough hills on the ride, so don't get discouraged.

0.5 *Turn left, continuing uphill. Go 0.9 mile to the first left, at signpost number 3.*

There's a spectacular view from the top of the hill, with Frenchman Bay in the distance.

1.4 *Turn left and go 1 mile to the next road on the left, which crosses a bridge. Signpost number 5 is at the intersection.*

At the beginning of this section, you'll pass Witch Hole Pond on your right. When you get to the road on the left, the bridge, a stone arched span high above tumbling Duck Brook, is worth a look.

2.4 *Bear slightly right and go 1 mile to the next left, at a large traffic island and signpost number 4.*

This section is mostly wooded, with a few clearings from which you can see the mountains in the distance. You'll climb and then descend gradually.

3.4 *Bear left and go 1.2 miles to a road on the right at signpost number 9, shortly after you go underneath a stone bridge.*

Eagle Lake is on your left at the intersection.

4.6 *Turn right and go 2.6 miles to a fork at signpost number 11.*

You'll climb steeply for the first 0.1 mile, and then gradually. At the top, Eagle Lake lies far below on your left, and just ahead you'll enjoy a sweeping view of Cadillac Mountain. A long, steady descent brings you to Aunt Betty Pond, with Sargent Mountain rising majestically behind it.

7.2 *Bear left at the fork and go 1.2 miles to the end, at signpost number 10.*

The last 0.7 mile is a steep climb—the worst hill of the ride. The road ascends over six small bridges that cross a rushing stream.

8.4 *Turn left at the end, go 50 yards (still marked by signpost number 10), and turn left again. Go less than 0.2 mile to the end, at signpost number 8.*

8.6 *Turn left and go 2 miles to a road on your right at signpost number 6, immediately before you go underneath a stone bridge.*

There's a long, gradual descent to Eagle Lake and a lovely ride along its shore.

When you come to the intersection the ride goes straight, but if you turn right for 50 yards you'll have a spectacular view along the full length of the lake, with hump-shaped North Bubble in the background.

10.6 *Continue straight, passing under the bridge. Go 1.1 miles to the end, at signpost number 4.*

11.7 *Turn left and go 1 mile to a road on your right at signpost number 2.*

Witch Hole Pond is on the right shortly before the intersection.

12.7 *Bear slightly left and go 0.2 mile to a narrower road on your left, at signpost number 1.*

12.9 *Turn left and go 0.5 mile to the visitors center parking lot.*

This is the same steep hill that you climbed at the beginning of the ride. **Caution:** The descent is steep and narrow; it's safest to walk.

Final mileage: 13.4

Bicycle Repair Services

Acadia Bike and Canoe, 48 Cottage Street, Bar Harbor (288-9605)

Bar Harbor Bicycle Shop, 141 Cottage Street, Bar Harbor (288-3886)

Northeast Harbor Bicycle Shop, Main Street, Northeast Harbor (276-5480)

Southwest Cycle, Main Street, Southwest Harbor (244-5856)

18
The Other Acadia: Schoodic Point

Distance: 29 miles
Terrain: Gently rolling, with two moderate hills.
Special features: Views of Mount Desert Island and Cadillac Mountain, Schoodic Point, fishing villages.

About 10 miles east of Mount Desert Island, on the far side of Frenchman Bay, lies an unspoiled peninsula that is ideal for a half day of bicycling. At the southern tip is Schoodic Point (pronounced "Skoodic"), a dramatic rockbound promontory that is part of Acadia National Park. There are few places in Maine off Mount Desert Island where the craggy coast is so powerfully presented. On windy days, the surf crashes onto the rocks, sending plumes of spray high into the air, in a spectacular display of nature's might. North of the point are quiet fishing villages on picturesque harbors. Another feature of the peninsula is the fine views of Cadillac Mountain across Frenchman Bay—better views than from Mount Desert Island itself.

The ride starts from West Gouldsboro, at the northwest corner of the peninsula. In the village is a bed & breakfast, the Sunset House (963-7156), a gracious wooden building where you might want to stay the night before the ride. Nearby are a stately white church and a handsome stone and concrete library. Halfway down the peninsula is Winter Harbor, a small fishing port at the head of an inlet filled with lobster boats. Beyond, the road clings to the coast as it works its way to Schoodic Point, and continues along the shore on the east side of the peninsula.

Halfway up the peninsula is Prospect Harbor, a classic Maine fishing village with lobster traps stacked neatly on docks with little red shacks at the far end. The last portion of the ride heads inland along the middle of the peninsula through a largely wooded area with a few small farms.

Distinctive ledges at the tip of Schoodic Point

Directions for the ride

Start from the small dirt parking area on the south side of US 1, across from a combined grocery store and gas station, near West Gouldsboro. It's about 2.5 miles east of ME 183, a mile west of ME 186, and 17 miles east of Ellsworth.

0.0 *Turn right out of the parking area, heading east, and go 1.1 miles to ME 186 (South Gouldsboro Road) on the right.*

You'll pass a distinctive A-frame house on your left near the beginning.

1.1 *Turn right and go 3.9 miles to Fire Road 270 on the right, shortly after a church on the left. It's the second of two roads on the right about 0.5 mile apart, and it immediately curves left.*

The beginning of ME 186 follows James Cove into West Gouldsboro.

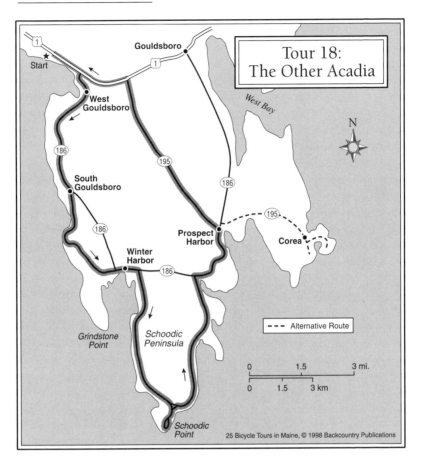

Tour 18:
The Other Acadia

5.0 *Bear right and go 4.5 miles to a road on the right that goes uphill (a sign says* TO ACADIA NATIONAL PARK, SCHOODIC POINT SECTION).

You'll dip down to a cove with attractive wooden houses at the water's edge, and then turn inland slightly, cutting across the top of Grindstone Neck, a wealthy summer colony. Shortly before the intersection you'll go through Winter Harbor, where there's a restaurant and a place to buy food.

9.5 *Turn right and go 4.6 miles to a fork (a sign points right to Schoodic Point).*

The road hugs Frenchman Bay, with fine views of Cadillac Mountain on the opposite shore.

14.1 *Bear right at the fork and go 0.6 mile to the tip, where the road makes a small loop.*

You'll pass a Navy communications station. On a calm day, the rocks and ledges are great for picnicking, relaxing, or exploring.

14.7 *Follow the main road away from the point and go 5.1 miles to the end (ME 186), following the ocean on your right.*

The first 3 miles cling closely to the coast. There's a grocery at the end.

19.8 *Turn right on ME 186 (a fairly sharp right) and go 2.1 miles to ME 195 (Pond Road) on the left, in Prospect Harbor.*

Side Trip: Here the loop route turns left, but if you go straight for 0.1 mile, then turn right and go 3 miles, you'll come to Corea, another unspoiled and untouristed lobster port. In the center of the village, a road on the left curls around tiny Corea Harbor. There is no place to buy food in the town.

21.9 *Turn left on ME 195 (right if you visited Corea) and go 5.1 miles to the end (US 1).*

The landscape is mostly wooded, with a few small farms. This is the hilliest section of the ride, but the hills are not difficult.

27.0 *Turn left on US 1 and go 2.3 miles to the parking area on the left, across from the grocery.*

This section of US 1 has a wide shoulder.

Final mileage: 29.3

Bicycle Repair Services

Bar Harbor Bicycle Shop, 193 Main Street, Ellsworth (667-6886)

19
Blueberries and Boats: Columbia Falls–Jonesboro–Jonesport–Addison

Distance: *43 miles*
Terrain: *Rolling, with a couple of tough climbs.*
Special features: *Ruggles House, blueberry barrens, fishing villages, bay views.*
Accommodations: *Since the starting point is rather isolated, you may want to stay overnight nearby before the ride. Some good spots: Ricker House, Cherryfield (546-2780); Pleasant Bay Bed & Breakfast, South Addison (483-4490); Red Barn Motel, Milbridge (546-7721).*

The southwestern corner of Washington County, midway between Ellsworth and the eastern tip of Maine, is outstanding for bicycling. South of US 1 lie unspoiled and untouristed lobster ports, and north of it is the blueberry capital of the United States, with vast blueberry fields, called barrens, stretching along broad hillsides. A pleasant feature of the area is its lack of traffic—few vacationers venture east of Ellsworth, even fewer explore the secondary roads off US 1, while through traffic to Canada passes to the north on ME 9 and I-95.

The ride starts from Columbia Falls, an attractive village of well-kept wooden houses. The Pleasant River cascades through the town and over a dam with a small hydroelectric plant next to it. A white church stands on the riverbank, and another one crowns a nearby hilltop. In the center of the village stands the Thomas Ruggles House, a superbly crafted mansion, built in 1818 for a wealthy lumber trader. The interior is splendid, with ornate woodwork and a delicate staircase which seems suspended in midair.

From Columbia Falls the ride heads northeast on a country road that

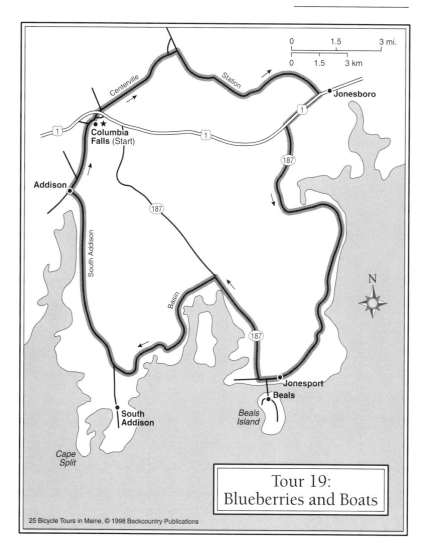

Tour 19:
Blueberries and Boats

25 Bicycle Tours in Maine, © 1998 Backcountry Publications

quickly leads into blueberry country, ascending onto a ridge with spectacular views. You'll run parallel to US 1 on another back road into
Jonesboro, a quiet village about 9 miles east of Columbia Falls. The
remainder of the ride follows the perimeter of the two-pronged peninsula, with Jonesport at the bottom of the eastern part and South Addison
at the tip of the western one. The ride along the eastern shore to

Jonesport is a delight, with numerous views of the bay across rolling fields of blueberries.

Jonesport is a rarely visited lobster port complete with a boat-filled harbor, wharves supported by tall pilings, and weathered lobstermen's sheds and fish processing plants. The shrill cry of seagulls pierces the air while you're pedaling through the town. For a side trip, you can cross the bridge to Beals Island, where the smaller village of Beals is another classic Maine fishing community.

From Jonesport you'll follow the western half of the peninsula to Addison, a sleepy, somewhat dilapidated village that is not as prosperous as Jonesport. From Addison it's a short hop back to Columbia Falls.

Directions for the ride

Start from the post office in the center of Columbia Falls, parking at the far end of the lot, near the river. Columbia Falls is about 45 miles east of Ellsworth and just south of US 1. From either the west or the east, a road bears off US 1 for about 0.5 mile into the village.

0.0 **Turn right out of the lot, crossing the bridge over the Pleasant River.**

If you'd like to visit the Ruggles House first, turn left out of the lot and go 0.1 mile; it will be on your right.

0.0 **Immediately after the bridge, turn left and go 0.2 mile to a crossroads and a stop sign at US 1.**

0.2 **Go straight for 3.3 miles to a fork where one road bears left and the other goes straight.**

You'll climb steadily through extensive blueberry barrens, followed by a sharp downhill with a great view.

3.5 **Go straight (don't bear left) for 0.3 mile to the end, at a yield sign.**

3.8 **Turn right and go 6 miles to the end (US 1), in Jonesboro.**

You'll traverse open blueberry fields with sweeping views. In the spring, some of the fields are burned to fertilize the soil and keep the bushes low.

9.8 **Turn right on US 1 and go 1.6 miles to ME 187 on the left.**

Church overlooking the Pleasant River in Columbia Falls

You'll pass a grocery store with a lunch counter on your right as soon as you turn onto US 1.

11.4 Turn left and go about 12.5 miles to the bridge to Beals Island (Bridge Street) on the left, in Jonesport.

There's a snack bar and grocery store in town. Fine views of the bay abound on this stretch. It's worth crossing the bridge to Beals Island. At the far end of the bridge, turn either right or left. If you follow (or chase, as the local people say) the road on the left for a mile, you'll come to a short causeway to Great Wass Island, which sports a network of hiking trails. If you're lucky, you may spot an osprey or even an eagle, both of which are occasionally seen in the vicinity.

24.0 *Continue on ME 187, which turns 90 degrees to the right after 0.25 mile. Stay on ME 187 and go 3.9 miles to an unmarked road on the left just before you would climb a hill. (As soon as you turn onto this road, a sign says TO SOUTH ADDISON).*

You'll go through the tiny hamlet of Indian River just before the intersection.

28.2 *Turn left and go 12.5 miles to the center of Addison, where the main road turns 90 degrees right.*

This section is not as prosperous as most of the Maine coast. The road hugs the bay as you approach Addison. Notice the old Masonic temple on your left just before the center of the village.

Side Trip: After 6 miles, a road on the left leads 1.5 miles to South Addison, a tiny settlement of weathered houses, a little church, and lobster traps everywhere.

40.7 *Turn right on the main road in the center of Addison. Go 0.4 mile to a fork where one road bears left and the other goes straight.*

41.1 *Go straight for 2.1 miles to the end, in Columbia Falls (merge right at a yield sign).*

The Ruggles House is on the left on the far side of the intersection.

43.2 *Bear right and go 0.1 mile to the post office on the right.*

Final mileage: 43.3

Bicycle Repair Services

None nearby

20
Washington County Tour

Distance: 147 miles in 3 days—48 miles the first day, 51 the second, and 48 the third.

Terrain: Gently rolling, with occasional hills. This is the easiest of the overnight tours.

Road surface: 3.2 miles of dirt road, which can be avoided.

Special features: Roosevelt summer home, lighthouse, highest tides in the United States, easternmost point in the United States, fishing villages.

Accommodations: For the night before the tour, in Machias: Sea Gull Motel (the most convenient, 255-3033); Bluebird Motel (255-3332); Maineland Motel (255-3334); Margaretta Motel (255-6500); Machias Motor Inn (255-4861).

For the first night, in Lubec: Home Port Inn (bed & breakfast, 733-2077); Eastland Motel (733-5501); Bayviews Bed & Breakfast (733-2181); Peacock House Bed & Breakfast (733-2403); Lubeckergasthaus Bed & Breakfast (733-4385); Breakers by the Bay (733-2487).

For the second night, in Calais: International Motel (454-7515); Calais Motor Inn (the fanciest, 454-7111).

Washington County, at Maine's eastern tip, embodies all that is associated with the phrase "Down East." It is a remote and unspoiled land of great natural beauty. Along its coast lie quiet fishing ports that rarely see visitors. Along the harbors are lobstermen's shanties and fish-processing plants, not boutiques and craft shops. Lobster boats and skiffs crowd the bays and inlets, not sailboats and yachts. Inland lies a nearly unpopulated wilderness of pristine lakes, endless forests, and blueberry fields.

Bicycling in Washington County is a pleasure. The traffic, even on US 1,

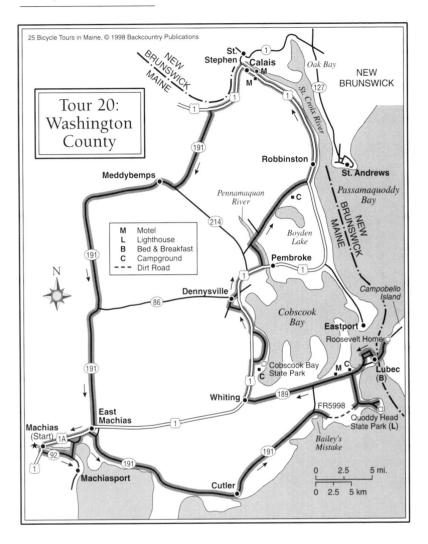

25 Bicycle Tours in Maine, © 1998 Backcountry Publications

Tour 20:
Washington
County

St.
Stephen Calais Oak Bay NEW BRUNSWICK

M Motel
L Lighthouse
B Bed & Breakfast
C Campground
--- Dirt Road

Meddybemps

Robbinston

St. Andrews

Pennamaquan River

Passamaquoddy Bay

Boyden Lake

Pembroke

Dennysville

Campobello Island

Cobscook Bay

Eastport
Roosevelt Home

Cobscook Bay State Park

Lubec (B)

Whiting

Machias (Start)

East Machias

Bailey's Mistake

Quoddy Head State Park (L)

Machiasport

Cutler

0 2.5 5 mi.
0 2.5 5 km

is never heavy because very few visitors to Maine come east of Ellsworth, and there are no cities or even big towns in the county. Calais, the largest town, has a population of only about 4000. Travelers on the way to New Brunswick generally take I-95 to Houlton or ME 9, which is not on the tour, east out of Bangor. The region's most visited attraction, Roosevelt Campobello International Park, is rarely crowded. Cyclists will also appreciate the fact that the land near the coast is not very hilly. People in the towns are friendly and may well start a conversation with you; this happened to me several times while I was exploring the area.

The tour starts from Machias (rhymes with "the bias"), an attractive town dominated by the graceful spire of the Congregational Church. The Machias River flows through the town, crashing over a waterfall just below US 1. The Burnham Tavern, a handsome yellow building with a gambrel roof that was built in 1770, is the oldest building in Maine east of the Penobscot River. A branch of the University of Maine is also located in town.

From Machias you'll follow the coast to Quoddy Head State Park, which contains the most easterly point of land in the United States. The park commands a pine-rimmed headland with footpaths winding along the jagged, rocky shoreline. Adjoining the park is the candy-cane-striped West Quoddy Head Light, which was built in 1808.

From the park it's about 7 miles to Roosevelt Campobello International Park, which is located on Campobello Island in New Brunswick. The island is linked to Lubec, Maine, by a bridge. In the park is Franklin Delano Roosevelt's summer "cottage," a graceful maroon mansion overlooking Cobscook Bay. The park, which is meticulously landscaped and shaded by stately groves of trees, exudes an aura of contentment and tranquillity.

From Campobello Island, the route crosses the bridge back to Maine and follows the state's easternmost coastline north to Calais (rhymes with "Dallas"), skirting Cobscook Bay and then the wide tidal estuary of the Saint Croix River, which separates Maine and New Brunswick. Calais is a busy little town with some fine old houses on US 1 overlooking the river and a traditional Victorian business block of three-story brick buildings. The last segment of the tour goes from Calais southwest back to Machias, passing through a primarily wooded landscape punctuated with undeveloped lakes and occasional blueberry fields.

Directions for the ride

FIRST DAY: Machias to Lubec (48 miles)

Start from the junction of US 1 and ME 92 in Machias, just west of the center of town. You'll probably stay at a motel the night before the tour.

When you make your reservation, explain that you'll be taking a bicycle trip and that you'd like to leave your car there for a few days. The Sea Gull Motel is closest to the start of the ride, just east of town, on US 1, and is reasonably priced. The Machias Motor Inn is just east of the Sea Gull Motel. The Bluebird Motel is a mile west of town on US 1. The Mainland Motel and the Margaretta Motel are a mile east of town on US 1.

A good spot to eat before and after the tour is Helen's Restaurant, which is a half mile east of town on US 1.

0.0 Head east on ME 92 and go 3.1 miles to the first left (a fairly sharp left).

ME 92 follows the south bank of the Machias River, south of US 1. As you start down this road, you'll see a small electric substation on the left. Immediately after it there's a good view of the falls from a footbridge.

Side Trip: When you get to the road on the left the tour turns here, but if you continue straight for a mile you'll come to Machiasport, a village of well-kept houses that overlook the mouth of the river. The Gates House, a Federal-style house built in 1807, is open to the public. A mile beyond Machiasport is Fort O'Brien, on the shore of Machias Bay, where the first naval encounter of the American Revolution took place, in 1775. Only the earthworks remain.

3.1 Make a sharp left and go 1 mile to the end (merge right at a yield sign).

4.1 Bear right and go 0.5 mile to the end (merge right on US 1).

The road hugs the East Machias River.

4.6 Bear right on US 1 and go 0.7 mile to the first right (a sign says TO THE NAVAL STATION, CUTLER).

5.3 Turn right. Just ahead, on the far side of the bridge, the main road curves right. Continue for less than 0.2 mile to the end (ME 191).

5.6 Turn right and go about 24 miles to a road on the right near the top of a steep hill.

There's a tiny, closed country store at the intersection. ME 191 is a nearly deserted road that is ideal for bicycling. After a few miles you'll hug the shore of Holmes Bay. The opposite shore is dominated by the forest of 26 radio towers belonging to the Naval Communications Unit, which is one of the most powerful radio stations in the world.

After about 12 miles you'll come to the lovely fishing village of Cutler, with its small harbor filled with lobster boats and lined with wharves propped up on tall pilings. Here, and on the rest of the tour as you work your way along the coast, these tall wharves are a standard feature of the landscape. Because the tides are so high, averaging over 15 feet, the docks have to be high enough so that the boats won't become grounded at low tide. There's a grocery in Cutler. Beyond the village, the road heads inland through an uninhabited landscape of scrubby evergreens and broad blueberry fields.

When you come to the road on the right, the ride turns here. This road contains a 3.2-mile section of dirt. If you want to avoid the dirt section (adding 4 miles to the ride, and covering ground over which you'll have to backtrack later), continue straight for 2.8 miles to the end (ME 189); turn right and go 4.2 miles to a road on the right with a grocery on the far corner (a sign will say TO QUODDY HEAD STATE PARK); turn right and go 2.7 miles to a fork; then bear left and go 2 miles to the state park and West Quoddy Head Light.

29.6 *Turn right. After 1.3 miles the road turns to dirt, a stretch that lasts for 3.2 miles.*

Caution: Watch for rough, loose spots, especially going up or down hills. When the road becomes paved again, continue 1.4 miles to the end (merge left at a stop sign). At the beginning of this road, you'll go along a small bay called Bailey's Mistake.

This colorful name commemorates a navigational error. According to legend, in 1830 a sea captain named Bailey was fogged in while sailing his schooner from eastern Maine to Boston. He attempted to land at Lubec but entered Bailey's Mistake instead and ran aground. Rather than face an embarrassing arrival in Boston, the crew settled along the shore, building houses from the ship's cargo of lumber.

35.5 *Make a sharp right, following the water on your left, and go 2 miles to a dirt fork.*

Straight ahead is West Quoddy Head Light, with its distinctive red and white candy stripes. To the right is Quoddy Head State Park, a superb picnic spot. Campobello Island lies across the channel.

37.5 *From the park and lighthouse, follow the main road for 4.7 miles to the end (ME 189), just outside of Lubec.*

The tour now heads to the Roosevelt home, which is 3 miles away, and open until 5 PM Eastern time (6 PM in Canada). If you don't have time to visit it now, go tomorrow.

42.2 *Turn right on ME 189 and go 0.8 mile to a fork where Main Street goes straight and ME 189 bears right.*

Just after you turn, a museum of the sardine industry, which was most active early in the century, is on the right.

43.0 *Bear right at the fork and go 0.4 mile to the bridge to Campobello Island.*

On the far side of the bridge, you will go through Canadian customs. Continue for 1.5 miles to the Roosevelt Campobello International Park on the left.

Roosevelt spent summers here from 1883, when he was a year old, to 1921, when he was stricken with polio. Behind the mansion a lawn slopes down to the bay, where there's a small dock. Next to the Roosevelt home is the Hubbard Cottage, a graceful mansion with a broad porch, built in 1891 for Gorham Hubbard, a Boston insurance broker.

45.4 *From the park, backtrack to the bridge.*

After 0.5 mile, a road on the right leads 0.3 mile to Friar's Head, a dramatic headland with a tall, detached pinnacle of rock at its outer end. Go through United States customs on the far side of the bridge.

47.4 *Turn sharply right immediately after the customs office, following the water on the right, and go 0.8 mile to the end (ME 189).*

The road loops counterclockwise around the small peninsula on which Lubec is located. At the beginning, you'll go through the center of town, which has a derelict, windswept look, and pass the Peacock Canning Company, one of the two sardine canneries in

Lubec. At the turn of the century there were 20 canneries in operation. Just ahead you'll pass some abandoned fish-processing plants and Lubec Packing Company, which is still alive and well. Bayviews Bed & Breakfast is on your right just before the end.

When you get to the end, the route turns right, but if you turn left and go a couple of blocks there are three more bed & breakfasts: the Home Port Inn, the Peacock House, and the Lubeckergasthaus. Breakers by the Bay is on ME 189 just before the bridge to Canada; you passed it earlier. The Eastland Motel is 2.3 miles to the right, on ME 189. The Seaview Restaurant, about a mile to the right on ME 189, is a good place to eat.

Final mileage (to ME 189): 48.2

SECOND DAY: Lubec to Calais (51 miles)

0.0 *From Lubec, head west on ME 189 and go about 11 miles to the end (US 1), in Whiting.*

From the Eastland Motel, it's about 8.5 miles to US 1.

11.0 *Turn right and go 4.3 miles to an unmarked road on the right (a sign says TO COBSCOOK BAY STATE PARK).*

As soon as you turn onto US 1, there's a grocery on the right.

15.3 *Turn right and go 3.8 miles to the end (US 1 again).*

After 0.5 mile you'll pass the entrance to Cobscook Bay State Park, a lovely wooded area with trails along the bay. Cobscook Bay boasts the highest tides in the country, averaging 24 feet. It's fascinating to stand by the water's edge and watch the tide come in; the water rises visibly, like a bathtub filling up. Farther along the road there's a marine research station, part of Suffolk University, not open to the public.

19.1 *Turn right on US 1 and go 1.8 miles to an unmarked road on the left (a sign says TO DENNYSVILLE).*

20.9 *Turn left and go 0.8 mile to the end, immediately after the bridge.*

21.7 *Turn right and go 0.9 mile back to US 1, at a stop sign.*

You'll go through Dennysville, a village with elegant houses and a war memorial statue on the hillside on the left, and the Dennys

165

River flowing along the road on the right. Just before US 1 on the left is the Lincoln House, a square yellow mansion that was built in 1787 and is now an inn.

22.6 *Turn left on US 1 and go 5.6 miles to the second crossroads, which comes up while you're going downhill. It's 1 mile after ME 214.*

There's a snack bar on your left at the intersection.

28.2 *Turn left and go 2.6 miles to the second right, which crosses a bridge.*

You'll follow the Pennamaquan River on your right. Just before the intersection there's a small dam on the right.

30.8 *Turn right, and just ahead curve left on the main road. Go 6.9 miles to the end (US 1).*

After going along Boyden Lake, you'll tackle a couple of short, steep hills and then a long, steady climb onto a ridge. At the top is a great view, with Passamaquoddy Bay far below. You'll enjoy a swooping descent from the ridge.

37.8 *Turn left on US 1 and go about 13.5 miles to the two recommended motels as you come into Calais.*

This is a beautiful stretch hugging the Saint Croix River. After 2 miles you'll go through Robbinston, a lovely town with some ornate Victorian houses and two fine churches.

About 3 miles beyond Robbinston you'll see a sign for the Saint Croix Island International Historic Site, an overlook on the riverbank. (To get there, turn right on the side road and immediately right down the steep driveway to the river.) The island, named because it is in the shape of a cross, was the site of one of the first attempts to set up a colony in the New World. In 1604 the French sent 120 colonists to the island, but during the severe winter 35 died, and the survivors resettled in Nova Scotia the following spring. As you come into Calais, gracious old houses stand above the riverbank on US 1.

Final mileage: 51.3

THIRD DAY: Calais to Machias (48 miles)

0.0 *From the motel, continue on US 1 for 0.6 mile to the traffic light in the center of Calais (US 1 turns left here).*

Bad Little Falls, Machias

167

You'll go past a park with an old wooden bandstand on the left. Just before the light, the attractive beige brick library, built in 1892, is on your right overlooking the river.

0.6 *Turn left at the traffic light (still US 1) and go 5.7 miles to ME 191 on the left (a sign says TO MACHIAS).*

The road skirts the Moosehorn National Wildlife Refuge, a 22,000-acre preserve of bogs, marshes, and forest.

6.3 *Turn left on ME 191 and go about 38 miles to US 1, in East Machias.*

After about 8 miles you'll pass through the tiny village of Meddybemps, which contains only a few houses and a country store. This is the last source of food and water for more than 30 miles. As you come into the village, Meddybemps Lake is on the right, about 100 yards off the road. Beyond Meddybemps the land is mostly wooded, with occasional blueberry fields. It also gets hillier.

About 8 miles after Meddybemps there's a long climb onto a ridge with a view of Lake Cathance in the distance. The road descends to the lake and follows it, but the view of the water is blocked by the trees. Beyond the lake the terrain is moderately hilly, and mostly wooded.

44.3 *Turn right on US 1 and go 4 miles into Machias.*

Final mileage: 48.3

Bicycle Repair Services

None nearby

21
Sebago Century

Distance: *99 miles in 2 days—59 miles the first day, 40 the second. You can also complete this ride in one day.*

Terrain: *Rolling, with several difficult hills.*

Special features: *Willowbrook at Newfield (living history museum), covered bridges, Hiram Falls, Jones Gallery of Glass and Ceramics, Douglas Mountain Preserve, Sebago Lake.*

Accommodations: *Cornish Inn, Cornish (625-8501); Mid-Way Motel, Cornish (625-8835); York County Campsite Park, Cornish (625-8808).*

When bicycling became popular around 1880, a ride of 100 miles, quickly dubbed a Century, became a challenge. Nearly every bicycle club in the country incorporates a Century into its ride schedule, and as a rule, the ride is done in 1 day. However, it's a lot more enjoyable in two, especially if there are places along the way that are worth visiting. If you really want to tackle this ride in one day, you can do it if you get into shape first, but you won't have time to see the attractions along the way.

The countryside between the western suburbs of Portland and the New Hampshire border is ideal for bicycling, with prosperous rolling farmland, unspoiled small towns, and quiet lakes. Dramatic mountain views unfold near the New Hampshire border. At the region's northern edge is the broad sweep of Sebago Lake, the second largest in Maine. The area contains a surprising number of places to see, including a restored 19th-century village, an outstanding museum of antique glass and ceramics, covered bridges, and a hilltop preserve with a spectacular view. With no cities or even large towns in the region, traffic is light, even on numbered roads. Although this portion of Maine is very rural, an extensive network of paved secondary roads, as fine as anywhere in the state, allows the bicyclist to come into intimate contact with the landscape.

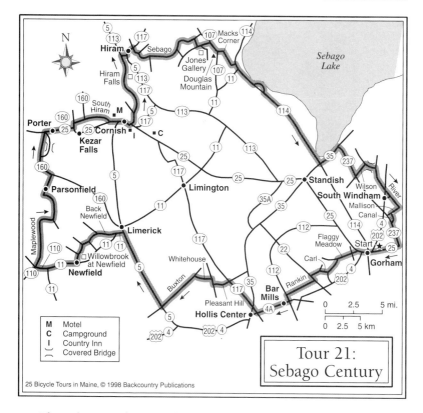

N

5
(113) (117)
Hiram Sebago
Hiram
Falls (113)
(117)

(160) South
Hiram **M**
160
Porter (25)
(25) **Cornish** ■ ■C
**Kezar
Falls**
I

(160)
5
Parsonfield
(160)
Back
Newfield

Maplewood
(110)
(110) **Limerick**
(11) (11)
(11) □ Willowbrook
at Newfield
Newfield
5

(11)

(107) Macks
Corner (114)

□
Jones
Gallery (107)
Douglas
Mountain (11)

*Sebago
Lake*

11
113

(113)
11
113

(25)
(117)
Limington
25
(25) ● **Standish**
Wilson
South Windham
Mallison
35A 35
Canal
(25)
(114)

(35)
(237)

River

202 (237)
4
● **Start** (25)
● **Gorham**

(112)
Flaggy
Meadow
Carl
(112)
22

(117)
Whitehouse

(117)

Buxton

35
(117)
Pleasant Hill
Hollis Center ●
(5)
(202) 4

**Bar
Mills** ●
4A
Rankin
202

0   2.5   5 mi.
0   2.5   5 km

(202) 4

M	Motel
C	Campground
I	Country Inn
⌣	Covered Bridge

Tour 21:
Sebago Century

25 Bicycle Tours in Maine, © 1998 Backcountry Publications

The ride starts from Gorham, a small rural town 10 miles west of Portland. As soon as you head west you will see prosperous farming country with big white farmhouses and rustic old barns. After passing through the attractive little towns of Bar Mills, Hollis Center, and Limerick, you'll arrive at Willowbrook at Newfield, a living history museum of a rural community during the late 1800s. Among its numerous restored buildings, staffed by guides in period costume and working at traditional crafts, are several houses with authentic furnishings, a machine shop, a cider mill, and a bicycle shop.

Beyond Willowbrook, the route turns north, paralleling the New Hampshire border about 3 miles away. This is the hilliest section of the tour, but you'll be rewarded by hillside views and exhilarating downhill runs. After crossing the old covered bridge into Porter, you'll follow the Ossipee River to the fine old town of Cornish, where you can spend the night at either a charming country inn, a standard motel, or a campground.

Just 3 miles from Cornish is Hiram Falls, a dramatic dam-plus-falls on the Saco River with a 75-foot drop. Above the falls stands a hydroelectric plant. The Saco, a favorite of canoeists, is southern Maine's major river, slicing from New Hampshire's White Mountains to the ocean at Biddeford and Saco. About 10 miles farther on is the Jones Gallery of Glass and Ceramics, a superb collection of antique glassware and china from all over the world and from all periods of history. An unusual feature of the gallery is a separate exhibit of items with imperfections or of limited artistic merit. Adding to the museum's charm is its location on a lonely mountain road. A footpath leads from the Jones Gallery to the top of Douglas Mountain, from which a magnificent view sweeps from Sebago Lake to the White Mountains.

A fast descent brings you to Sebago Lake, which is about 7 miles across and 10 miles long. Only 25 miles northwest of Portland, it is a favorite spot for vacationers, with hundreds of cabins nestled in the woods along its shore. The lake is also the source of Portland's water supply, which has prevented the onslaught of development. The route runs parallel to the lake for several miles along its southwest shore. From Sebago Lake it's about 11 miles back to Gorham. Once again you'll roll through wide expanses of farmland and cross another covered bridge.

Directions for the ride

FIRST DAY: 59 miles
Start from the Gorham Municipal Center on ME 25 in Gorham. It's 0.8 mile east of the center of town, and 1.5 miles west of ME 237.

From the Maine Turnpike, take exit 8. Go straight at the traffic light immediately after the toll booth, following the sign to Westbrook. At the next traffic light continue straight, and follow ME 25 West for 6 miles to the starting point on your right. Park in the lot to the left of the driveway. The police station is in the building; you should tell the police that you'll be leaving your car overnight.

0.0 Turn right out of the parking lot, heading west, on ME 25. Go 0.8 mile to ME 114, at the traffic light in the center of Gorham.

0.8 *Go straight for 0.4 mile to Flaggy Meadow Road, which bears left.*

1.2 *Bear left and go 0.6 mile to a crossroads (Cressy Road), at the blinking light.*

1.8 *Go straight for 1.7 miles to Waterman Road, which bears left. It's immediately after Webster Road on the right, just before the top of the hill.*

The road ascends onto a low ridge with a good view and passes through a mixture of woods and farmland.

3.5 *Bear left and go 1.2 miles to a fork where the main road bears left and Carl Road goes straight.*

4.7 *Go straight on Carl Road for 0.7 mile to the end.*

5.4 *Turn left and go 0.8 mile to the end (ME 22).*

6.2 *Turn left and go 0.2 mile to the first right (Rankin Road).*

6.4 *Turn right and go 1.9 miles to the end (ME 112), passing through farmland.*

8.3 *Turn left and go 0.4 mile to the traffic light (ME 4A), in Bar Mills.*

There's a grocery on the corner.

8.7 *Turn right on ME 4A and go 0.4 mile to a fork where the main road bears left across the bridge over the Saco River.*

Notice the traditional wooden schoolhouse on your right, and the little brick library on your left.

9.1 *Stay on the main road and go 2.2 miles to a crossroads (ME 117).*

Notice the old factory on the right while crossing the bridge.

11.3 *Turn right. Just ahead you'll cross ME 35. Continue on ME 117 for 2.6 miles to a crossroads (Haley Road on the right, Pleasant Hill Road on the left).*

14.0 *Turn left on Pleasant Hill Road and go 1.3 miles to the end.*

There's a steep hill at the beginning.

15.3 *Turn right and go less than 0.2 mile to Whitehouse Road on the left.*

15.5 *Turn left and go 1 mile to the end.*

You'll have a tough hill 0.25 mile long, followed by a well-earned descent.

16.5 *Turn left and go 3.9 miles to a crossroads (ME 5) and a stop sign.*

20.4 *Turn right and go 8.5 miles to ME 11 on the left, at a blinking light, as you come into Limerick.*

There's a grocery as soon as you turn onto ME 5, and another grocery after 3 miles. At the beginning of this stretch you'll follow the shore of Little Ossipee Pond. Just past the second grocery store, notice the fine stucco church on the left.

When you get to ME 11 the ride turns left, but just ahead is the center of Limerick and a food store. At the intersection, notice the Federal-style house and the Gothic-style church.

28.9 *Turn left on ME 11 and go 0.4 mile to the point where ME 11 curves left and a smaller road (Back Newfield Road) goes straight.*

29.3 *Go straight on the smaller road for 1.2 miles to a fork where Owls Head Road bears right.*

30.5 *Bear left and go 2.9 miles to the end (ME 11), in Newfield.*

Several roads bear off the main road on both the right and the left, but stay on the main road at each intersection. Shortly before the end is Willowbrook at Newfield. The main building, the William Durgin Homestead, built in 1813, is on the left.

33.4 *Turn right on ME 11 and go 3.1 miles to the intersection where ME 11 turns left and ME 110 goes straight.*

36.5 *Go straight for 0.9 mile to the crossroads where ME 110 turns left.*

There's a country store on the corner.

37.4 *Turn right at the crossroads and go 5.3 miles to a fork where the main road curves sharply left and a smaller road bears right.*

There's a church on your left at the intersection. This stretch is very hilly but beautiful, with fields crisscrossed by stone walls, old barns and rambling farmhouses, and views of wooded hills across the pastures. You'll pass through the tiny community of Maplewood, with just a few houses and a cemetery.

42.7 *Continue on the main road for 5.1 miles to the end (ME 160).*

Caution: Watch for bumps and cracks on a steep descent after about 1.5 miles. The hilly but inspiring landscape continues through the township of Parsonfield. After 3 miles, you'll see a stately white church on the left. There's a difficult climb after the church, but you will be rewarded by a sweeping view and a wild descent to ME 160.

47.8 *Turn left on ME 160. After 1.2 miles, the main road curves 90 degrees right. Continue for 2.6 miles to the end (ME 25), in Porter.*

Just after the 90-degree turn, the graceful white buildings of the Parsonfield Seminary will be on your right. Shortly before the end, you'll cross the Ossipee River. To your right is the Porter Bridge, a covered bridge built in 1876. If you wish, you can bear right just before the river and cross the covered bridge instead of the new one, carrying your bicycle over cement barriers at each end of the bridge.

51.6 *Turn right on ME 25 and go 2.6 miles to the crossroads, where ME 160 turns left and ME 25 turns right, in Kezar Falls.*

There's a country store on your left near the beginning. The road hugs the Ossipee River on the right. At the crossroads the loop tour turns left, but if you turn right you'll cross the river into the center of Kezar Falls, an attractive small town. As you cross the river there's a dam on the right and an old mill on the left. Just past the bridge is a store and a snack bar.

54.2 *Turn left on ME 160 and just ahead turn right, staying on ME 160. Go 0.8 mile to the point where ME 160 turns left and another road goes straight.*

55.1 *Go straight for 3.4 miles to the end (merge left on ME 25).*

The Mid-Way Motel is on the left just before the end.

58.5 *Bear left on ME 25 and go 0.7 mile to Bridge Street, which bears left opposite the Cornish Inn.*

Notice the handsome brick library on the left on the far side of the intersection and the distinctive white church on the right just beyond the inn. If you'd like to camp, continue on ME 25 and go about 2 miles to the York County Campsite Park on the left.
Final mileage to the Inn: 59.2

SECOND DAY: 40 miles

0.0   *Bear left on Bridge Street opposite the Cornish Inn, passing the library on your right. Go 0.6 mile to a fork.*

0.6   *Bear slightly right and go 5.5 miles to the end, at a stop sign (ME 5 and ME 113), in Hiram.*

After 3.2 miles, look for a dirt path on the right just as you start to go uphill. The path leads about 200 yards to Hiram Falls, also called Great Falls. At times the dam prevents the water from flowing over the falls.

6.1   *Turn right, cross the bridge, and turn left on ME 117 North. Go 0.5 mile to a crossroads.*

There's a country store here.

6.7   *Turn right at the crossroads and go 0.3 mile to a fork. Ignore a very small road that bears right shortly before the fork.*

7.0   *Bear slightly right and go 5.3 miles to the third paved right, Orchard Road, almost at the top of a hill.*

12.3   *Turn right and go 0.7 mile to the end.*

This road climbs steadily through orchards. As you're climbing, look back for a great view.

13.0   *Turn left and go 100 yards to Douglas Mountain Road, which bears right.*

13.1   *Bear right and go 0.1 mile to the Jones Gallery of Glass and Ceramics on the right.*

If it's a clear day be sure to walk the half mile to the top of Douglas Mountain, from which there's an inspiring view of Sebago Lake and the White Mountains. From the gallery, continue up the road for a quarter mile to a small dirt parking lot on the left. (It's easier to walk than to bicycle up the steep grade.) Turn left onto a footpath and go a quarter mile to the top. At the top there's a stone observation tower and a monument inscribed NON SIBI SED OMNIBUS—Latin meaning "Not for one but for all."

13.2   *From the gallery, backtrack 0.1 mile to the main road.*

13.3   *Make a sharp right and go 0.8 mile to the end, at the bottom of the hill (merge right on ME 107).*

A dam on the Ossipee River, Kezar Falls

Caution: This is a steep downgrade that ends suddenly while you're still going downhill.

14.1   Bear right on ME 107 and go 0.5 mile to a fork where ME 107 bears right.

14.6   Bear left and go 2.3 miles to the end (ME 114).

You'll enjoy a gentle descent with a view of Sebago Lake in the distance.

16.9 *Turn right and go 2.1 miles to Wards Cove Road, a smaller road that bears left along the shore of Sebago Lake.*

Notice the fieldstone library on the right shortly after you turn.

19.0 *Bear left on Wards Cove Road and go 0.6 mile to the end (ME 114 again).*

Caution: Watch for bumps and sandy spots. This is a delightful ride along the lake, passing rustic cottages.

19.6 *Turn left on ME 114 and go 6.7 miles to a crossroads (ME 35) and a blinking light.*

A grocery store and a pizza shop are at the corner.

26.3 *Turn left on ME 35 and go 1.6 miles to ME 237 (White Rock Road) on the right.*

The road follows the lakeshore through pine groves.

27.9 *Turn right on ME 237 and go 2.2 miles to a crossroads (Wilson Road) at the top of a short hill.*

30.1 *Turn left and go 1.2 miles to the end (Hurricane Road).*

Notice the old Grange hall on the right as soon as you turn. The road rolls past large farms.

31.3 *Turn right and go 1 mile to the end.*

You'll cross the covered bridge, called Babb's Bridge, that spans the Presumpscot River. It is a replica of the original one, which was built in 1864 and burned in 1973. **Caution:** There are bumps getting on and off the bridge.

32.3 *Turn right and go 1.7 miles to a crossroads (US 202 and ME 4), at the traffic light.*

There are two short, steep hills on the first half of this section, and a pizza shop at the crossroads.

34.0 *Go straight (**Caution** here) for 1.2 miles to the second right (Mallison Street), at the bottom of the hill.*

This is a pleasant ride through broad sweeps of farmland.

35.2 *Turn right and go 0.6 mile to Canal Street (unmarked) on the left, immediately after the bridge.*

You'll pass the Maine Correctional Center. At the bridge, notice the dam and the old brick mill on the left.

35.8 *Turn left and go 0.4 mile to the end (merge left on ME 237).*
There's a nasty little hill on this road, the last tough hill of the tour.

36.2 *Bear left on ME 237 and go 2.7 miles to the end (ME 25), at a large traffic island.*

38.6 *Turn right and go 1.5 miles to the Gorham Municipal Center on the right.*
Final mileage: 40.1

Bicycle Repair Services

Gorham Bike & Ski, 12 Main Street, Gorham (839-2770)

Ernie's Cycle Shop, 105 Conant Street, Westbrook (854-4090)

Gearheads, 83 Warren Avenue, Westbrook (854-6253)

Seger's Cycle, 865 Bridgton Road, Westbrook (854-5108)

Speed Cycle, US 302, Naples (693-6118)

Sanford-N-Sun Cyclery, 480 Main Street, Sanford (490-3994)

179

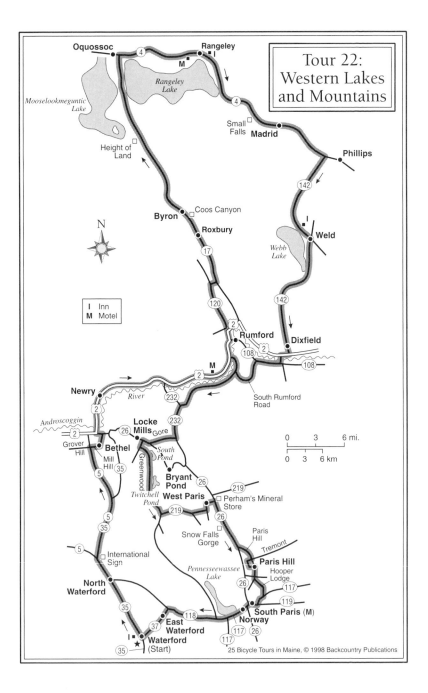

Oquossoc

Rangeley

4

M

I

*Rangeley
Lake*

*Mooselookmeguntic
Lake*

4

Tour 22:
Western Lakes
and Mountains

Small
Falls

Madrid

□

Phillips

Height of
Land

□

142

N

Byron

Coos Canyon

Roxbury

Weld

I

17

*Webb
Lake*

142

I   Inn
M   Motel

120

2

Rumford

Dixfield

108

2

108

M

2

Newry

River

232

South Rumford
Road

2

Androscoggin

2

Locke
Mills

26

Gore

232

Grover
Hill

Bethel

*South
Pond*

26

219

Mill
Hill

35

Greenwood

Bryant
Pond

26

219

5

*Twitchell
Pond*

West Paris

Perham's Mineral
Store

□

5

219

Snow Falls
Gorge

Paris
Hill

35

Tremont

5

International
Sign

□

*Pennesseewassee
Lake*

26

Paris Hill

North
Waterford

Hooper
Lodge

117

35

119

118

South Paris (M)

East
Waterford

37

Norway

26

Waterford
(Start)

I

★

117

117

35

26

0   3   6 mi.

0   3   6 km

25 Bicycle Tours in Maine, © 1998 Backcountry Publications

22
Western Lakes and Mountains

Distance: 194 miles in 4 days—40 miles the first day, 46 the second, 55 the third, and 53 the fourth.

Terrain: Generally rolling, with about 10 long, steep hills. This is a fairly challenging tour.

Special features: Gracious New England towns, spectacular mountain and lake views, upper Androscoggin River, gorges and waterfalls, Rangeley Lake, Wilhelm Reich Museum, mineral museum.

Accommodations: For the night before the tour, in Waterford, recommended start: Kedarburn Inn (583-6182); Lake House Inn (583-4182).

Alternative start: Goodwin's Motor Inn, South Paris (743-5121).

First and third nights: Linnell Motel, Rumford (the most convenient, 364-4511); Madison Motor Inn, Rumford (364-7973); Blue Iris Motor Inn, Rumford (364-4495).

Second Night: Rangeley Inn, Rangeley (864-3341); Northwoods Bed & Breakfast, Rangeley (864-2440); Farmhouse Inn, Rangeley (864-5805); Saddleback Inn, Rangeley (864-3434).

West-central Maine, stretching between Sebago and Rangeley Lakes near the New Hampshire border, is a region dotted with classic New England towns, rugged mountains and soft green hills, pristine lakes, and swift streams. Bicycling in the region is challenging, but you'll be amply rewarded by sweeping views, soaring downhill runs, and quite possibly the thrill of a deer poised at the edge of a field or a hawk nose-diving through the sky. There are many fewer tourists here than along the coast, and they are mostly hikers and fishing enthusiasts instead of beachgoers and boutique browsers. Traffic is light to moderate, even on the numbered roads, and nearly nonexistent on the unnumbered byways.

The tour starts from the village of Waterford, a New England jewel, which is a National Historic District. Large white houses with dark green shutters and a stately church cluster around the small green. Two of the houses are country inns—intimate affairs with a warm and cozy atmosphere and home-cooked meals. If you've never experienced the charm of an old-fashioned inn, here is a good excuse to do so.

From Waterford, the route heads north for about 18 miles to Bethel, going up and down hills with spectacular views of the neighboring hills and mountains. This type of scenery will repeat itself many times during the tour. The land is partly forested and partly farmed, with rough-hewn barns and big wooden farmhouses.

Bethel is another classic New England town, larger than Waterford, with fine old homes gracing its tree-shaded streets. Across from the green is the elegant Bethel Inn, a golden, 65-room landmark. Just down the street is the center of town, with wooden Victorian commercial buildings and the handsome campus of Gould Academy, a preparatory school. As you glance across the green or the broad lawns of the campus, mountains pierce the horizon in all directions.

The 20-mile stretch from Bethel to Rumford is the easiest part of the tour, hugging the Androscoggin River. The river is calm here, held back by the dam in Rumford, as it curves gracefully between wooded hills and narrow farms along its banks.

Rumford is a small manufacturing city which lacks the charm and fine architecture found in so many other Maine communities. The massive Boise-Cascade paper mill dominates the town and its odor fills the nostrils. Fortunately, Rumford is compact and as soon as you leave US 2 you get back into the countryside.

Most of the 35-mile section from Rumford north to Rangeley Lake follows the Swift River, a small stream hemmed in by a narrow wooded valley. The population density drops dramatically; only an occasional house and the two tiny hamlets of Roxbury and Byron break the isolation until the cabins and cottages along the lake. In Byron is Coos Canyon, a narrow gorge through which the river surges forcefully. Beyond Byron the road climbs steadily to the crest of the divide between the Androscoggin River and the lakes to the north. From the divide, called Height of Land, an inspiring view unfolds across Mooselookmeguntic Lake to the White Mountains and Canada. A thrilling descent brings you to Rangeley Lake.

The Rangeley Lake region has long been a favorite for hikers, hunters, fishermen, and families spending their vacation in lakeside cottages. Visually, the lake is striking; it's fairly large (about 7 miles long) and ringed by mountains. The town of Rangeley is attractively located on a small cove. Next to the center of town is the gracious yet reasonably priced Rangeley Inn.

After climbing out of town, you'll enjoy a long, gentle descent along the Sandy River. Like the Swift River, it flows through a narrow, nearly uninhabited valley. You'll pass Smalls Falls, a series of four cascades in quick succession, plummeting through a pine-rimmed gorge. Ahead lies the antique village of Weld, with a charming old general store and the turn-of-the-century Weld Inn standing guard above Webb (not Weld) Lake.

From Weld, 14 miles of gentle downhill grade bring you back to the Androscoggin River. You'll follow it on the opposite bank and then weave your way on back roads through the cluster of ponds that dot the landscape just east of Bethel. The West Paris area is rich in minerals and dotted with abandoned mines and quarries. A fascinating landmark is Perham's Maine Mineral Store, which is not only a store but also a museum displaying every mineral to be found in Maine and a scale model of a working feldspar quarry. Some of the minerals are displayed in ultraviolet light to best bring out their fluorescent colors and internal structure.

South of West Paris is Paris Hill, which is the finest traditional New England village that I've encountered in Maine, and one that is nearly undiscovered. The large, semicircular green crowns a high ridge with magnificent views of the rugged mountains to the west. Fronting on the green are elegant white houses with dark shutters and fanlights above the doors and an exceptionally elegant church. The route descends into the twin towns of South Paris and Norway, which form the commercial center for an extensive rural area between Lewiston and North Conway, New Hampshire. At South Paris, the route turns west for about 13 miles back to Waterford through a mostly wooded landscape dotted with ponds.

Directions for the ride

FIRST DAY: Waterford to Rumford (40 miles)

Start from the junction of ME 35 and ME 37 in Waterford (the inns

183

cluster around this intersection). Waterford is about 50 miles northwest of Portland.

An alternative starting point is Goodwin's Motor Inn, on ME 26 and
ME 117 in South Paris. If you start here (which adds about 12 miles to
the first day, and subtracts it from the last day), turn right (west) from
the motor inn onto ME 117 and follow it for about 3 miles to the intersection where ME 117 turns left and ME 118 goes straight. Go straight
for 5.8 miles to ME 37 on the left. Turn left and go 3 miles to ME 35 in
Waterford, and turn right.

0.0   *Head north out of Waterford on ME 35 and go 4.6 miles to
the end (merge left at the stop sign at the bottom of a long
hill), in North Waterford.*

Caution here. There's a steady climb out of Waterford with a good
view from the top across fields stretching to forested hillsides, followed by a long, fast descent into North Waterford. Watch for
bumps on the descent.

4.6   *Bear left at the stop sign (staying on ME 35) and go 1.1 miles
to the intersection where ME 35 turns right and ME 5 South
goes straight.*

At the intersection, on the right, is an often-photographed sign
indicating the direction and distance to nine Maine towns that bear
the names of foreign countries and cities. The sign is aimed at traffic coming the other way, so you'll have to look back to see it.

5.7   *Turn right on ME 35 (also ME 5 North) and go 6.4 miles to
the point where ME 35 turns right and ME 5 goes straight.*

12.1   *Go straight for 6 miles to a crossroads where Grover Hill Road
turns left and Mill Hill Road turns right. A sign points right to
Bethel Area Health Center.*

The road goes along Songo Pond, lined with rustic, tree-shaded
cottages.

18.1   *Turn right and go 0.2 mile to the Bethel town green, at the
top of the steep hill. The main road curves sharply left here.*

On your right is the elegant Bethel Inn. Also fronting on the green
is the Moses Mason House at 15 Broad Street, a stately Federal-era
mansion built in 1813.

18.3 *At the green, stay on the main road and go 0.1 mile to a stop sign (Broad Street on your right), in the center of town.*

18.4 *Turn 90 degrees left and go 0.4 mile to the end (ME 26).*

You'll pass a graceful white church on your right and the handsome redbrick buildings of Gould Academy. It's worth spending some time in Bethel to stroll past the fine old houses along the green and the Victorian commercial buildings in town. There are several restaurants in town, and if you'd like a touch of class, the Bethel Inn serves excellent meals.

18.8 *Turn left on ME 26. After 0.1 mile, ME 26 bears to the left. Bear left and go 100 yards to the end, at the stop sign.*

18.9 *Turn left, and immediately bear left along an overpass onto US 2 East.*

19.0 *Stay on US 2 East for about 21 miles to the Linnell Motel on the left, on the outskirts of Rumford. (You'll come to the other motels first.)*

US 2 is fairly busy, but there's a good shoulder for most of this section. This is a flat ride along the Androscoggin River, with farmland along its banks and views of the mountains in the distance.

Side Trip: After about 3 miles, if you bear left on a side road toward the Sunday River Ski Area and go about 4 miles, you'll come to the Artist's Bridge. This unusually picturesque covered bridge, built in 1872, spans the Sunday River.

Final mileage: 40.0

SECOND DAY: Rumford to Rangeley (46 miles)

0.0 *Go east toward Rumford on US 2 for 2.8 miles (from the Linnell Motel) to the traffic light where US 2 turns right and ME 120 goes straight.*

US 2 makes several turns in Rumford, but fortunately they are well marked. The road stays on the north bank of the river; if you cross it you've gone off the route. As you start down the long hill into Rumford, you have a dramatic view of the city, river, arched bridge and mountain backdrop. Eat a hearty breakfast in Rumford and carry some extra food and liquids, as there is no place to get food between here and Rangeley Lake, about 39 miles ahead.

The International Sign in Lynchville is a landmark in western Maine.

2.8 Go straight on ME 120 for 3 miles to an unmarked road on the right.

The land becomes pastoral shortly after you get onto ME 120. The Swift River is on your right.

5.8 Turn right across the bridge and go 0.1 mile to the end (ME 17).

5.9 Turn left and go about 33 miles to the end (ME 4).

The first half of this long section is gently rolling, following the Swift River upstream as it cascades alongside the road. In Byron, about 11 miles along ME 120, the river roars through Coos Canyon, a deep gorge where gold has been found. The picnic area is a great spot for a rest.

After the road diverges from the river, there's a steady climb for 2 miles to Beaver Pond, and some sharp ups and downs for the next 3 miles to the highest point, called Height of Land, which has an elevation of 2400 feet. To the left is a spectacular view of Mooselookmeguntic Lake and the northern White Mountains.

From here it's all downhill to Rangeley Lake, which you'll follow for the last few miles. **Caution:** The first 2 miles of the descent are very bumpy; then the road smooths out. At the end, in the village of Oquossoc, a grocery and restaurant are on the left.

39.0 *Turn right on ME 4 and go 7 miles into Rangeley.*

You'll have two steep hills about 0.5 mile long on this stretch. Panoramic views of the lake and of distant mountains unfold across broad, sloping fields. Some of the peaks are more than 4000 feet high.

After about 3 miles, a dirt road on the left leads 0.8 mile uphill to one of Maine's more unusual attractions, the Wilhelm Reich Museum. Reich was a psychoanalyst and natural scientist with controversial theories of physical, biological, and sexual energy. He died in 1957 in prison, having been convicted of fraud for selling boxes in which one would sit to absorb the energy, which Reich called orgone. He is buried on the property.

In Rangeley, the Town and Lake Motel is on the right just before the town. Northwoods Bed & Breakfast and the Rangeley Inn are on your left in the center of town. The Saddleback Inn is 0.5 mile past town, and the Farmhouse Inn is 1.5 miles past town. There are several restaurants in town. One of them, Doc Grant's, has a sign in front saying that Rangeley is halfway between the North Pole and the Equator.

Final mileage: 46.0

THIRD DAY: Rangeley-Weld-Rumford (55 miles)

0.0 *From Rangeley, continue on ME 4 for about 21 miles to ME 142 on the right.*

Be sure to eat a hearty breakfast in Rangeley and stock up on food, as there is no food until Weld, 33 miles away. There are a couple of steep hills to get out of Rangeley; then it's mostly downhill as you follow the Sandy River downstream.

About 12 miles out of town, Smalls Falls will be on your right, at a rest area. It's a spectacular chain of four waterfalls in quick succession that plunge through a pine-fringed gorge. A trail leads for about 200 yards to Chandlers Mill Stream Falls, which is also worth seeing.

21.0 *Turn right on ME 142 and go about 12 miles to the cross-roads where ME 142 turns right, in Weld.*

This is the most difficult section of the tour, with several long, steep hills. Shortly before Weld you'll go along Webb Lake. The Weld Inn, across the road from the lake, is a good spot for lunch. There's also a country store at the crossroads.

33.0 *Turn right on ME 142 and go about 14 miles to the end (US 2), in Dixfield.*

Most of this section is a gentle downhill grade, following the Webb River. There's a food store halfway along in the hamlet of Carthage, and another food store shortly before the end.

47.0 *Turn right on US 2 and go 0.4 mile to the first left (the sign says* TO PERU*).*

There's a snack bar on your left just before the intersection.

47.4 *Turn left, crossing the Androscoggin River, and go 0.3 mile to the crossroads (ME 108) and a stop sign.* **Caution:** *You'll cross diagonal railroad tracks.*

47.7 *Turn right on ME 108 and go 2.4 miles to an unmarked road that bears left. A sign saying* REDUCED SPEED AHEAD *is at the intersection.*

50.1 *Bear left. After 2.2 miles you will merge head-on at a stop sign into a larger road. Continue straight for 0.9 mile to the end (US 2).*

53.2 *Turn left and go 1.4 miles to the Linnell Motel on the right. The other motels are farther along US 2 .*

Final mileage: 54.6

FOURTH DAY: Rumford–South Paris–Waterford (53 miles)

0.0 *Go east toward Rumford on US 2 for 1.4 miles (from the Linnell Motel) to South Rumford Road on the right (a sign says* TO SOUTH RUMFORD*).*

1.4 *Turn right and go 0.9 mile to a fork where the main road curves right and a smaller road goes straight.*

2.3 *Curve right on the main road and go 8.6 miles to the end (ME 232), at a stop sign and a grassy traffic island.*

This is a lovely run along the Androscoggin River.

10.9 *Bear left on ME 232 and go 3.9 miles to Gore Road on your right.*

There is a redbrick house on the far corner.

14.8 *Turn right and go 3.1 miles to the end (merge right on ME 26).*

Caution: Bumpy sections. The narrow road winds along the shore of North Pond.

17.9 *Bear right on ME 26 and go 0.2 mile to Howe Hill Road on your left.*

You'll pass a restaurant on the left, and there's a variety store on the far left corner.

18.1 *Turn left and go 100 yards to Greenwood Road on the left, immediately after the railroad tracks.*

18.2 *Turn 90 degrees left on Greenwood Road (don't bear left uphill on Knoll Road). Go 7 miles to ME 219 on the left (a sign says TO WEST PARIS).*

Caution: Bumpy sections. At the beginning of this stretch you'll hug the shore of unspoiled South Pond; just ahead you'll ride alongside Twitchell Pond.

25.2 *Turn left on ME 219 and go 4.3 miles to the end (ME 219 turns left).*

Two smaller roads bear off to the right on this section, but stay on the main road. This is a relaxing ride, mostly a gentle descent, along the Little Androscoggin River.

29.5 *Turn left at the end (still ME 219) and go 1.2 miles to the end (ME 26).*

You will go through West Paris, a town with fine rambling houses and a big yellow schoolhouse. At the end, Perham's Maine Mineral Store, a landmark since 1919, is 100 yards to the left. Across the road is a general store and a restaurant.

30.7 *Turn right on ME 26 (if you visited Perham's, turn left when you leave) and go 4.2 miles to Paris Hill Road, which bears left. It's 0.5 mile after a crossroads.*

189

Smalls Falls, near Madrid

After 2.2 miles, you will pass Snow Falls Gorge on the right. Here the Little Androscoggin River sluices through narrow passages between boulders. It's a great picnic spot.

34.9 *Bear left on Paris Hill Road and go 1.7 miles to a crossroads (Tremont Street), in Paris Hill.*

The road climbs steeply, but you will be rewarded with a sweeping view and a long, fast descent.

36.6 *Turn right at the crossroads and go 0.2 mile to the end, which is the same road you were on before the crossroads.*

Paris Hill is a classic, elegant New England village. When you ride behind the church, you will pass the pillared Hannibal Hamlin House (a private residence) perched on the brow of the hill on the right. Hamlin was vice-president under Abraham Lincoln. Next door is the Paris Hill Library and Museum, a square, granite building that looks more like a jail, and, indeed, it was the Oxford County Jail from 1822 to 1896. From behind the museum, an inspiring view extends west to the White Mountains.

36.8 *Turn right at the end. Stay on the main road for 0.7 mile to Hooper Ledge Road, which bears left at a five-way intersection.*

37.5 *Bear left on Hooper Ledge Road (don't turn 90 degrees left). Go 1.3 miles to the end, where you merge right on ME 117 at the bottom of the hill (**Caution** here).*

This is a wonderful downhill ride with some fine views.

38.8 *Bear right on ME 117, and follow it for 5.1 miles to the intersection where ME 117 turns left and ME 118 goes straight, opposite Pennesseewassee Lake on the right.*

ME 117 turns several times as it threads through the twin towns of South Paris and Norway, but it is well marked. **Caution:** You will cross two diagonal railroad tracks a half mile apart—walk across them. As you come into South Paris, notice the dam on the right as you cross the Little Androscoggin River. If you started from Goodwin's Motor Inn, it's on the right after 2.2 miles.

43.9 *Go straight on ME 118 for 5.8 miles to ME 37 on the left, in East Waterford.*

You'll climb steadily away from the lake for 0.8 mile. There's a restaurant on the right 0.5 mile before the intersection.

49.7 *Turn left on ME 37 and go 3 miles to the end (ME 35), back in Waterford.*

You'll pass a wonderful old general store on the right after 0.5 mile. Just before the end, you'll go along wooded Keoka Lake on the left.

Final mileage: 52.7

Bicycle Repair Services

Bicycle Barn, 108 Main Street, Norway (744-0377)

Mahoosuc Mountain Sports, ME 26, Locke Mills (875-3786)

Rangeley Mountain Bike Touring, Main Street, Rangeley (864-5799)

Wallace's Wheels, US 2, Rumford (364-7946)

TNS Cyclery, ME 10, Jay (897-6834)

Northern Lights Health & Sports, 2 Front Street, Farmington (778-6566)

Speed Cycle, US 302, Naples (693-6118)

23
Androscoggin Valley: Lewiston–Auburn–Turner–Greene

Distance: *40 miles (35 with shortcut)*
Terrain: *Gently rolling, with one long, steep hill and a few short ones.*
Special features: *Bates College, Lake Auburn, ridge with spectacular views, lovely rolling countryside.*

Just north of the twin cities of Lewiston and Auburn lies a rural area, bisected by the Androscoggin River, that provides some superb cycling. The region's most attractive feature is its tranquillity—it is virtually unvisited by tourists and not on the way to any center of population. This means that the secondary roads are nearly traffic free.

The ride starts from Bates College, which is located on the northern edge of Lewiston. The twin cities, with a combined population of about 65,000, form the second-largest metropolitan area in the state. The powerful falls on the Androscoggin, which flows between the two communities, sparked the development of shoe and textile manufacturing during the 1830s. These two industries still form an important part of the area's economy. The tour stays north of the downtown and manufacturing areas—which are not very pleasant to bicycle through—and instead heads quickly into the countryside.

Bates College (the author's alma mater, '69) is a small, academically rigorous liberal arts institution with a well-manicured campus shaded by towering elms. The centerpiece of the campus is Hathorn Hall, a handsome brick building with a bell tower. Built in 1856, it is the original academic building of the college and is listed on the National Register of Historic Places. Opposite the campus, on the corner of College Street and Mountain Avenue, is Mount David, a rocky hill from which there's a fine

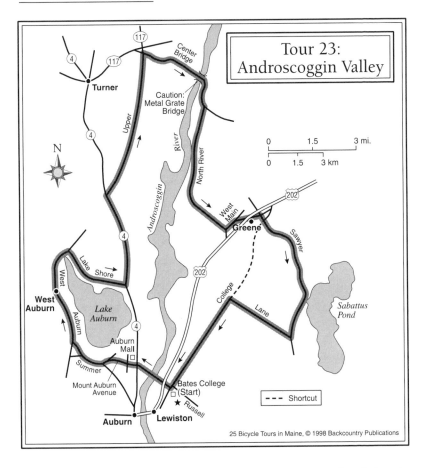

Tour 23:
Androscoggin Valley

25 Bicycle Tours in Maine, © 1998 Backcountry Publications

view of the college and the city of Lewiston. Dominating the skyline is Saints Peter and Paul Church, which looks like a cathedral and can hold 2000 worshipers.

From Bates, the ride heads west across the new bridge over the Androscoggin River into Auburn. The bridge is only a half mile from the campus. Once in Auburn, you'll quickly enter rural countryside. The route skirts most of Lake Auburn, which is the water supply for the twin cities and nearly undeveloped. Quiet secondary roads lead through gently rolling farmland, which slopes down to the lake about a quarter mile away. You'll ride through West Auburn, an unspoiled New England village with a few fine old houses and a small church. Beyond, the route descends steeply to the lake and hugs its shore.

North of Lake Auburn, you'll climb onto a magnificent open ridge with panoramic views of the hills and mountains of western Maine. While cycling along the ridge, you'll see horses and cows grazing contentedly on broad expanses of pasture. At the northernmost point of the route, you'll descend into the valley of the Androscoggin and cross the river to the eastern bank. The route turns south, following the river past farmland, and then curving inland through forest.

After a few miles you'll pedal through Greene, another attractive little town with a Gothic-style church and a fine old Grange hall. From Greene, you'll follow a winding road past Sabattus Pond, climb onto a hillside with a sweeping view, and descend to College Road, a pleasant secondary road that passes through gently rolling farmland as it heads toward the campus.

Directions for the ride

Start from Bates College, which is a mile north of downtown Lewiston and just east of US 202.

From the Maine Turnpike, take the Lewiston exit (exit 13). Turn left at the end of the ramp (right if you were heading south). Go 0.5 mile to the end, where you merge right onto ME 196. Go 1.2 miles to East Avenue on the right, at a traffic light (a sign points to US 202 East and ME 126 East). Turn right and go 0.9 mile to Webster Street, at the second traffic light. Turn left and go 0.8 mile to College Street, at the third traffic light. Turn right and go 0.5 mile to the campus on your right. Park where legal on College Street or on Mountain Avenue, which is on the left opposite the campus.

The college snack bar, called the Den, is an inexpensive place to eat before or after the ride. It's in the student union building, Chase Hall, which is on Campus Avenue, the street bordering the campus on the south. (College Street borders the campus on the west.)

0.0 Head north on College Street, with the campus on your right, and go 0.2 mile to Russell Street, at the traffic light.

0.2 Turn left and go 0.3 mile to US 202, at the traffic light.

0.5 *Go straight for 1.1 mile to ME 4, at the next traffic light.*
It's at the far end of the bridge across the Androscoggin River.

1.6 *Continue straight onto Mount Auburn Avenue (**Caution** here). Go 0.4 mile to a traffic light (Turner Street, unmarked).*
You go past Auburn Mall, the area's largest, on the right.

2.0 *Go straight for 1.1 miles to the end, at a yield sign (merge right on Summer Street).*
The road passes through farmland, with Lake Auburn in the distance on the right.

3.1 *Bear right on Summer Street and go 0.7 mile to a fork where Youngs Corner Road bears left and Summer Street bears right.*

3.8 *Bear right and go 0.4 mile to the end, at a yield sign (merge right).*

4.2 *Bear right and go 3.3 miles to Lake Shore Drive on the right, just past the bottom of the big hill. A grocery is on the left at the intersection.*
On this stretch are two forks where a smaller road bears right and then left, but stay on the main road. This is a lovely, rolling ride, passing pastures, fields, and farms with rambling connected buildings in the New England tradition. You'll climb gradually to West Auburn; then a flying downhill run brings you to the shore of Lake Auburn.

7.5 *Turn right on Lake Shore Drive and go 2.7 miles to the end (ME 4).*
The road hugs the lakeshore, passing a snack bar on the right about halfway along.

10.2 *Turn left on ME 4 and go 3.4 miles to an unmarked road that bears right uphill immediately after a True Value hardware store on the right.*
There's a concrete traffic island in the intersection. ME 4 is heavily traveled, but it has a wide shoulder.

13.6 *Bear right and go 5.2 miles to the crossroads at the bottom of the steep hill, just before Cobb Road on the right. A convenience store is on the far right corner.*

Hathorn Hall, built in 1856, graces the elm-shaded campus of Bates College.

Caution: The crossroads comes up suddenly, while you are descending a steep grade. The road climbs steadily, with one very steep section, onto a high ridge with splendid views. You'll pass rambling old farmhouses attached to their barns, a hallmark of rural Maine architecture.

18.8 *Turn right at the crossroads, passing the store on your left. (**Caution:** It's a fairly sharp right.) Go 3.1 miles to a fork where North River Road bears right, about a mile after the metal-grate bridge across the Androscoggin.*

Caution: The metal grating is very slippery when wet; there's a very real danger of falling and hurting yourself. If the road is wet, or even if the metal may be wet from condensation, please walk across.

21.9 *Bear right on North River Road and go 5.1 miles to the end (West Main Street).*

This is another lovely back road, passing farms with views of the river in the distance.

27.0 *Turn left and go 0.3 mile to a fork where the main road bears slightly right.*

Just after you turn left, the back of an IGA supermarket, a corrugated metal building, is on the right.

27.3 *Bear right and go 0.4 mile to a diagonal crossroads (US 202).*

27.7 *Cross US 202 diagonally onto Main Street (**Caution** here). Go 0.6 mile to a crossroads (Sawyer Road on the right).*

You'll go through Greene. Notice the Gothic-style church, the Grange hall, and the little library.

28.3 *Turn right on Sawyer Road and go 0.1 mile to the crossroads (College Road).*

Here the ride goes straight, but if you want to cut 4.5 miles off the route, turn right on College Road and go 6.7 miles to Bates College on your left, just after the traffic light.

28.4 *Go straight for 4.6 miles to Lane Road on your right.*

You'll climb gradually through prosperous farmland and descend to Sabattus Pond.

33.0 *Turn right and go 2.4 miles to the end (College Road).*

You'll climb steeply to the top of a hill with a good view, and enjoy a fast descent down the other side.

35.4 *Turn left and go 4.2 miles to Bates College on the left, just after the traffic light.*

There are several short hills on this stretch. You'll pass a small grocery on the right after about 2 miles.

Final mileage: 39.6

Bicycle Repair Services

Moe's Bicycle Shop, 54 Sabattus Street, Lewiston (783-2641)

Mountain Bike Service, 39 Winter Street, Auburn (782-7412)

Pedal Power, 570 Washington Street, Auburn (753-1334)

Rainbow Bicycle Center, 1225 Center Street, Auburn (784-7576)

Roy's Bicycle Shop, 51 Farwell Street, Lewiston (783-9090)

Ski & Bike Service Center, 9 North River Road, Auburn (784-0103)

Twin City Cyclery, 199 Bartlett Street, Lewiston (783-0622)

24
Lakes of Central Maine:
Augusta–Hallowell–Litchfield–Winthrop

Distance: *38 miles*
Terrain: *Rolling, with a few steep hills.*
Special features: *Antiques shops and fine architecture in Hallowell, lakeshore scenery, side trip to Monmouth Museum (open 1–4 PM).*

The region just west of Augusta, dominated by a cluster of lakes, is ideal for bicycling. A network of lightly traveled back roads leads along and between the lakes, passing through rolling farmland and rustic small towns.

The ride starts from the western edge of Augusta, a compact city that slopes gradually along both banks of the Kennebec River. After about 2.5 miles, the route plunges steeply down to Hallowell, a riverfront town that abounds in 19th-century architecture and is a center for antiques dealers. From Hallowell, the road climbs more gradually out of the Kennebec Valley and heads through farms and woodlots to Cobbosseecontee Lake (usually shortened to Cobbossee), the largest of the three lakes you'll see on the ride.

After going along Cobbossee, it's not far to Lake Annabessacook. The ride curves north along the lakeshore and heads into Winthrop, a scenic town sandwiched between Lake Annabessacook on the south and Maranacook Lake on the north. Leaving Winthrop, you'll hug the shore of Maranacook Lake for several miles before turning east back to Augusta. The last section of the tour leads primarily through open farming country, ascending onto several ridges with fine views.

Augusta itself is worth a visit after the ride. The granite-domed State House, designed by Charles Bulfinch, is easily the most impressive building in town. It is located just south of US 202, near the river on the west

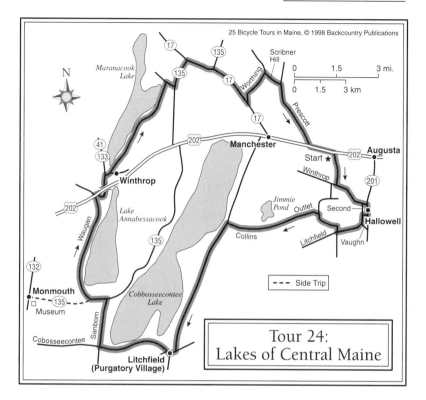

25 Bicycle Tours in Maine, © 1998 Backcountry Publications

Tour 24:
Lakes of Central Maine

bank. Adjacent to the State House is the Maine State Museum, with an outstanding collection of exhibits relating to Maine's history, industry, and cultural life. Across the street from the State House is the elegant Blaine House, originally built for a sea captain and now the governor's residence. Tours are offered on weekday afternoons. On the east bank of the Kennebec, just north of US 202, is a restoration of Fort Western, a trading post built in 1754 for protection from hostile Indians.

Directions for the ride

Start from Sears, Turnpike Mall, on US 202 in Augusta. It's just west of the Maine Turnpike and I-95.

0.0 Turn right out of the east side of the parking lot, paralleling

*the Maine Turnpike on your left. (Don't get on US 202.) Go
1.3 miles to the end at Winthrop Street.*

1.3 *Turn left and go 1.3 miles to the end (US 201), in Hallowell.*

Caution: There is a long, steep downhill into Hallowell—take it easy. The town, on the Kennebec River about 2 miles south of Augusta, boasts some superb 19th-century commercial and domestic architecture and is worth exploring. The downtown area consists of three- and four-story brick buildings, constructed during the late 1800s, which face each other across US 201. The three streets closest to US 201 and running parallel with it (on your right as you're heading down the hill into town), are lined with fine Victorian, Federal-era, and Georgian houses. Just before the bottom of the hill, notice the handsome yellow-brick town hall, built in 1898, on your left. You'll also pass the Maine Publicity Bureau, which operates the visitors center at the southern end of the Maine Turnpike.

2.6 *Turn right at the bottom of the hill on US 201 (Water Street)
and go 0.2 mile to Temple Street on the right. It runs one
short block to a stone church.*

You'll go through downtown Hallowell, passing a cluster of antiques shops and restaurants.

2.8 *Turn right on Temple Street and go one block to the end
(Second Street).*

2.9 *Turn left and go 0.25 mile to a fork where Vaughn Street
(unmarked) bears left and the main road goes straight.*

Caution: There are treacherous diagonal railroad tracks shortly after you turn left. Please dismount.

3.1 *Continue straight on the main road and go 1 mile to a crossroads, shortly after the bridge over the Maine Turnpike.*

This is a steady but moderate climb away from the river, not nearly as steep as the descent into Hallowell.

4.1 *Turn right and go 1.3 miles to Outlet Road, which bears left
uphill. The main road curves 90 degrees left after 0.2 mile.*

5.4 *Bear left and go 3.5 miles to the end.*

This is a lovely back road through mostly wooded landscape, passing some rambling farmhouses. Jimmie Pond will be on your right after 2 miles, nestled in the woods. At the end, Cobbosseecontee Lake is in front of you.

8.9 *Turn left and go 5 miles to the end, where you merge to the right at a stop sign.*

The road parallels the lake about half a mile from its shore, winding past woods and small farms. Only a few dirt roads lead to the lake, which is pleasantly undeveloped.

13.9 *Bear right and go 0.1 mile to the fork, in the village of Litchfield (also called Purgatory Village).*

Notice the small dam in the middle of the fork. Litchfield is a tiny community with just a few houses and no store.

14.0 *Bear right, and immediately bear right again at another fork, uphill. Go 3 miles to a crossroads (South Monmouth Road on your left, Sanborn Road on your right).*

This is the most difficult section of the ride, with several short steep hills and one long one. After 2 miles, the road descends steeply to the southern end of Cobbosseecontee Lake, where you'll have a nice view. At the top of each hill, look back for additional good views.

17.0 *Turn right at the crossroads and go 1.8 miles to the end (ME 135).*

Caution: The first half of this stretch is bumpy. The road runs parallel to a stream that flows between Lake Annabessacook and Cobbosseecontee. Notice the little dam on your right just before the end.

18.8 *Turn left on ME 135 and go 0.6 mile to Waugan Road, which bears right.*

Side Trip: Here the ride bears right, but if you continue straight for 2.6 miles to ME 132, at the end, you'll see the Monmouth Museum on the left. This is a living history museum of rural life in Maine during the 19th century, including a blacksmith shop, country store, house with period furnishings, and other buildings.

19.4 *Bear right on Waugan Road (turn sharp left if you're coming from the museum) and go 4 miles to a crossroads (US 202) and stop sign.*

This is an inspiring stretch, rolling through prosperous farms, with views of Lake Annabessacook in the distance across the fields. When you come to US 202, there is a fine Victorian house and a grocery store on the far side of the intersection.

23.4 *Turn right on US 202 and go 100 yards to ME 41 and ME 133, which bear right.*

23.5 *Bear right and go 0.7 mile to Main Street, which bears right (a sign says TO WINTHROP).*

24.2 *Bear right and go 0.2 mile to Bowdoin Street on the left just before the center of town. It's your first left.*

There's a restaurant in Winthrop.

24.4 *Turn left and go 4 miles to the end, at a T-intersection and a stop sign.*

Caution: Watch for bumps and potholes. This is a lovely ride hugging the shore of Maranacook Lake, passing cozy cottages nestled in the woods on the lakefront.

28.4 *Turn right and go 0.5 mile to the end (ME 135).*

28.9 *Turn left and go 1.2 miles to the end (ME 17).*

At the end there's a good view to your left. On a clear day you can see Mount Blue, 30 miles away.

30.1 *Turn right, and stay on ME 17 for 2.6 miles to the second left, Worthing Road (unmarked). It's a sharp left that comes up while you're going downhill.*

After turning right on ME 17, you'll climb a long, steady hill with a church on top. As you're climbing, look back for a spectacular view across sweeping farmland. On the far side of the hill, you can see Cobbosseecontee Lake on your right, in the distance across broad fields.

32.7 *Make a sharp left on Worthing Road and go 1.2 miles to the end.*

33.9 Turn right and go 0.8 mile to the end (Prescott Road, unmarked).

You'll pass a small isolated meetinghouse on the left, dating from 1795, followed by an exhilarating downhill run.

34.7 Turn right on Prescott Road and go 2.5 miles to the end (merge left on US 202).

The road passes through large farms and ascends onto a hillside with inspiring views.

37.2 Bear left on US 202 and go 0.8 mile to Turnpike Mall on the right.

Caution: Watch for potholes.

Final mileage: 38.0

Bicycle Repair Services

Auclair's Cycle & Ski, 64 Bangor Street, Augusta (623-4351)

Hilltop Ski & Bike, US 202, Manchester (623-6219)

CM Cycle, 209 College Avenue, Waterville (873-5490)

All Season Sports, 109 Main Street, Waterville (873-7300)

Mathieu's Cycle and Sport, 10 Main Street, Oakland (465-7564)

Holden Cyclery, 317 Madison Avenue, Skowhegan (573-3732)

Skowhegan Bicycle, 317 North Avenue, Skowhegan (474-0334)

25

Bangor–Hermon–Levant

Distance: 26 miles
Terrain: Pleasantly rolling, with a few moderate hills.
Special features: Prosperous farming country, ridges with good views.

The best bicycling in the Bangor area is west of the city. To the north and east are relatively few paved roads, and most of these go through miles of woodland without much variation in the scenery. To the south, a loop ride will inevitably involve pedaling on US 1A or ME 15, both of which are heavily traveled and not particularly attractive. To the west, fortunately, lies rolling open farm country and quiet villages linked by a network of back roads with very little traffic.

The ride starts from the western edge of Bangor, across from Maine's largest airport. With a population of about 33,000, Bangor is the only real city in the northern two-thirds of the state. The next largest community to the north, Presque Isle (population 11,000), is 150 miles away. Heading west from Bangor, the route immediately heads into open farm country traversed by low ridges. Most of the landscape has a prosperous, well-trimmed appearance, with rambling farmhouses, big barns, and woodpiles neatly stacked beside them. Many of the pastures are home to horses and cattle that graze contentedly. Following the style unique to northern New England, many of the houses and barns are connected into one elongated habitat.

Most of the westward leg of the ride passes through Hermon, a farming community that has not been despoiled by suburban development. The village center lies a mile south of the route. After about 10 miles, the route turns north along a ridge between two small streams. You'll dip into a valley and then climb gradually to the summit of another ridge, where a sweeping view and a glorious downhill run will reward your

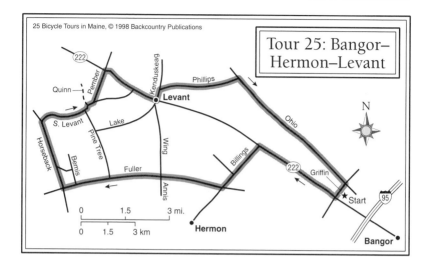

25 Bicycle Tours in Maine, © 1998 Backcountry Publications

Tour 25: Bangor–Hermon–Levant

efforts. At the bottom lies Levant, another undeveloped farming village, which borders Bangor on the northwest. The homestretch, from Levant back to Bangor, continues through gently rolling farmland with some extensive views.

Directions for the ride

Start from Airport Mall in Bangor. It is on ME 222 (Union Street), a mile west of I-95. Take exit 47 and go 1 mile to the mall on your right. Park at the western end of the mall (farthest from I-95), near Griffin Road.

0.0 *Turn left from the western end of the mall onto Griffin Road (not ME 222), and just ahead turn right at the traffic light on ME 222. Go 3 miles to Billings Road on the left, as you start to go uphill.*

3.1 *Turn left and go 1.9 miles to the second crossroads, Fuller Road.*

There is a gradual climb onto a ridge with a panoramic view from the top, followed by a swooping descent.

5.0 *Turn right on Fuller Road and go 5.5 miles to a crossroads and a stop sign at Horseback Road.*

207

Bicycling is a pleasure on the back roads west of Bangor.

The road passes through a harmonious mix of woods and farmland, up and over a few small hills.

10.5 *Turn right at the crossroads and go 2.3 miles to a fork.*

Currently there are two barricades near the beginning to keep out cars because a gravel pit on your right is eroding, but you can go through on your bike. The road traverses a low ridge with rolling farmland on both sides. Just before the fork, a small white church will be on your left.

12.8 *Bear right at the fork and go 1.9 miles to Pember Road (unmarked), which bears left.*

It's 0.2 mile after Quinn Road, a dirt road that also bears left.

14.7 *Bear left on Pember Road and go 1.2 miles to ME 222, at the stop sign.*

The road climbs gradually through farmland onto a ridge. You may spot a deer bounding across the road on this stretch.

15.9 *Turn right on ME 222 and go 2.1 miles to a crossroads in the village of Levant (Kenduskeag Road on your left).*

Enjoy the long, steady descent from the ridge, and the magnificent view unfolding before you as you start to go down.

18.0 *Turn left at the crossroads and go 0.3 mile to Phillips Road, which bears right.*

18.3 *Bear right and go 2.5 miles to the end (Ohio Street), at a stop sign.*

20.8 *Turn right and go 5.1 miles to Griffin Road, at a traffic light.* There's a convenience store on the far left corner.

25.9 *Turn right at the traffic light and go 0.3 mile to the mall on your left, just before ME 222.*
Final mileage: 26.2

Bicycle Repair Services

Ski Rack Sports, Maine Square Mall, Hogan Road, Bangor (945-6474)

Wight's Sporting Goods, 930 Stillwater Avenue, Bangor (945-4455)

Pat's Bike Shop, 373 Wilson Street, Brewer (989-2900)

L & J's Bike Shop, 1074 School Street, Veazie (945-9932)

Rose Bicycle, 9 Pine Street, Orono (866-3525)

The Bike Shop of Old Town, 27 North Main Street, Old Town (827-5450)

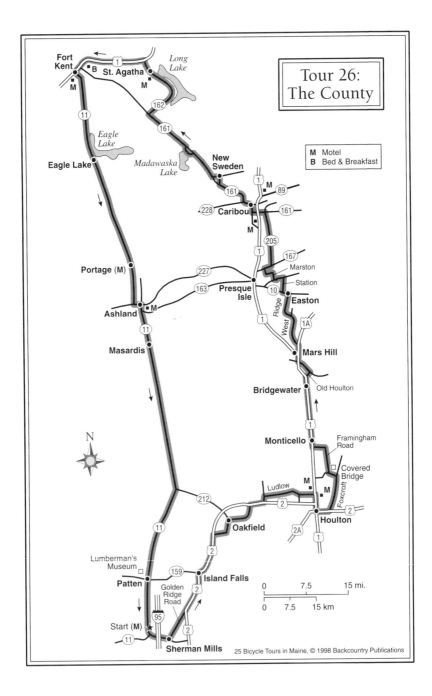

Fort Kent
■ B St. Agatha
■ M
■ M
Long Lake

11

Eagle Lake

Eagle Lake
Madawaska Lake

162

161

New Sweden

Tour 26:
The County

M Motel
B Bed & Breakfast

161
228 Caribou
■ M

1 M■ 89
161

205
1
167

227
163 Presque Isle
Marston
Station
10 Easton

Portage (M)
Ashland ■ M
11

1
Ridge
West
1A

Masardis

Mars Hill

Bridgewater
Old Houlton

1

Monticello
Framingham Road

Covered Bridge
M
M
Foxcroft

N

Ludlow
212
2
2

11
Oakfield
2A
1

Houlton

Lumberman's Museum
159
Patten
Golden Ridge Road
95
Start (M) ★
11
2
Sherman Mills

Island Falls
2

0   7.5   15 mi.
0   7.5   15 km

25 Bicycle Tours in Maine, © 1998 Backcountry Publications

26
The County: Touring the Top of Maine

Distance: *270 miles in 5 days—41 the first day, 63 the second, 58 the third, 50 the fourth, and 58 the fifth.*

Terrain: *Hilly. This is a challenging tour.*

Special features: *Wide open potato country, covered bridge, unspoiled lakes, Saint John and Aroostook Rivers, museums of vintage fashion and lumbering, views of Mount Katahdin.*

Accommodations: *For the night before the tour: Katahdin Valley Motel, Sherman (365-4554).*

For the first night: Shiretown Motor Inn, Houlton (532-9421); Ivey's Motor Lodge, Houlton (532-4206).

For the second night: Crown Park Inn, Caribou (493-3311); Russell's Motel, Caribou (less fancy, 498-2567); Old Iron Inn, Caribou (a bed & breakfast, 492-4766).

For the third night: Daigle's Bed & Breakfast, Fort Kent (very nice, 834-5803); Rock's Motel, Fort Kent (a bit rundown, 834-3133).

For the fourth night: Four Seasons Inn, Ashland (435-8255).

Be sure to arrange your accommodations in advance.

Caution: *This tour has some long, isolated stretches with no stores or restaurants. Be sure to carry extra food and water. Bring at least three water bottles and keep them filled. The last two days of the tour follow ME 11, which has heavy lumber-truck traffic on weekdays. Try to finish the tour on a Saturday and Sunday.*

Northern Maine has a landscape unlike anything else in New England. Its dominant feature is its expansiveness. Near the eastern border, vast treeless fields stretch to the horizon, sweeping up and over broad rolling hills. Farther west, uninhabited forests extend for dozens of miles, traversed by only a few logging roads. Wild rivers and pristine lakes, undeveloped except for a few summer cottages (locally called "camps"), abound. Towns are small and, with the exception of the ones along US 1, far apart. The largest town, Presque Isle, has only about 11,000 people.

Aroostook County is to Maine what Texas is to the United States, but with none of the Lone Star State's flash and swagger. Residents of Aroostook refer to it simply as "The County," implying that Maine's 15 other counties don't quite measure up; and in size, this is certainly true. Aroostook covers a fifth of Maine, an area the size of Rhode Island and Connecticut combined—but with one-fortieth of the population.

Another of the County's superlatives is the friendliness and honesty of the people. People in Aroostook frequently started conversations with me as if I were an old friend. In every town, the sight of my bicycle would prompt people to ask where I was headed and how long I'd been on the road, wish me good luck, and express the wish that they were doing the same thing. In Fort Kent, I paid for groceries with two $10 bills that were stuck together. The clerk, not noticing this until after I'd left the store, chased me down the road to return one of the bills. When I asked a police officer in Houlton about points of interest for cyclists, he went into detail about every back road in the area and interesting spots to see.

The County is host to several old-fashioned local festivals and agricultural fairs. The two largest are the Potato Blossom Festival, held in late July in Fort Fairfield (10 miles east of Presque Isle and Caribou), and the Northern Maine Fair, held in early August at the Presque Isle Fairgrounds. Keep in mind that if your tour coincides with a festival, accommodations will be difficult to find unless reserved far in advance.

The County boasts a surprising number of museums for such a rural and remote area. On the tour you'll pass a museum of vintage fashion in Island Falls, a railroad museum in Oakfield, a natural history museum in Caribou, and museums of the lumber industry in Ashland and Patten. You can also visit museums of local history in Houlton, Caribou, New Sweden, Saint Agatha, and Fort Kent.

The tour starts from Sherman, a small village in the southeastern corner of the County. Within a couple of miles, the route ascends onto a long, high ridge, the first of dozens that undulate across the landscape.

From its flank, panoramic views unfold to the horizon across large farms. On a clear day you can see the distinctive hump of Mount Katahdin, the highest peak in Maine, about 25 miles away. As you approach Houlton, about 40 miles northeast of the start, you start to see potato farms that comprise most of the land in the eastern part of the County. Houlton is an attractive town of about 7000 with a wide central square. A unique fountain, with a statue of a young boy holding a leaking boot, stands just east of town.

From Houlton, the tour heads north to Caribou through the heart of the potato-growing region. The potato barns, large buildings nearly buried by earth embankments to protect the harvest from the cold, are a distinctive feature of the landscape. The potatoes blossom in late July, covering the fields with a delicate carpet of pink and white flowers. In October, when the potatoes are harvested, the schools close so that the children can help. In Caribou, the second-largest town in the County (population 10,000), the Nylander Museum is worth a visit. It has exhibits of local history, geology, vegetation, and Indian artifacts.

On the third day of the tour, you'll continue through the potato-growing region in a northwesterly direction to Fort Kent, on the New Brunswick border near Maine's northern tip. The route passes through New Sweden, a village where most of the residents are of Swedish descent—an ethnic oasis in a predominantly French Canadian area. The New Sweden Historical Museum is excellent. Ahead, the road follows the shore of two large, unspoiled lakes, Madawaska Lake and Long Lake, and descends to the banks of the Saint John River, which separates Maine from Canada at the top of the state. The last 12 miles hug the river into Fort Kent. Overlooking the river near the center of town is the Fort Kent Blockhouse, built in 1840 during the bloodless Aroostook War, a boundary dispute between New Brunswick and Maine's lumber interests.

From Fort Kent, the remainder of the tour heads due south through hilly countryside that becomes progressively more forested. The area and the vast expanses of woodland to the west are dominated by the lumber industry and a few scattered hunting and fishing camps. About 10 miles south of Fort Kent there's a lovely run alongside Eagle Lake. Beyond Ashland is a nearly unbroken 30-mile stretch of forest. In Patten, 9 miles from the end of the tour, the Lumberman's Museum is one of the outstanding attractions of Northern Maine. Its nine buildings, crammed

213

with tools and other artifacts, are an authentic restoration of a lumber camp, including the bunkhouse, cooking quarters, sawmill, and blacksmith shop. The last stretch from Patten to Sherman affords magnificent views of Mount Katahdin on the western horizon.

Directions for the ride:

FIRST DAY: Sherman to Houlton (41 miles)

Start from the Katahdin Valley Motel on ME 158 in Sherman, immediately west of I-95. Sherman is about 80 miles north of Bangor. It's okay to leave your car here if you stay at the motel the night before your tour. The restaurant next to the motel is a logical spot for breakfast.

0.0 *Turn left (east) from the motel on ME 158 and go 1.5 miles to a fork where ME 158 bears right and a smaller road bears left.*

This is the village of Sherman Mills. Notice the fine church at the fork. Just before the fork is a wonderful Victorian house on the left, with a seemingly infinite number of gables.

1.5 *Bear left at the fork and go 5 miles to the end (merge head-on into US 2).*

The road climbs gradually onto a ridge with sweeping views across dairy farms. Look back over your left shoulder for a view of Mount Katahdin. You'll pass a couple of partially buried potato barns, the first of hundreds that are a hallmark of the potato-growing region.

6.5 *Go straight on US 2 for about 7 miles to a crossroads where US 2 turns right, in Island Falls.*

You'll cross a stream with rapids on the right just before the crossroads. Immediately after the bridge, the fascinating Webb Museum of Vintage Fashion, open Monday through Thursday, is on your right.

13.5 *Turn right (still US 2) and go about 7 miles to a road that bears right immediately before a railroad overpass (a sign says TO OAKFIELD).*

Just after you turn, there's a bell tower on your left. It was originally on top of the high school, built in 1902. You'll pass Upper

Mattawamkeag Lake on your right, across from the May Mountain ski area. May Mountain is really a round grassy hill.

20.5 *Bear right and go 2.3 miles to an unmarked road on the right, in the village of Oakfield.*

22.8 *Turn right and go about 6 miles to the end (US 2).*

A grocery is on the left just after you turn right. If you turn right just before the grocery and go 0.2 mile you'll come to the Oakfield Railroad Museum (open weekend afternoons), housed in the old depot. A pink caboose stands next to it.

There's a tough hill heading out of town after the grocery. Beyond, the road winds through lovely rolling farmland with wooded hills in the distance, passing big old barns and farmhouses. **Caution:** Be careful when crossing the diagonal railroad tracks after about 4 miles. Please dismount.

28.8 *Turn right on US 2 and go 2.1 miles to Town Line Road on the left, about a mile beyond I-95.*

There's a snack bar on your left at the intersection with I-95.

30.9 *Turn left and go 0.3 mile to the first right.*

31.2 *Turn right and go 10.2 miles to the end (US 1), on the outskirts of Houlton.*

The road traverses a long, open hillside with great views. When you come to US 1, the Shiretown Motor Inn is on your left at the intersection, and Ivey's Motor Lodge is to your right on the far side of US 1.

Final mileage: 41.4.

SECOND DAY: Houlton to Caribou (63 miles)

0.0 *Head south on US 1 (toward the center of Houlton) and go 1 mile to US 2 East on your right, at a traffic light.*

1.0 *Continue straight for 0.2 mile to the next traffic light, at the far end of the bridge.*

1.2 *Turn left and go 0.7 mile to the end (merge left on US 2, Military Street).*

You'll ride through the center of town at the beginning. Just before the end, the leaking-boot fountain is on your right on a green.

1.9   Bear left on US 2 and go less than 0.4 mile to Foxcroft Road on your left, just as US 2 starts to climb a long hill.

2.2   Turn left on Foxcroft Road and go 6 miles to Framingham Road on the left, at the bottom of a steep little hill. A sign may say COVERED BRIDGE.

8.2   Turn left and go 0.5 mile to a fork where one road bears right and the other goes straight.

The road parallels the Watson Bridge, Maine's newest covered bridge, built in 1902.

8.7   Bear right (still Framingham Road) and go 6 miles to a crossroads and a stop sign (US 1).

After you bear right, the large round hill directly ahead of you in the distance is Mars Hill. You'll see it for the next 20 miles.

14.7 Turn right on US 1 and go about 12 miles to Bridgewater Corner Road on the right, about 2 miles beyond Bridgewater (a sign says TO CENTERVILLE AND FLORENCEVILLE, NEW BRUNSWICK). You will continue straight here.

US 1 is so straight here that you can see it stretch ahead for miles as it goes up and down long, gradual hills. The towns of Monticello and Bridgewater are strung out along the highway with no real centers, but there are grocery stores and snack bars.

26.7 Continue on US 1 for 0.2 mile to Old Houlton Road, which bears right.

26.9 Bear right and go 1.5 miles to the end, at a yield sign.

This road, and the next one, are narrow byways threading through potato farms.

28.4 Turn left and go 2.5 miles to the diagonal crossroads (US 1), in the village of Blaine.

30.9 Bear right and go 0.8 mile to the point where US 1 turns left and US 1A goes straight, in the town of Mars Hill.

The hill towers several hundred feet above the town. There's a food store and a snack bar here.

31.7 Go straight on US 1A for 0.7 mile to West Ridge Road, which bears left.

32.4 *Bear left and go 5.8 miles to a fork where Bangor Road bears right and the main road bears left.*

You'll pass a small airport on your left at the beginning. Beyond, the road climbs onto a broad ridge with panoramic views across the wide open countryside.

38.2 *Bear left at the fork and go 3.6 miles to the end (ME 10), in the village of Easton.*

41.8 *Turn left and go 0.1 mile to Station Road on your right.*

There's a grocery on the far side of the intersection.

41.9 *Turn right and go 3 miles to the end (Conant Road).*

You'll pass an attractive wooden church with a bell tower at the beginning, and then a lumber mill.

44.9 *Turn left and go 1.3 miles to Marston Road on your right. It comes up while you're going downhill.*

46.2 *Turn right and go 2.7 miles to the end (ME 167).*

You'll enjoy a glorious descent through large farms toward the end. Marston Road becomes Burlock Road. At the end, Presque Isle is about 3 miles to your left.

48.9 *Turn right on ME 167 and go 0.9 mile to ME 205 on the left.*

There's a snack bar on your right at the intersection.

49.8 *Turn left and go about 11 miles to a crossroads and a stop sign (ME 161, Fort Street).*

ME 205 is a beautiful road following the Aroostook River, with rolling fields on both sides sloping down to the water.

60.8 *Turn left on ME 161, crossing the river, and go 0.3 mile to a traffic light (US 1), in Caribou.*

Caution: You cross railroad tracks just before the bridge. Also, watch out for the expansion joints as you cross the bridge.

61.1 *To get to Crown Park Inn, turn right on US 1 and go 1.3 miles to ME 89. The motel is on ME 89, on your left, just past the intersection.*

To get to Russell's Motel, go straight across US 1 and go 0.2 mile to the end (Main Street, ME 164), then turn left and go 1.2 miles. Russell's Motel is on your left. To get to the Old Iron Inn (155 High

217

Street), turn right on US 1 and go 0.5 mile, then left on High Street and go 0.2 mile to the inn on your left.

Final mileage: 62.4

THIRD DAY: Caribou to Fort Kent (60 miles)

0.0 *Head into the center of Caribou, which is on ME 161, 0.25 mile west of US 1. You will be heading northwest out of town on ME 161.*

The downtown area consists of several one-way roads that form a counterclockwise loop. Fortunately, ME 161 is well marked.

1.0 *(Approximate mileage—the distance from the motels to downtown varies slightly.) From downtown, head out of town on ME 161 North and go 8 miles to Capitol Hill Road, which bears right (a sign says TO NEW SWEDEN). ME 161 turns several times as you leave downtown Caribou.*

You pass through wide open potato country.

9.0 *Bear right on Capitol Hill Road and go 0.7 mile to the end (Station Road).*

You'll pass a handsome concrete church built in 1871. The New Sweden Historical Museum, an attractive white building with a clock tower, is in front of you at the end.

9.7 *Turn left on Station Road and go 0.6 mile to a crossroads and stop sign (ME 161 again).*

There's a grocery on the corner.

10.3 *Bear right on ME 161 and go about 8 miles to Lake Shore Drive, a small road on the left that parallels the main road. It's about a mile after the bottom of a long, fast descent.*

18.4 *Turn left and go 1.4 miles to the end (ME 161 again).*

As soon as you turn onto the side road you'll see Madawaska Lake. The road runs along its shore, passing a ramshackle country store on your left. You'll climb steeply for 0.5 mile at the end.

19.8 *Turn left on ME 161 and go 8.4 miles to ME 162 on the right (a sign says TO SINCLAIR, SAINT AGATHA).*

There's a grocery shortly before the intersection in Guerette—it's the only building in town—and a snack bar at the intersection.

28.3 *Turn right on ME 162 and go 4 miles to the stop sign, in Sinclair. ME 162 turns left here.*

There's a grocery on your left at the intersection.

32.3 *Turn left (still ME 162) and go about 13 miles to the end (US 1), in Frenchville.*

This is a delightful ride along the shore of Long Lake, passing cozy cottages and cabins. Wooded hills rise from the opposite shore. As you continue along the lake, the land opens up into large farms with big, weathered barns. Saint Agatha, at the far end of the lake, is a town of trim white houses spread out along the road, with a large, handsome brick church at the top of the hill. There's also a motel in town. Beyond Saint Agatha, rolling potato fields descend to the Saint John River.

45.3 *Turn left on US 1 and go about 12.5 miles to ME 11 on the left, in Fort Kent.*

Caution: There are three dangerous railroad crossings on this section—two after Upper Frenchville, and one as you come into Fort Kent at the bottom of a hill. Please dismount.

The road follows the Saint John River, which curves gently through a narrow valley with wooded hills on both sides. Shortly after turning onto US 1 you'll go through Upper Frenchville, which, like Saint Agatha, is a small town dominated by an impressive Catholic church. The Fort Kent Blockhouse is on your right, about 100 yards off the road, just before ME 11. Daigle's Bed & Breakfast is on the left as you come into town, just past the hospital. Rock's Motel is on US 1 0.4 mile after the intersection with ME 11.

Final mileage: 57.8

FOURTH DAY: Fort Kent to Ashland (50 miles)

Be sure to eat a hearty breakfast in Fort Kent and bring food with you, as the terrain will now become very hilly, and sources of food are few and far between.

0.0 *Head south out of Fort Kent on ME 11 and go about 50 miles to the crossroads where ME 11 turns right, in Ashland.*

The road climbs a series of steplike hills to get out of Fort Kent. Beyond, the terrain is demanding, with vigorous ascents and

Mount Katahdin rises dramatically above a field in Patten.

delightful descents. You'll climb steeply onto a ridge with spectacular views of rolling hillsides and Eagle Lake in the distance, and then you will descend to the lake and follow its shore.

There's a grocery in Eagle Lake about 16 miles from Fort Kent; the next food is 22 miles ahead, in Portage (there's a motel here also). Beyond Eagle Lake the land is mostly wooded, with an occasional view from a ridge. There are several steep climbs before Portage.

Just before Ashland, ME 11 turns left across the Aroostook River and a smaller road goes straight. If you go straight for 0.3 mile, you'll come to the Ashland Logging Museum, which contains several buildings and sheds, and some massive felled trees. The hill into Ashland is a steady, half-mile grind. As you're climbing it, look back for a great view.

50.0 *Turn right at the crossroads in Ashland (still ME 11) and go 0.25 mile to ME 163 on the left.*

50.2 *Turn left and go 0.2 mile to the Four Seasons Inn on the left. The motel has a restaurant.*

Final mileage: 50.4

FIFTH DAY: *Ashland to Sherman (58 miles)*
Again, eat heartily in Ashland, and stock up on groceries and liquids.
There is no food on the 38-mile stretch between Masardis and Patten.

0.0 From the motel, backtrack 0.2 mile to ME 11.

*0.2 Turn left on ME 11 and go about 48 miles to ME 159 on the
right as you come into Patten.*

The road out of Ashland follows a high, mostly open ridge to the
lumber-mill town of Masardis, 10 miles south. The grocery store
here is the last source of food for 38 miles. Beyond Masardis is
nearly unbroken woodland almost to Patten. The 17 miles
between ME 212 and Patten are very hilly, with the worst climb
(0.7 mile long) a few miles before Patten.

*48.2 Turn right on ME 159 and go 0.3 mile to the Lumberman's
Museum, and backtrack to ME 11.*

*48.8 Turn right on ME 11, continuing south. After about 9 miles ME
11 turns right, but continue straight for 0.2 mile to the
Katahdin Valley Motel on the left.*

There's a steep climb about a mile long when you leave Patten, but
you'll be rewarded by magnificent views of Mount Katahdin, 25
miles away, on the right. There's a grocery in Sherman Station,
about 2 miles from the end.

Final mileage: 58

Author's note: I'd like to know how many riders take this tour. If you
tackle it, could you please let me know? You can contact me in care of
Backcountry Publications, PO Box 748, Woodstock, VT 05091.

Bicycle Repair Services

Cunliffe's Sales & Service Center, Bangor Road, Houlton (532-6056)

Aroostook Bicycle & Sport, 690 Main Street, Presque Isle (764-0206)

Vicious Cycle, 95 Parkhurst Siding Road, Presque Isle (764-5728)

Andre's Ski and Sport Shop, 27 West Main Street, Fort Kent (834-5188)

27
The Linear Tour:
Kittery to Bar Harbor and Back

Distance: *About 240 miles each way*
Terrain: *Generally rolling, with occasional difficult hills.*
Special features: *A continuous tour along the Maine coast using secondary roads whenever possible.*

The tour from the southern tip of Maine up the coast to Bar Harbor, or from Bar Harbor down the coast to Kittery, is one of the most popular bicycling excursions in the East. Unfortunately, nearly every bicycle tourist follows US 1 for all or most of the distance—a road that is at best boring and unattractive and at worst unsafe. Every time I've driven along US 1 I've seen bicycle tourists, their bikes loaded with panniers and sleeping bags; but I've never seen a touring cyclist on the wealth of secondary roads that parallel US 1, because many of these roads do not show up on the standard highway maps that most bicyclists use to plan their routes. The East Coast Bicycle Trail, a popular linear tour on back roads, runs from Virginia to Boston; northeast of Boston, the touring cyclist is on his or her own.

The tour starts from the bridge between Portsmouth, New Hampshire, and Kittery, Maine. For the most part, it follows the coast to Bar Harbor, using secondary roads whenever possible. The route is fairly direct, except for a slight semicircle to the west that bypasses Portland. The northbound and southbound routes are the same except for about a quarter of the tour where, for variety, the southbound route runs farther inland.

Food stores, restaurants, and accommodations are plentiful on the tour, and the choice is yours. In nearly every coastal town you'll find

motels, inns, and bed & breakfasts. Campgrounds, indicated by a triangle on the maps, occur along or very close to the route at least every 30
miles. Lists of accommodations and campgrounds may be obtained from
the Maine Publicity Bureau, PO Box 2300, Hallowell, Maine 04347.
During the off-season, indoor accommodations are inexpensive and usually do not fill up. During the summer, the opposite situation prevails;
it's a good idea to set an end-of-day goal each morning, call an accom-
modation there, and reserve a spot. If it is full, often an innkeeper will
call other places nearby (especially if you explain that you're on a bicycle tour), and you can call back in a few minutes to see if another spot
was found. Personally I prefer to camp on bicycle tours and avoid the
daily hassle of finding indoor accommodations.

Because the tour is long, I have kept the descriptions of points of
interest brief, or have referred to other tours in the book where the place
is described in more detail. The map is divided into sections, because it
is obviously impossible to put the entire tour on one sheet of paper.

Directions for the Ride

LINEAR A: Kittery to Bar Harbor

Most cyclists enter Maine from Portsmouth, New Hampshire, on US 1,
crossing the most easterly of the three bridges between Portsmouth and
Kittery. From the Boston-Brookline-Cambridge-Somerville area, the best
bicycle route to Portsmouth is to cross the MA 99 bridge into Everett. Go
two-thirds of the way around the rotary at MA 16 onto Main Street,
heading due north. Follow Main Street through Malden, Melrose,
Wakefield (where Main Street becomes Haverhill Street when you cross
MA 128 at the rotary), and North Reading. At the end, bear left on MA
114 (there is camping nearby at Harold Parker State Forest) and go about
3 miles to MA 125 North on the right. Follow MA 125 to Haverhill.
Continue north on MA 108 to Exeter, New Hampshire. (There is a campground 1.1 miles south of town.) Beyond Exeter, bear right on NH 101
to US 1 in Portsmouth, and turn left on US 1.

From Boston's western suburbs, pick up MA 62, follow it northeast
to MA 28, turn left and go about 2 miles to MA 125 North, and follow it
to Haverhill.

0.0 From the bridge on US 1 between New Hampshire and Maine, go 0.4 mile to the traffic island where US 1 curves left.

0.4 Go straight along the right side of the island for 50 feet to the end, then turn right and go 0.3 mile to the traffic light, in the center of Kittery.

0.7 Go straight onto ME 103. Follow it for 8 miles to the end (US 1A), in York Harbor.

Historic York Village is 0.5 mile to the left on US 1A (see Tour 1).

8.7 Turn right on US 1A and go 3.5 miles to Nubble Road (unmarked), which bears right uphill, following the ocean. A sign points to Nubble Light.

12.2 Bear right on Nubble Road. After 0.5 mile the main road curves right, following the water. Continue for 0.4 mile to a fork where Sohier Park Road bears right.

13.1 Bear right and go 0.1 mile to the dead end. Enjoy the view of Cape Neddick Light (also called Nubble Light), and backtrack 0.1 mile to the main road.

13.3 Turn right and go 0.6 mile to Kendall Road on the right, immediately after Fort Hill Avenue on your right.

13.9 Turn right and go 0.5 mile to the stop sign at US 1A (unmarked).

Caution: There is a steep, winding downhill shortly after you turn onto Kendall Road.

14.4 Turn right at the stop sign, following the ocean, and go 0.3 mile to the end (US 1A), in the center of York Beach. US 1A turns right here.

14.7 Turn right and go 0.6 mile to a fork where US 1A bears left and Shore Road goes straight.

Caution: Shore Road, which you will take to Ogunquit, is very narrow, very curvy, and, on beach days, very busy. On busy days, there is not enough room for a car to pass a bicycle safely without either risking a head-on collision or squeezing the cyclist off

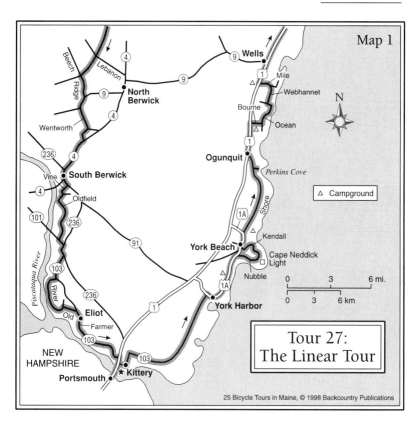

Map 1

△ Campground

0   3   6 mi.

0   3   6 km

Tour 27:
The Linear Tour

25 Bicycle Tours in Maine, © 1998 Backcountry Publications

the road. If the traffic looks bad, it's safer to bear left on US 1A to US 1, and turn right on US 1 to Ogunquit.

15.3 *Go straight on Shore Road for 4.8 miles to a small road that turns sharply right at a stop sign and a traffic island. The main road curves left at the intersection. A sign in the traffic island says* PERKINS COVE.

20.1 *Make a sharp right and go 0.3 mile to the tip of the small peninsula bordering Perkins Cove. Backtrack to Shore Road.* Marginal Way (see Tour 2) is worth exploring.

20.7 *Bear right and go 1 mile to the end (merge right on US 1), in the center of Ogunquit.*

The beach is 0.25 mile to the right.

21.7 *Bear right on US 1 (there's no escaping it in places) and go 1.8 miles to Bourne Avenue on the right, at a traffic light. It's immediately after the Wells-Moody Motel on the right.*

23.5 *Turn right on Bourne Avenue and go 0.7 mile to the end.*

24.2 *Turn left along the ocean and go 1.3 miles to Webhannet Drive on the right.*

25.5 *Turn right, following the ocean, and go 1.2 miles to the end.*

26.7 *Turn left and go 0.9 mile to the end (US 1).*

27.6 *Turn right and go about 6 miles to the traffic light (Water Street on the right) as you come into downtown Kennebunk, immediately after the bridge.*

Caution: For the first 3 miles, US 1 is a busy 3-lane road with no shoulder. Keep to the right. There is a campground between Wells and ME 9. Of interest are the Wells Auto Museum and the Brick Store Museum in Kennebunk (0.2 mile north of the traffic light—see Tour 3).

33.6 *Turn left at the light and go 0.4 mile to the end (merge left on ME 35 at the stop sign).*

34.0 *Bear left and go 1.4 mile to the fork, just after the bridge over the Maine Turnpike, where one road goes straight and the other road (ME 35) bears right.*

The Turnpike Motel is on your right just before the bridge over the Maine Turnpike.

35.4 *Go straight (don't bear right on ME 35) for 3 miles to a fork where Old Falls Road bears left and the main road bears right.*

You'll pass Mousam River Campground and Yankeeland Campground, good spots away from the beach traffic, on the left.

38.4 *Bear right on the main road and go 2.5 miles to ME 35 North on your left, at a traffic island and a stop sign. (ME 35 South goes straight at the intersection.)*

40.9 *Turn left and go about 32 miles to ME 302, at a traffic light in the center of North Windham.*

Caution: The metal-grate bridge across the Saco River, after about 18 miles, is very slippery when wet; it's safest to walk across. The Daniel Marrett House in Standish, built in 1789, is open to the public.

73.0 *Go straight at the traffic light onto ME 115 and go 3 miles to the end (ME 202 and ME 4).*

76.0 *Turn left (still ME 115) and go 3.8 miles to the traffic light in the center of Gray.*

79.8 *Bear right on ME 115 and go 1.6 miles to Depot Road, which bears left.*

81.4 *Bear left and go 2.8 miles to the end (ME 231).*

84.2 *Turn left and go 100 yards to a crossroads (Pownal Depot Road, unmarked, on the right).*

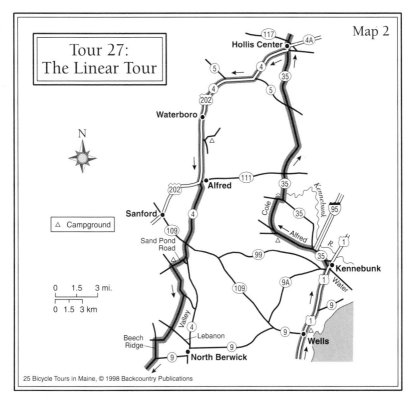

Map 2

Tour 27:
The Linear Tour

△ Campground

N

0   1.5   3 mi.
0 1.5 3 km

25 Bicycle Tours in Maine, © 1998 Backcountry Publications

On the left is Pineland Center, a state institution for the severely handicapped.

84.3 *Turn right and go 1.8 miles to the second right, Elmwood Road, at the top of the steep hill.*

86.1 *Turn right and go 2.4 miles to a crossroads and a stop sign (ME 9).*

If you turn left on ME 9 and go 0.5 mile you'll come to Bradbury Mountain State Park, where a trail leads 0.25 mile to the top of a hill with a sweeping view. Just beyond the picnic area is the park campground, on the right.

88.5 *Cross ME 9 and go 4.5 miles to ME 125 and ME 136 on the right.*

93.0 *Turn right and go 0.6 mile to the end (US 1).*

93.6 *Turn right and go 0.3 mile to Bow Street on the left, opposite L.L. Bean.*

93.9 *Turn left and go 1.6 miles to a fork where Pleasant Hill Road bears left.*

95.5 *Bear left and go 4.4 miles to a diagonal crossroads (Casco Road), at a yield sign.*

99.9 *Go straight for 1.8 miles to the end.*

101.7 *Turn left and go 1.2 miles to ME 24, which bears right immediately before a large, Gothic wooden church on the right.*

This is the center of Brunswick. Just before the intersection you'll pass Bowdoin College on the right (see Tour 5). The Bowdoin College Museum of Art and the Peary-MacMillan Arctic Museum are excellent.

102.9 *Bear right, and follow ME 24 South for 2.4 miles to the traffic light where ME 24 turns right (shopping center on corner).*

You'll pass Brunswick Naval Air Station on your right.

105.3 *Go straight for 4.8 miles to Western Avenue on your right, immediately before merging into US 1.*

110.1 *Turn right and go 0.4 mile to the end (High Street).*

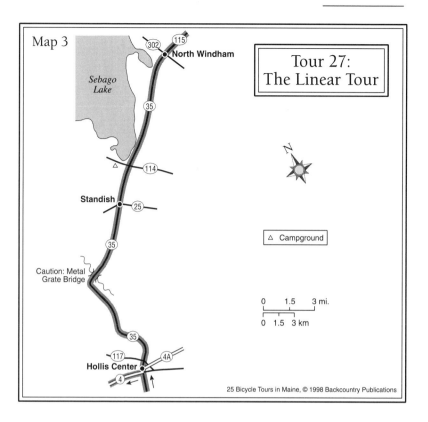

Map 3

North Windham

Sebago Lake

Standish

Caution: Metal Grate Bridge

Hollis Center

△ Campground

0 1.5 3 mi.
0 1.5 3 km

Tour 27:
The Linear Tour

25 Bicycle Tours in Maine, © 1998 Backcountry Publications

110.5 *Jog left and immediately right on South Street. Go 0.3 mile to the end (Washington Street). Bath Iron Works is in front of you.*

The Maine Maritime Museum, about a half mile to your right on Washington Street, is worth seeing.

110.8 *Turn left and go 0.25 mile to a traffic light.* **Caution:** *There are diagonal railroad tracks at the light, where you will turn right.*

111.0 *Turn right onto a ramp to the long bridge across the Kennebec River (US 1). Cross the bridge. (It's safest to use the sidewalk if traffic is heavy.) At the far end, continue for 0.4 mile to ME 127 on the left.*

111.9 *Turn left and go 4 miles to the third right, Old Stage Road. It's just after the second right, which is a short dead-end road.*

115.9 *Turn right and go 2 miles to a fork where Gray Corner Road bears right and the main road goes straight.*

117.9 *Go straight for 1.5 miles to a stop sign where you merge left on Mountain Road.*

119.4 *Bear left and go 0.2 mile to a fork where Mountain Road bears left and Old Stage Road bears right.*

119.6 *Bear right and go 1.5 miles to another stop sign where you merge left.*

121.1 *Bear left and go 0.8 mile to the end (US 1).*

121.9 *Turn left and go 0.8 mile to ME 218 on the left, in the center of Wiscasset.*

Of interest are the Nickels-Sortwell House (1807), Castle Tucker (also 1807), and the Musical Wonder House. (See Tour 7 for more detail.)

122.7 *Turn left on ME 218 and go 4.4 miles to a road on the right opposite a small electric substation.*

After 0.3 mile, the Lincoln County Museum and Old Jail (1811) will be on the right.

127.1 *Turn right and go 4 miles to the end (US 1), passing through Sheepscot. The main road curves 90 degrees right after 0.8 mile.*

131.1 *Turn left and go 0.8 mile to the first right (a sign says* TO NEWCASTLE, RIVER ROAD*).*

131.9 *Turn right and go 1 mile to the intersection where ME 215 goes straight and Business US 1 curves right, in Newcastle.*

132.9 *Curve right and go 2 miles to Back Meadow Road, which bears right.*

The intersection is 0.5 mile after a McDonald's on the right. You'll go through downtown Damariscotta and past the Chapman-Hall House (1754).

134.9 *Bear right on Back Meadow Road and go 2.9 miles to a wide crossroads and stop sign (US 1).*

137.8 *Turn right and go 5 miles to a road that bears right at a small traffic island after the* WELCOME TO WALDOBORO *sign.*

This section of US 1 has a wide shoulder.

143.8 *Turn right and go 2.3 miles to US 1 again, at a traffic light.*

There's a long descent into Waldoboro followed by a long climb out of it. At the top of the hill, the main road curves left at a fork. The Waldoboro Historical Society Museum is on the left just before US 1 (see Tour 9). Moody's Diner, a great food stop, is on the right when you get to US 1.

145.1 *Turn right on US 1 and go 5.6 miles to ME 90 on your left.*

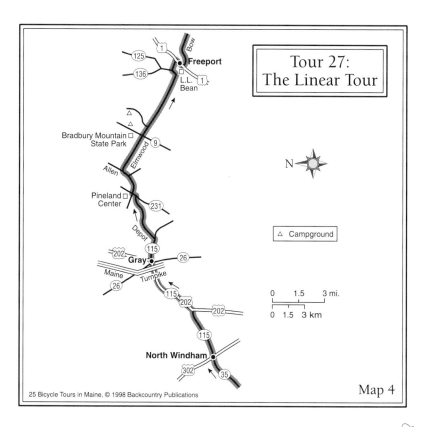

Tour 27:
The Linear Tour

Map 4

There's a good shoulder on this part of US 1.

150.7 *Continue straight and go 0.3 mile to a crossroads at the top of the hill (a sign points left to Warren).*

Caution: No shoulder on this brief stretch.

151.0 *Turn left and go 0.2 mile to the end, at a grassy traffic island.*

151.2 *Bear left and go 0.2 mile to a fork with a monument in the middle (Western Road bears left, Main Street bears right).*

151.4 *Bear right and go 1 mile to the end (ME 131, Oyster River Road).*

There's a steep drop into Warren and a tough climb out.

152.4 *Turn left and go 0.2 mile to the crossroads (ME 90).*

152.6 *Turn right and go 6.7 miles to a traffic light (ME 17).*

159.3 *Cross ME 17 and go 2.8 miles to US 1, at another light.*

162.1 *Cross US 1 and go 0.2 mile to the end.*

162.3 *Turn left and go 0.3 mile to the end, on the far side of the bridge, in Rockport.*

162.6 *Turn right and go 0.2 mile to the intersection at the top of the hill, where Union Street turns left and Russell Avenue bears right.*

162.8 *Bear right and go 1 mile to Bay View Street on the right.*

163.8 *Turn right and go 1.7 miles to the end (merge right on US 1), in the center of Camden.*

165.5 *Bear right and go 0.2 mile to the fork where US 1 bears right and ME 52 bears left, at a blinking light.*

For a side trip to Mount Battie, bear right on US 1 and go 1.5 miles, then go left into Camden Hills State Park (campground here also) for 1.3 miles to the summit. (See Tour 12.)

165.7 *Bear left on ME 52 and go about 17 miles, through lovely rolling farmland, to US 1, at a traffic light.*

ME 52 turns left at a stop sign after about 6 miles, and right at a crossroads about a mile farther on.

182.7 Turn left on US 1 and go about 28 miles to ME 176 on the right, approximately 8 miles beyond Bucksport.

This section of US 1 has a good shoulder (except for the bridges in Belfast and Bucksport), fine views of Penobscot Bay, and several campgrounds. After about 7 miles, in Searsport, is the excellent Penobscot Marine Museum, housed in a group of six buildings. If you bear left on ME 174 immediately before the first suspension bridge, just ahead is Fort Knox, a fascinating spot with ramparts, turrets, narrow corridors, and some of its original cannon. It was built in 1844 after the Aroostook War, a bloodless border dispute with Canada.

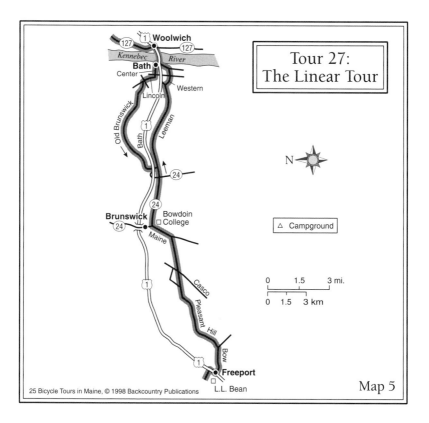

210.7 *Turn right on ME 176 and go about 9 miles to the end (ME 172), at a stop sign.*

This is the village of Surry.

219.7 *Turn left on ME 172 and go about 6.5 miles to the end (merge right on US 1 and ME 3).* **Caution:** *The intersection comes up while you're going downhill.*

Just before the end on the left, set back from the road on a large tract of land, is the Colonel Black Mansion (also called Wood-lawn), an opulent Federal-era mansion built in 1826.

226.2 *Bear right on US 1 and ME 3. Go 0.3 mile to the traffic light (ME 230 on the right).* **Caution:** *Steep descent.*

Here the tour turns right, but if you want the services of the Ellsworth commercial strip (motels, shopping mall, fast food, and the like), continue along ME 3 directly to Mount Desert Island. The strip is a four-lane, shoulderless highway extending for about a mile.

226.5 *Turn right on ME 230 and go 6.5 miles to Goose Cove Road (unmarked) on your left.*

233.0 *Turn left and go 1.9 miles to the end (ME 230 again).*

234.9 *Turn left and go 1.4 miles to the end (ME 3).*

236.3 *Turn right and go 1.4 miles to the fork where ME 3 bears left and ME 102 goes straight, just beyond the bridge to Mount Desert Island.*

At the intersection is Barcadia Campground, a conveniently located spot. ME 3 is very heavily traveled, but there is a good shoulder.

237.7 *Go straight on ME 102 for 2.2 miles to Crooked Road on the left. It's 100 yards after the Town Hill Market on the left.*

239.9 *Turn 90 degrees left on Crooked Road (don't turn sharp left on Knox Road), and go 4.9 miles to the end (ME 3).*

244.8 *Turn right and go 0.4 mile to the entrance to the Acadia National Park Visitor Center on the right.*

If you want to head into Bar Harbor, continue as follows instead of fighting the traffic on ME 3. (For the Nova Scotia ferry terminal, continue on ME 3 for 1.5 miles.)

245.2 *As you leave the parking lot of the visitors center, turn right on Park Loop Road. Go 1.8 miles to the first left (a sign says* TO BAR HARBOR).

There's a sweeping view of Frenchman Bay from the top of the hill beyond the visitors center.

247.0 *Turn left and go 0.8 mile to ME 3. Turn right on ME 3, and take the first left on Cottage Street into downtown Bar Harbor.*

The Bar Harbor Bicycle Shop is at the corner of ME 3 and Cottage Street.

Final mileage: 247.8

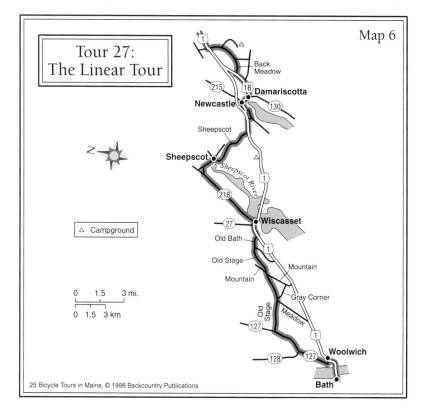

Tour 27:
The Linear Tour

Map 6

△ Campground

0 1.5 3 mi.
0 1.5 3 km

25 Bicycle Tours in Maine, © 1998 Backcountry Publications

LINEAR B: Bar Harbor to Kittery

The southbound tour follows the same route as the northbound tour for about three-quarters of its length. The other quarter runs parallel to the northbound tour, but farther inland. For the sake of conciseness, I have not repeated descriptions of points of interest along the northbound route.

Start from the junction of ME 3 and West Street in Bar Harbor, at the northwest edge of town. The intersection is one block north of the Bar Harbor Bicycle Shop.

0.0 *Bear left on West Street Extension (unmarked), heading west, and go 0.8 mile to the end (Park Loop Road).*

0.8 *Turn right and go 1.8 miles to the crossroads and stop sign immediately before the visitors center parking lot, and go right for 100 yards to the end (ME 3).*

2.7 *Turn left and go 0.4 mile to Crooked Road on the left, opposite Hulls Cove.*

3.1 *Turn left (**Caution** here) and go 4.9 miles to the end (ME 102).*

8.0 *Turn right and go 2.2 miles to the end (ME 3).*

10.2 *Turn left (**Caution** here) and go 1.4 miles to ME 230 on your left.*

11.6 *Turn left and go 1.4 miles to Goose Cove Road (unmarked) on your right.*

13.0 *Turn right and go 1.9 miles to the end (ME 230 again).*

14.9 *Turn right and go 6.5 miles to US 1 and ME 3, at a traffic light.*

Downtown Ellsworth is to your right at the intersection.

21.4 *Turn left and go 0.3 mile to ME 172, which bears left while you're climbing a steep hill.*

21.7 *Bear left (**Caution** here) and go about 6.5 miles to ME 176 on the right, just past the village of Surry.*

At the beginning of ME 172, you'll pass the Colonel Black Mansion (also called Woodlawn) on the right.

28.2 *Turn right on ME 176 and go about 9 miles to the end (US 1).*

37.2 *Turn left and go about 28 miles to ME 52 on your right, at a traffic light on the outskirts of Belfast.*

This section of US 1 has a good shoulder (except for the bridges in Bucksport and Belfast). The Penobscot Marine Museum is located in Searsport.

65.2 *Turn right on ME 52 and go 1.3 miles to a fork where Back Belmont Road bears right.*

There's a country store at the intersection.

66.5 *Bear right. After 2.6 miles bear slightly right at a fork, staying on the main road. (The Belmont town line is just ahead.)*

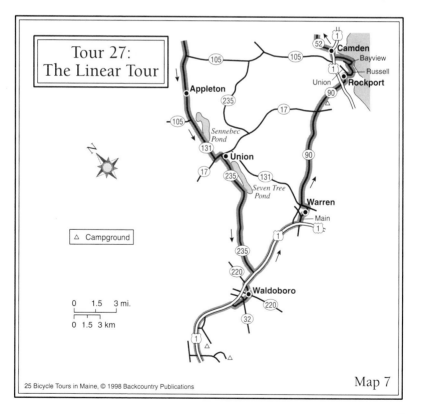

Tour 27:
The Linear Tour

△ Campground

0   1.5   3 mi.
0 1.5 3 km

25 Bicycle Tours in Maine, © 1998 Backcountry Publications

Map 7

Continue for 3 miles to a crossroads and stop sign at Lincolnville Road.

72.1 *Go straight for 0.7 mile to the end (merge left at a stop sign).*

72.8 *Bear left. After 0.8 mile you'll merge head-on into ME 173 (no stop sign). Continue straight and go 1.8 miles to the end (ME 131).*

75.4 *Turn left and go about 12.5 miles to the end (ME 17), passing through magnificent rolling countryside.*

There are groceries in Searsmont and Appleton. Sennebec Pond is on your left toward the end.

87.9 *Turn left on ME 17 and go 0.5 mile to ME 235 on the right, at a blinking light.*

There's a restaurant and convenience store at the intersection.

88.4 *Turn right on ME 235 and go about 9 miles to the end (US 1).*

After 0.25 mile you'll go through Union, a lovely New England town built around a large, sloping green (see Tour 10). **Caution:** In Union, a crossroads and stop sign come up suddenly while you're going downhill. Beyond Union, you'll follow Seven Tree Pond on your left. Look back over your left shoulder for views of the Camden Hills across the pond.

97.4 *Turn right on US 1 and go 0.9 mile to a crossroads (ME 220), at a blinking light.*

Moody's Diner, on the left at the intersection, is a great food stop.

98.3 *Turn left on ME 220. After 0.6 mile, ME 220 turns left while you're going down a steep hill, but continue straight for 1.6 miles to the end (US 1 again).*

There's a long, fairly steep climb up to US 1.

100.5 *Turn left on US 1 and go about 5 miles to a crossroads (Back Meadow Road; a sign says TIDEWATER TELECOM).*

The road on the left goes up a short, steep hill. This section of US 1 has a good shoulder.

105.5 *Turn left at the crossroads and go 1.8 miles to a fork where*

the main road bears right.

107.3 Bear right and go 1.1 mile to the end (Business US 1).

108.4 Turn left. After 2.1 miles the main road curves sharply left at a blinking light, shortly after downtown Damariscotta. Continue for 0.2 mile to a smaller road that bears left as you start to go uphill.

110.7 Bear left and go 0.6 mile to a fork (a sign points right to US 1).

111.3 Bear right and go 0.2 mile to the end (US 1).

111.5 Turn left and go 0.8 mile to Sheepscot Road, which turns right up a short hill.

112.3 Turn right. After 3.1 miles the main road curves 90 degrees left as you come into Sheepscot. Continue for 0.8 mile to a fork where the main road bears left.

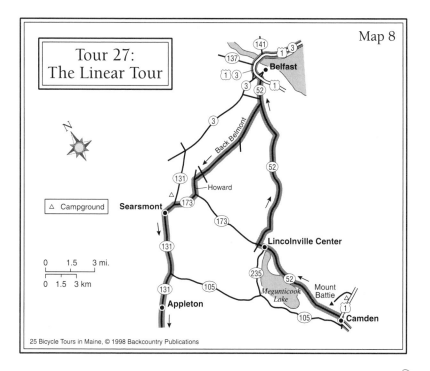

Tour 27:
The Linear Tour

Map 8

△ Campground

Searsmont

Howard

Belfast

Back Belmont

Lincolnville Center

Mount Battie

Megunticook Lake

Camden

Appleton

0   1.5   3 mi.
0   1.5   3 km

25 Bicycle Tours in Maine, © 1998 Backcountry Publications

116.2   *Bear left and go 0.2 mile to the end (ME 218).*

116.4   *Turn left and go 4.4 miles to the crossroads (US 1) and stop sign in Wiscasset.*

Shortly before the end, the Lincoln County Museum and Old Jail is on the left. For other historic buildings, see Tour 7.

120.8   *Turn right and go 0.8 mile to Old Bath Road on the right, after Bradford Road.*

121.6   *Turn right and go 0.8 mile to a fork where Old Stage Road bears right.*

122.4   *Bear right and go 1.5 miles to the end (merge left at the stop sign).*

123.9   *Bear slightly left and go 0.2 mile to the fork, 100 yards after the cemetery on the right. Old Stage Road bears right at the fork.*

124.1   *Bear right at the fork (don't turn right immediately after the cemetery). Go 1.5 miles to another fork (Meadow Road bears left).*

125.6   *Bear right and go 2 miles to the end (ME 127, Middle Road).*

127.6   *Turn left and go 4 miles to the end (US 1).*

131.6   *Turn right and go 1 mile to the first right on the far side of the bridge (Front Street), in Bath.*

It's safest to use the sidewalk on the left side of the bridge.

132.6   *Turn right and go 1 block to the first left (Centre Street), opposite the town hall.*

132.7   *Turn left and go 0.3 mile to Lincoln Street on the right, at the top of the hill, immediately after the redbrick courthouse on the left.*

Lincoln Street is just after High Street, the crossroads at the top of the hill.

133.0   *Turn right on Lincoln Street and go 0.5 mile to a crossroads with a combined gas station and grocery on the corner.*

133.5   *Go straight at the crossroads, and then immediately bear left*

on *Old Brunswick Road* and go 5.4 miles to the end, at a traffic light.

138.9 Turn right and go 0.5 mile to the second traffic light.

There's a shopping center on the far left corner.

139.4 Go straight on ME 24 for 2.2 miles to another traffic light (ME 123 on the left).

141.6 Go straight for 0.2 mile to the stop sign immediately after the large, Gothic-style church, in the center of Brunswick. (Don't bear right at the church onto ME 24 North.)

You'll pass Bowdoin College on the left (see Tour 5).

141.8 Turn left and go 1.3 miles to *Pleasant Hill Road* on your right, just past the hospital on the left.

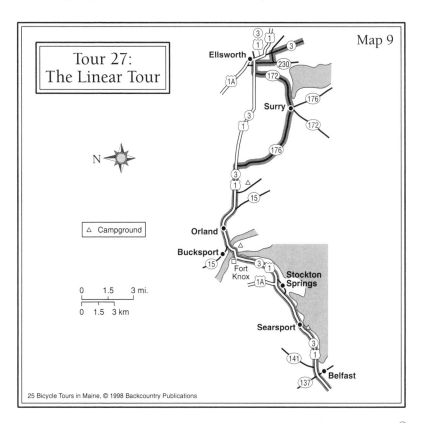

Tour 27:
The Linear Tour

Map 9

Ellsworth

Surry

N

△ Campground

Orland

Bucksport

Fort Knox

Stockton Springs

Searsport

Belfast

0   1.5   3 mi.

0   1.5   3 km

25 Bicycle Tours in Maine, © 1998 Backcountry Publications

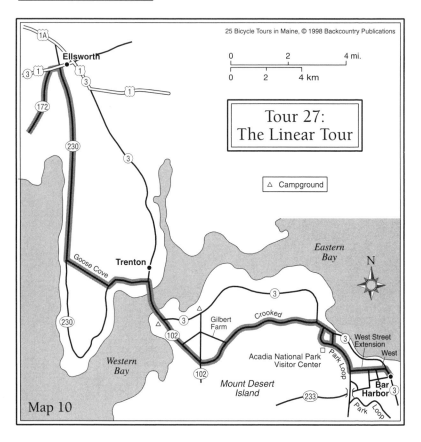

25 Bicycle Tours in Maine, © 1998 Backcountry Publications

Tour 27:
The Linear Tour

△ Campground

Map 10

At the beginning of this stretch, Bowdoin College will again be on your left.

143.1 *Turn right on Pleasant Hill Road and go 1.8 miles to a diagonal crossroads, Casco Road.*

144.9 *Go straight for 4.4 miles to the end (merge right at the yield sign).*

149.3 *Bear right and go 1.6 miles to the end (US 1).*
L.L. Bean is in front of you.

150.9 *Turn right and go 0.3 mile to ME 125 on the left, at a blinking light (a sign says TO I-95).*

151.2 *Turn left and go 0.6 mile to the end (ME 125 turns right).*

151.8 *Turn left and go 4.5 miles to the crossroads and stop sign (ME 9).*

If you turn right on ME 9 and go 0.5 mile you'll come to Bradbury Mountain State Park, where a trail leads 0.25 mile to the top of a hill with a panoramic view. A campground is just past the picnic area.

156.3 *Cross ME 9 and go 2.4 miles to the end (Allen Road).*

158.7 *Turn left and go 1.8 miles to a crossroads (ME 231) and a stop sign.*

Pineland Center, a state institution for the severely handicapped, is on the far side of the intersection.

160.5 *Turn left on ME 231 and go 100 yards. Then bear right on Gray Depot Road (unmarked) and go 2.8 miles to the end (ME 115). **Caution:** There are railroad tracks at the bottom of a steep hill.*

163.4 *Turn right on ME 115 and go 1.6 miles to the traffic light, in the center of Gray.*

165.0 *Bear slightly left (still ME 115, also US 202 and ME 4), and go 3.8 miles to the point where ME 115 bears right.*

168.8 *Bear right (still ME 115) and go 3 miles to US 302 at the traffic light in the center of North Windham.*

171.8 *Go straight at the light onto ME 35. Follow ME 35 for about 22 miles to ME 4, at a stop sign and blinking light.*

Caution: After about 14 miles, you'll come to the metal grate bridge over the Saco River. The bridge is very slippery when wet. It's safest to walk across.

194.1 *Turn right on ME 4 and go about 18 miles to ME 109, at a traffic light.*

212.1 *Continue straight on ME 4 and go 0.9 mile to Country Club Road 2, which bears right.*

213.0 *Bear right and go 0.4 mile to a fork where Sand Pond Road bears right.*

243

213.4 Bear right and go 1 mile to a crossroads and a stop sign. You'll pass a campground on your right.

214.4 Turn left and go 2.1 miles to Valley Road on the right.

216.5 Turn right and go 2.6 miles to a crossroads and a stop sign (Lebanon Road on the left). It's the third crossroads.

219.1 Go straight for 1.5 miles to the next crossroads (Beech Ridge Road).

220.6 Turn left and go 1.5 miles to the end (merge right on ME 9).

222.1 Bear right and go 0.5 mile to Wentworth Road on the left.

222.6 Turn left and go 1.5 miles to the end.

224.1 Turn right and go 0.5 mile to the end (ME 4).

224.6 Turn right and go 2.3 miles to the end, where ME 4 turns left, in South Berwick.

On the right at the intersection is the Georgian house of the writer Sarah Orne Jewett, built in 1774.

226.9 Turn left (still ME 4) and go 0.2 mile to ME 236 on the left.

227.1 Turn left and go 0.5 mile to Vine Street on the right.

227.6 Turn right and go 1 mile to the end (Oldfield Road on the right).

228.6 Turn right and go 3 miles to the end (ME 101).

As soon as you turn, the Hamilton House, an elegant Georgian mansion with extensive grounds along the Salmon Falls River, is on the right, set back from the road. Just past the mansion is the Vaughan Woods Memorial, a lovely picnic area along the river.

231.6 Turn left on ME 101 and go 0.1 mile to the traffic light (ME 236).

231.7 Bear right and go 0.5 mile to ME 103 (State Road) on the right.

232.2 Turn right and go 1.5 miles to River Road on the right, shortly after a small bridge over an inlet.

233.7 Turn right on River Road and go 3 miles to Old Road, which bears right at a traffic island. (Signs may also say RIVER ROAD and FORE ROAD.)

The author after completing the linear tour. Portland Head Light, Cape Elizabeth, is in the background.

236.7 *Bear right and go 0.7 mile to the end, at the Eliot town green (merge slightly right on ME 103).*

237.4 *Bear right and go 0.5 mile to Moses Gerrish Farmer Road (also ME 103) on the right.*

237.9 *Turn right (still ME 103) and go 3.2 miles to the end (Dennett Road), at a stop sign.*

241.1 Turn right (still ME 103) and go 0.7 mile to US 1, at the traffic light.

You're in Kittery. ME 103 bears right and left several times, but it is well marked.

241.8 Turn right on US 1 and go 0.5 mile to the bridge to Portsmouth, New Hampshire.

Final mileage: 242.3

Bicycle Repair Services

Goodrich's Bicycle Shop, 111 School Street, Sanford (324-1381)

Sanford-N-Sun Cyclery, 480 Main Street, Sanford (490-3994)

Birgfeld's Bicycle Shop, US 1, Searsport (548-2916)

Also consult bike shop listings for Tours 1–17 and 21.

Let Backcountry Guides Take You There

Our experienced backcountry authors will lead you to the finest trails, parks, and back roads in the following areas:

50 Hikes Series

50 Hikes in the Maine Mountains
50 Hikes in Southern and Coastal Maine
50 Hikes in Vermont
50 Hikes in the White Mountains
50 More Hikes in New Hampshire
50 Hikes in Connecticut
50 Hikes in Massachusetts
50 Hikes in the Hudson Valley
50 Hikes in the Adirondacks
50 Hikes in Central New York
50 Hikes in Western New York
50 Hikes in New Jersey
50 Hikes in Eastern Pennsylvania
50 Hikes in Central Pennsylvania
50 Hikes in Western Pennsylvania
50 Hikes in the Mountains of North Carolina
50 Hikes in Northern Virginia
50 Hikes in Ohio
50 Hikes in Michigan

Walks and Rambles Series

Walks and Rambles on Cape Cod and the
    Islands
Walks and Rambles in Rhode Island
More Walks and Rambles in Rhode Island
Walks and Rambles on the Delmarva
    Peninsula
Walks and Rambles in Southwestern Ohio
Walks and Rambles in Ohio's Western
    Reserve
Walks and Rambles in the Western Hudson
    Valley
Walks and Rambles on Long Island

25 Bicycle Tours Series

25 Bicycle Tours in Maine
30 Bicycle Tours in New Hampshire
25 Bicycle Tours in Vermont
25 Mountain Bike Tours in Vermont
25 Bicycle Tours on Cape Cod and the
    Islands
25 Mountain Bike Tours in Massachusetts
30 Bicycle Tours in New Jersey
25 Mountain Bike Tours in New Jersey
25 Bicycle Tours in the Adirondacks
30 Bicycle Tours in the Finger Lakes Region
25 Bicycle Tours in the Hudson Valley
25 Mountain Bike Tours in the Hudson Valley
25 Bicycle Tours in the Twin Cities and
    Southeastern Minnesota
30 Bicycle Tours in Wisconsin
25 Bicycle Tours in Ohio's Western Reserve
25 Bicycle Tours in Eastern Pennsylvania
25 Bicycle Tours in Maryland
25 Bicycle Tours on Delmarva
25 Bicycle Tours in and Around Washington,
    D.C.
25 Bicycle Tours in Coastal Georgia and the
    Carolina Low Country
25 Bicycle Tours in the Texas Hill Country
    and West Texas

We offer many more books on hiking, fly-fishing, travel, nature, and other subjects. Our books are available at bookstores and outdoor stores everywhere. For more information or a free catalog, please call 1-800-245-4151 or write to us at The Countryman Press, PO Box 748, Woodstock, Vermont 05091.